D1590655

CORPORAL CANNON

CORPORAL CANNON

A Female Marine in Afghanistan

A Memoir

Savannah Cannon

CASEMATE

Philadelphia & Oxford

Published in the United States of America and Great Britain in 2022 by
CASEMATE PUBLISHERS
1950 Lawrence Road, Havertown, PA 19083, USA
and
The Old Music Hall, 106–108 Cowley Road, Oxford OX4 1JE, UK

Copyright 2022 © Savannah Cannon

Hardback Edition: ISBN 978-1-63624-166-1
Digital Edition: ISBN 978-1-63624-167-8

A CIP record for this book is available from the British Library

All rights reserved. No part of this book may be reproduced or transmitted in any form or by any means, electronic or mechanical including photocopying, recording or by any information storage and retrieval system, without permission from the publisher in writing.

Printed and bound in the United States of America by Integrated Books International

Typeset in India by Lapiz Digital Services, Chennai.

For a complete list of Casemate titles, please contact:

CASEMATE PUBLISHERS (US)
Telephone (610) 853-9131
Fax (610) 853-9146
Email: casemate@casematepublishers.com
www.casematepublishers.com

CASEMATE PUBLISHERS (UK)
Telephone (01865) 241249
Email: casemate-uk@casematepublishers.co.uk
www.casematepublishers.co.uk

This publication has been cleared for publication by the Department of Defense. The views expressed in this publication are those of the author and do not necessarily reflect the official policy or position of the Department of Defense or the U.S. government.

Note from the author: I have tried to recreate events, locales, and conversations from my memories of them. In order to maintain their anonymity, in some instances I have changed the names of individuals and I may have changed some identifying characteristics and details.

Cover image © Sarah Tirza

To those who are still fighting, and to those who support them.

Foreword

2017, San Diego, California

I began writing this book largely as a form of self-therapy, one that forces the trauma victim (me) to walk through a difficult experience in as much detail as possible in a non-stressful environment.

It took me a long time and several panic attacks (one putting me in the hospital with what I thought was a heart attack) to understand that I needed help.

So, I tried to get help.

I requested PTSD help from Veterans Affairs (VA) six months ago but never heard back.

I requested help from an outside organization that took four months to get back to me, at which point I was turned off by their lack of professionalism (they had promised same-week assistance).

I requested help from my doctor who prescribed a sedative to which I eventually became addicted.

I tried talking to a therapist who said Jesus would help me if I stopped doing such horrible things. I walked out of his office.

I have lost friends to suicide. One hung himself in the garage and left three children fatherless. I have thought about swerving my car into oncoming traffic just to escape my own mind. But I have a son, and he deserves more than that.

Depression is like standing in a pitch-black room full of dangerous objects that you cannot see. You know you should move around, live life normally, but the darkness is so heavy and pain follows any action. Even fumbling around for a light switch can hurt because you may stumble into one of those dangerous objects. So, you become immobile.

People always said, "Just come to me if it gets that bad." But when the pain is inside your head and radiates to your toes, no one can help.

So, in a last-ditch effort to get better and have nightmares less often, I finally understood that what I really needed to do was write.

If this story is descriptive in parts, and blank in others, it is because I wrote it as I remembered it. The language used in my account can be rough and in some places, considered offensive.

Today, I have a great life, and I am safe. But I think it's time to address what happened during my Afghanistan deployment in 2010. Perhaps my words will help some of you realize that you're not alone in your pain; that you can also get better.

1

August 2010, Camp Delaram, Afghanistan

I stepped into the tent and walked across the dusty floor to my bunk. My boots left imprints in the sand, so fine that they looked and felt like moon dust. No matter how often I swept, the desert always came back.

My bunk bed was in the back-left corner of an empty tent that was designed to hold over 30 bunks. The tents were giant containers shaped like soup cans that had been cut in half vertically and turned with the cut side on the ground. The metal frame was covered in a sandy-colored canvas designed to "protect" its inhabitants from the sun and other elements. The canvas did nothing to protect us from mortars.

I slept in the same tent as the only other female Marine at Delaram, Lance Corporal Sandwith. Her bunk was in the back also, and we had both hung extra sheets from our top bunks to enclose our sleeping areas on the bottom. Not that it mattered—we never saw each other. She and I were doing different jobs, saw different people, slept at separate times—if we did sleep—and patrolled different bases with different enemies.

I took off my rifle and sat down on the bed. A blank wall stared back at me. Everything was the same color as the desert—a weird yellow-tan; even things that weren't that color were covered in the powdery sand and eventually melted into the never-ending landscape. I Googled pictures of fields when I was at work just to see some green.

Sweat dripped from my face. If I sat too close to the edge of the tent, the canvas radiated 140-degree heat from outside. But the edge of the tent was also where the air-conditioning tube ran, which blew sometimes-cooler-than-140-degree air. I say 140 degrees because after 120 degrees, does it even matter how hot it really is? It was August, in the Middle Eastern desert, with no natural shade; it felt like Satan's asshole.

Gazing listlessly at the wall, I fumbled for the 30-round magazine I kept in the right cargo pocket of my cammie bottoms, on my calf. We had to have ammo on us at all times, and since we weren't supposed to have our rifles loaded on base, most people kept their cartridges in that pocket. As I pulled the mag out, I looked at the scrape marks on the cartridge from the constant insertion and retraction that we practiced. The portion of the mag that had been scraped was a shiny, silvery color; the rest of it was black.

Flipping the mag around in my hands a few times, I felt the familiar weight of 30 bullets. I picked my rifle off the ground and inserted the magazine.

With a firm pull, I racked back the rifle's charging handle. It slid forward, and the bullet moved into place. I knew that when I pulled the trigger, the bullet would travel up through the chamber and meet its target. The mag would be lighter than usual to the person who picked up my rifle, and the casing for that bullet would be cast to the side, falling under my gear until the staff non-commissioned officer who would inventory my personal effects found it.

After flipping the rifle's safety from SAFE to SEMI with a quick snap, I gently placed the buttstock of the rifle between my legs and onto the ground. I slid both of my hands around the top of the barrel. As my right hand slid down the rifle and toward the trigger, I felt the dust scrape against my fingers on the ridged plastic and metal.

I placed the muzzle of the rifle into the bottom of my jaw and held the buttstock between my boots. Then I reached for the trigger. It was just barely out of reach, and my entire body was shaking as my arm strained downwards, trying to get to it.

The seconds ticked by.

I couldn't reach the trigger.

Frustrated, I carefully, slowly laid the loaded rifle back onto my bed and slid to the ground. Opening my flight bag, I rummaged through my silkies until I found what I was looking for.

Still shaking, I leaned against the edge of the bed, sitting in the sand on the tent floor, and looked at the positive pregnancy test in my hand.

2

Three months earlier: May 2010, Camp Leatherneck, Afghanistan

In 2010, when I was 20 years old and a corporal in the United States Marine Corps, I deployed to Afghanistan. My military occupational specialty (MOS) was 0656—a tactical data networking specialist, aka a "data dink." It was my job to give Internet capabilities to Marine units as they invaded and occupied different areas of war.

I'd been at Camp Leatherneck—a huge base in Helmand Province—for almost four weeks when a bunch of Data Marines were asked for volunteers to go "do some things" that would take us away from Leatherneck's eternal and predictable boredom. We were to be the network liaisons for a Georgian battalion that was trying to prove to NATO that they were allies so NATO would protect them from Russia. Because Georgians didn't know how to operate the equipment that NATO had given them, we were to be sent in teams of two, to be embedded in the Georgian units and work the equipment for them.

My hand shot up ... that stupid little hand.

Those last days before we left for the much smaller base at Delaram marked the last time I remember feeling innocent. I had done lots of things that would not be considered innocent, but I was still innocent in my heart. What took place in Delaram shot-gunned me down a path that forced me to grow up. I ache now to think of who I was when I volunteered for the network liaison job and how unprepared I was for the rest of that deployment.

Within 48 hours, ten of us, eight men and two women, loaded our bags into an Osprey helicopter. We left at night, with 180 rounds of ammunition—a full combat load—in the flak jackets we carried on our bodies. The Kevlar helmet on my head pressed my tightly made hair bun down the back of my neck, straining my scalp and giving me a slight tension headache. I was excited and I was naive.

I spent the entirety of the hour-long flight watching the machine gunner hang out the back of the helo, swiveling the weapon back and forth in the darkness, while he and another Marine used night vision goggles to look for attackers on the ground. As we approached Delaram, the tension increased.

The turret gunner hung out of the lowered ramp:

"Hold on tight, we have to avoid some hadjis."

Suddenly, the whir of the engine became a squeal and the Osprey tilted back with its nose in the air. Our unsecured bags in the center shot out the back of the helicopter and disappeared into darkness.

The machine gunners were pissed as they dodged the falling bags we had lunged to try and save. The Osprey swung back and forth, faster and faster, left and right. The squeals got louder and louder.

There was a reverberating thud as the Osprey hit the ground.

"Get the fuck out and hurry," someone on the flight crew yelled at us.

The ten of us grabbed what was left of our gear and exited the back of the Osprey. The helicopter took off swiftly, dusting up clouds of sand that momentarily blinded us. I clenched my eyes closed and put my head down. Once the dust cleared, we looked up and peered into the darkness. We had been dropped off on a giant rock with nothing around. I didn't know if we were inside the base or outside, or whether we should have our weapons raised. I asked the sergeant what to do. I was the only corporal, and the lance corporals were looking at the sergeant and me, ready to follow our lead.

"Fuck if I know."

There were no lights. We were alone, on a rock, in the darkness, without any idea of where we were or what we were supposed to do.

"Hey, Corporal! Here are our bags!"

We followed the voice through the darkness and gathered the lost bags from around the rock. There was movement off to the right. My heart jumped into my throat and I began to raise my weapon, my finger ready to switch off the safety, until I saw a Marine coming toward us.

"Hello, gents. Welcome to Delaram."

3

May 2010, Camp Delaram, Afghanistan

We were brought to a can to drop off our gear, and we left everything except our weapons. Leaving the flak, Kevlar, combat load, and multiple bags made me feel a billion times lighter. I grabbed a single magazine with 30 rounds of ammo and placed it in the cargo pocket of my right leg before leaving the can. The Marine who had walked out to the "landing rock" gestured for us to follow him up a hill toward another set of tan tents. I ran to keep up with his long stride. Antennas of all different shapes and sizes stuck out of the ground, some haphazardly held up with bits of wire and tied to stakes. I noticed a lightweight multiband satellite terminal behind one of the tents, and tons of cables ran across the ground from tents into other tents; sometimes piles of sand covered the cables.

These tents were located inside a secure compound within the base, where access was restricted to Communications Marines, contractors, and higher-ranking officers. The compound covered about two acres and was surrounded by 12-foot-tall concrete barriers. There was a wooden building immediately to the right within the entrance to the compound. It had a wide porch that had become a smoke pit for the nicotine-addicted.

A tall, dark-haired contractor stood on the porch, leaning on his elbow, with his right foot up on a bench, steadily dragging on his cigarette as he watched us walk by in the darkness. He met my curious gaze and I held it longer than socially acceptable, partially looking over my shoulder at him as we crossed in front of his building. The contractor smiled at me, and I quickly looked away. I hadn't seen many other contractors in civilian clothes, and this attractive one caught me by surprise. Weeks of seeing only Marines had made me unused to anything other than men in cammies with high and tights; their faces all ran together. But this man, with his longer hair and khakis, stood out.

We were used to the check-in ordeal that every Marine endured when checking into a new unit. All of us had secret clearances and dealt with access restrictions regularly. We were escorted through the compound to a larger tent called the Command Operations Center (COC) to meet the Marine major in charge of the base and unit. His blue eyes scanned the ten of us lined up in front of him. When he saw the female lance corporal and me, he sighed in disappointment and studied me sternly.

"You're a girl."

"Yes, sir."

"You're not supposed to be here. This is a regimental combat team. There are no women here."

The lance corporal and I stared at him blankly.

What could we say? *Sorry about that, sir. We'll start walking?*

"We can't get the Ospreys back now. You're stuck here. But you two listen very carefully. You were never here. You will not bother the men. You will, under *no* circumstances, do anything unprofessional."

The male Marines in the tent—my *subordinate* male Marines—looked at us out of the corners of their eyes as they stood at ease in front of the Marine major. I felt my face getting hot.

"Yes, sir."

"As soon as we get some assistance from Camp Leatherneck, you two girls are going back where you belong. Do not talk to anyone."

With that said, the ten of us were dismissed.

Well, that's stupid. They had our names on the roster that was sent to them before we came here. Does "Savannah" sound like a masculine name? What a waste, because I'm a girl … don't they just need trained Marines?

We left the tent, and I saw the contractor was still on the wooden porch. He lit another cigarette as we passed; the red tip glowed in the darkness.

Over the next few days, Lance Corporal Sandwith and I watched the eight male Marines who had traveled with us get ready to be inserted into the Georgian battalions. She and I were placed in a "temporary" tent on the back edge of the living quarters, which had multiple empty tents surrounding it. No one could approach our tent without a solid three minutes of exposure in a "known empty" part of the living quarters and certain questioning about their intentions and gossip.

The other Marines were getting acquainted with the Georgians. They were busy day in and day out, attempting to learn the Georgian language (a dialect of Russian). They questioned the Georgians on what they knew and what the plans were for the next few months. When the Georgian Liaison Marines saw the lance corporal and me, they'd boast: "Hey, we're super busy, but this operation is going to be awesome!" Then they'd dash away. She and I weren't allowed to meet the Georgians or to see the equipment we had been sent to work on.

We ate alone, with the combat team Marines watching our every move.

We waited for the Ospreys.

I read in my tent, laying on my bottom bunk that had the most heavenly mattress. Rumors were that the Air Force had extra mattresses and somehow, they had ended up on this tiny Forward Operating Base. Either way, that mattress was better than mine at home, and infinitely better than the thin hard pads we had in Camp Leatherneck. The white comforter was just fluffy enough to add some softness to the harsh desert environment. I was too conditioned to be combat-ready to remove my boots when I lay on the bed (you can't be too comfortable, you know). So, I dangled my feet over the metal end of the bottom bunk and propped my book on my legs to read.

Three days into this stupor of boredom, we were awoken by a loud knock on the door of our can.

"Get up. You're wanted in the COC."

The lance corporal and I shuffled to the door and began to trudge up the sandy hill to the protected compound. I glanced at the smoke pit as we walked by; it was empty.

We were led into a room with the major and two higher staff members.

"The Ospreys aren't coming. You won't be going back to Camp Leatherneck. You will be placed in respective sections to your jobs, and you will work here."

He seems pretty upset to have to keep us here. This is exactly like when Gunny Brown removed me from the MEU. He was known to remove girls from his units' deployments because he didn't want trouble. I bet this major asked for different (and male) Marines and was told to pound sand. Good.

The major looked disgruntled as he gestured to the two men.

"Lance Corporal, you will be with Staff Sergeant Wilkins working on satellite communications."

He looked at me. "Corporal, you will be with Staff Sergeant Rambo in the networking section."

Looking back and forth between us, he grew even firmer in his next statement. "Remember what I said about behaving."

It looked like we were there to stay.

4

May 2010, Camp Delaram, Afghanistan

My second week on Delaram was a blur of faces, numbers, and equipment. Getting accustomed to a new network is always overwhelming, and this newly implemented and ever-growing network was no exception. The combat team had reached this base a few months earlier. It was completely empty when they arrived. Over the past few months, the Marines had erected a lot of tents and the Navy Seabees, aka Construction Battalion (CBs), had constructed a few buildings.

The network team was small, maybe only five men total. They were forever roving to other combat bases where broken communications needed fixing. With so few knowledgeable people and an ever-expanding base, the network team was overworked. I was necessary.

One of the men on the team, Wiśniewski, remembered me from communications school in 2008. I remembered him only vaguely, because he was in a different class, and there were about 200 men to every girl, but comradeship was slim in the desert, and we became fast friends. "Ski" made me laugh, caught me up on the network and things I needed to know, and essentially set me up for professional success.

The platoon was offering an opportunity to get a gray belt in Marine Corps Martial Arts by training sessions held at various times of the day. I was stoked and immediately signed up to be tossed around by men twice my size. I needed some way to stay in shape and running was almost impossible on the small base, unless you wanted to run in tiny circles. I missed the miles of road on Leatherneck where I regularly ran at night.

The martial arts training was in a giant green tent with a tall ceiling. Torn-up rubber and, of course, sand covered the ground. Everyone dropped their blouses, and in our boots, cammie bottoms, and green skivvy shirts, we practiced take-downs and hand-to-hand combat. On the first day of practice, my partner, who was over 6 feet tall, threw me from his shoulder. The person getting thrown is supposed to land properly to prevent injury.

I did not land properly. Besides having the wind knocked out of my lungs for what felt like eternity and feeling like I was going to vomit, I had landed sharply on my elbow. I felt a snap and excruciating pain.

Years later, it would be discovered that I had shattered a bone in my elbow. But a combat zone doesn't have time for frivolous injuries. Less than two weeks in this unit and I would be going to medical? Heck no, I wouldn't let them see me seek medical assistance and shake their heads: "Typical broken female Marine, worthless unless they are on their backs." I gingerly got up and kept training, occasionally wiggling a shard of bone across my elbow and feeling the pain grow.

Later in the week, the black belt instructor grappled with every single person attempting to get their gray belt. It was part of the program, and I was nervous. Mr. Black Belt had about 5 inches in height and 50 pounds on me. Not too bad, right? Well, he was skilled. It took approximately ten seconds before I was down and pinned with my head squarely between his thighs. He began squeezing harder and harder, and as I began to black out, I turned my head to the right … and bit the shit out of his leg. He yelped and released me, shoving me away from him and springing to his feet.

Everyone circled around us flipped out, shouting and jumping up and down in excitement, mocking the instructor for getting beat by a girl.

"She won!"

"That's complete bullshit and inappropriate, Corporal!"

He was furious. If I'd been a man, he would have decked me. As it was, he scolded me and went on and on about how inappropriately I had acted in front of about 20 male Marines.

I left that session, alone. Everyone, even Ski, avoided me, as if the instructor's fury at me would rub off on them.

I walked back to my can; my rifle smacking my leg with every step. I was furious with myself; my actions had isolated me further from the men who were supposed to be my brothers. Every smack on my leg felt deserved and painful, yet not painful enough.

5

May 2010, Camp Delaram, Afghanistan

"INCOMING!"

Ski and I jumped up and grabbed our rifles. Panicking, I tripped over my folding chair and began sprinting to the entrance of the tent.

"Quick, this way!"

We ran into concrete bunkers that were immediately next to the networking tent. The bunkers had two long sides and a roof made of a slab of concrete; the sides were lined with green sandbags to our shoulders. I leaned against the edge of the bunker, gasping for breath as other Marines and contractors piled inside.

A lean whistle began, growing louder and louder, shriller and shriller until it hit. The explosion was very close. The ground shook and dust fell from the concrete slab over our heads.

"Bet they missed. Those motherfuckers are shooting shitty mortars out of the back of trucks and can't hit the broad side of a barn," someone joked from the other side of the bunker.

Everyone chuckled nervously.

The contractor from the smoke pit was standing beside me; we tried to keep some space between us in the crowded bunker. His white collared shirt was a sharp contrast to the tan cammies we were wearing. When more Marines showed up on the edge of the bunker, everyone pressed closer together to give them room. The contractor and I leaned against each other; my face extremely close to his chest. He smelled like warmth and man, the kind that makes you hunger for more.

I gazed up at the slab overhead. *If we get hit, that two-ton slab is going to land on us.* The contractor watched me, correctly interpreting my fear and suspicion of the engineering design of the bunker.

"It's an illusion of safety. If we get hit, they can report that we had 'taken cover.'"

"Oh. Fantastic."

Another whistle and explosion. More dust settled on our heads.

When your life is in danger, the environment becomes strange, almost surreal as you look around and become hyper-aware. You can't do anything to protect yourself, so you laugh. You make inappropriate jokes about the Marines who came to the bunker half-dressed. My fear of dying in a bunker under a roof collapse drove me to press up against the tall and strong man right in front of me. I wanted to feel his chest rise and fall with mine as we awaited our fate.

When the people around me shifted, the cute contractor looked down at me as I was pushed closer to him.

"I'm William," he said.

"And I can barely breathe," I said as I gasped for air in the tight space.

Afterwards, everyone trudged back to their individual working areas. The explosions had hit the compound directly next to ours, about 100 meters from where I was sitting when the first mortar struck. That compound was the Afghan National Army (ANA) base, where the Marines were supposed to train the Afghans to fight against the Taliban. The mortarmen had hit the attackers' own countrymen.

At the end of my workday, I walked back to my sleeping tent and took a detour to the ANA compound to see the damage. An ANA soldier told me what had happened when I walked up. He wouldn't let me see the area that had been attacked, forcibly shoving me away. Two men had died, hit by the mortars, while in the porta-shitter. Their legs had been blown off while they were squatting to take a crap.

The ANA soldier spoke to me scornfully. "They were aiming for your tent. They wanted to take out the—" He gestured to the satellite antennas. "They would never have killed these men. They are our brothers. Fuck you, and fuck America."

He spat at my feet.

Shaken, I walked to my tent.

6

May 2010, Camp Delaram, Afghanistan

After the mortar attack, I was extremely jumpy. The Afghan National Army soldiers glared at the Marines when we walked by. We were encouraged to walk with a "battle buddy," after reports came in of a member of the ANA stabbing a Marine in the neck on Camp Leatherneck. But ever since the MCMAP incident, I walked alone.

The ANA was a complicated unit of men. Many of the soldiers were known affiliates of the Taliban, whom we were fighting. They made no attempt to hide their meetings with the Taliban before casually walking onto our base, going to our tiny chow hall, and sitting down at the tables next to us as we ate the same food. However, American policy was to train them and teach them to build up their own forces, knowing that they were passing information to our enemy.

I don't believe these men were bad. They needed a job, and the ANA provided the means for them to earn a living. And we Americans were in their country and trying to kill their family members. War is not black and white, especially when it has twisted politics and purposes over hundreds of years.

I had known nothing of the war in Afghanistan when I was sent to fight it. Like most Marines, my job was to support the few Marines who would kill the enemy. These men were called "grunts" and I was a POG (derogatory term for "personnel other than grunt," pronounced pogue). Not only was I a POG, I was a girl.

I wanted to call home after the attack, hoping my husband Adam could reassure me. I hadn't called home since arriving at Camp Delaram, nearly two weeks before.

It was extremely difficult to place a phone call in a combat zone, even as a Communications Marine. I was lamenting to Ski about the lack of contact with my husband, who hadn't emailed or sent me anything during my entire deployment. Ski led me to a tent filled with communications gear stacked high in green tactical boxes. On one of the boxes, there was a single phone going into the equipment.

"Don't tell anyone about this phone. We don't have it registered to be taken down during River City."

River City is a state of communications that the command imposes when it doesn't want information leaving an area of operation. This state can be implemented during times of serious operations, or ... death. When an American dies in combat, all communication with the outside world stops. No email, no Internet, no phone, no contact. This is to protect American families from learning that their family member has died from anyone other than the death detail who knocks on their front door. This dreaded knock is how families are to be notified—*not* by some shell-shocked lance corporal who was a family friend.

So, this phone was "off the grid." It was a fantastic secret.

"Make it quick."

I reached for the piece of paper in my pocket that had the 14-digit phone number to a call center in Germany. I dialed, and then waited with static in my ear for the operator to pick up.

"I'd like to connect to an American phone center."

I had been told to ask specifically for a center in Ohio that allowed calls from a combat zone and didn't charge international fees.

"Please hold."

Five minutes went by as my call was connected to another operator. I shuffled uncomfortably on the floor of the tent.

"I would like to call area code 760 ...."

When I heard the dial tone, I dialed my husband's number.

He picked up on the fifth ring, and I heard sounds of a party in the background.

"Hey, I haven't heard from you in a while."

There was a horrible ten-second lag before I heard him respond. "Yeah, I've just been relaxing after my deployment."

He had gotten back from his eight-month-long deployment aboard a naval ship two days before I left for mine. We'd been married in December 2008. An open marriage was his idea, and I'd agreed. The idea intrigued me as a Southern-raised Christian. There was a lot of cheating anyway in military relationships because of the long years spent apart. So the idea of ethical non-monogamy with a solid base of trust and love appealed to me. It reassured me that we could do this and come out the other side. But as time went on, I became less sure of this and expressed my doubts to him as my jealousy of his actions had grown.

"Well, things have been pretty rough here."

"I bet."

Giggles from a girl came through the phone.

"Adam, I thought we said we weren't going to swing anymore."

"Yeah, I'm not sure I want to not swing."

"Oh."

"Well, I'm going to go jump in the hot tub. Talk to you later." *Click.*

I had a horrible heavy feeling in my stomach. I set down the phone and got up from the uncomfortable position I had been in on the floor.

When Ski asked if everything was okay, I just shook my head as hot tears collected dust down my face. I walked past him and out of the tent.

Later that day, mail was delivered. Everyone's names were called out by some random lance corporal in charge of mail; letters and packages were tossed to their recipients. Some 50 names were called out, and mine was not one of them.

"Here's one for William."

My ears perked up. I waited for him to walk by.

He came from the back of the room, grabbed his package, and grinned at me as he passed. I turned beet-red and looked at my boots. His smile made my heart skip.

When my 12-hour shift was over, I was leaving the compound and saw William sitting on the porch of the operations center, smoking. He waved at me and I walked over to him.

"Hey, William! Hope you got some cool stuff from home!"

You know what? Fuck Adam. Fuck him and that bitch he's fucking.

"Yeah, come here. I'll show you!"

I walked toward him.

7

May 2010, Camp Delaram, Afghanistan

William and I became extremely close over the next few days. We sat on the porch in front of his workspace where I had seen him smoking that first day and talked until two in the morning about life, politics, religion, our families, and our upbringings. I told him about my husband and how I didn't want to swing anymore, but he was indulging in whatever he wanted while I was gone. When I told William, my head sank, and my eyes drooped to my lap. I didn't talk for a few minutes. He looked down at me, seeming to ponder something. "Wait here."

He walked over to his work building, unlocked the door, and walked in, leaving me outside. I had no reason to be inside of his work area, so I waited patiently.

Deployment teaches you a lot about yourself and those you are deployed with. There aren't any cell phones to pull out in times of the slightest boredom. If you want to read a book to pass the time, you need to carry that book with you at all times, because boredom is a random occurrence. Books were uncommon on base and limited to the few that people passed around, like the copy of *World War Z,* which was dog-eared after being read by every single person in Communications. I had brought a few books from Camp Leatherneck and had read them all within the first week. My e-book reader needed a firmware update that I couldn't download in another country so I couldn't access those books. Losing books felt like losing my best friends.

Without distractions, you are subject to a lot of introspection. If you are lucky enough for someone else to be around, you get to know each other pretty well. Theories about the world's purpose, religious arguments, and discussions about which celebrity's dirty bathwater you would drink from after a bad bout of diarrhea were all too common. (The right answer is Natalie Portman, not Taylor Swift, Norred.) No topic is left untouched in a group of Marines.

Remember a time before cell phones? People would rely on television to zone out when they were gathered in groups. Well, in Afghanistan, we had our personal laptops, if we were lucky enough to have brought one, but laptops broke after so much exposure to sand and being thrown around in our packs. Without an electronics store around, even the Communications Marines couldn't keep their computers operational. As it was, my laptop barely lasted the deployment after the fan broke. We didn't have Internet access beyond what the military allowed us to have, which was extremely slow and not worth using, so we watched videos on the universal sharedrive. That sharedrive was where everyone dumped their copies of shows like *Weeds*, music like 3OH!3, and all their porn (in the folder named "Pron"). When everyone had uploaded what they had, they downloaded what they wanted to see. To this day, I can't listen to 3OH!3 without getting transported to the desert sands of Afghanistan.

William walked back from his work area and showed me a picture of a baby. "This is my daughter, Amelia. We call her Amy."

She had the most adorable rolls of fat around her ankles. He looked down at her proudly and asked if I wanted children.

"Of course, I can't wait to have a baby of my own."

"Good."

I turned red and changed the topic back to Amy, cooing over those adorable rolls.

8

May 2010, Camp Delaram, Afghanistan

A few hours after my conversation with William, I was walking out of the network tent toward the exit of the compound to eat lunch by myself when I heard the thud of boots come up quickly behind me. I wheeled around in alarm, just in time to see a flash of Ski's face before he picked me up and threw me over his shoulder. Laughing and smacking him, I screamed at him to put me down. Some other Marines joined him when he set me down.

"Wanna go eat with us?"

"Yeah."

We set off toward the tent that doubled as a chow hall.

"HEY, MARINES!"

We immediately stopped in our tracks and turned toward the voice of a very angry major.

"What is going on here?"

"What do you mean, sir?"

"Why are you laughing?"

Ski stepped forward.

"Uh, I was playing around with her and we—"

"Stop." The major snapped at me, "You, keep walking."

I turned around and headed toward the exit, confused and embarrassed, while the three male Marines were reprimanded by the Major. William came out of his building and asked if I was heading to eat. I said yes and joined him on the walk down the hill. My thoughts of the others were dispelled until I saw them in the chow hall later. "Ski, what was that all about?"

"Go away. We can't talk to you."

"What? Why?"

"Just go away."

Ski refused to meet my eyes as he spoke. He turned around and left me standing in the center of the tent with my food tray in my hands.

When I went back to work, Staff Sergeant Rambo called me next to his desk. "So, uh, yeah, some changes have to be made, and uh, it's been decided that you will work nights from now on."

"Alone, Staff Sergeant? Why? What did I do?"

"Yes, alone. And it's just because of … circumstances …."

He trailed off and shuffled papers on his desk. This was clearly a conversation he didn't want to have. "So, take off now and be back at 1900 to start your shift."

"Yes, Staff Sergeant."

As I left the tent, I heard the other Marines complaining.

"Man, I wanted night shift! Skate life!"

"Fuck her, girls always get special treatment."

I assumed Ski would catch me up later on what the major had said to them after our episode of laughter. I went to my shift, conducted changeover with the guy I was relieving, and began my work. Around nine at night, Ski walked in and mumbled at me to meet him in the martial arts tent. As he swiftly exited the tent, I gazed around at the other Marines working nearby to see if I'd be missed. No one was paying any attention to me, as they were indulging in Season 4 of *Weeds*.

I walked out into the clear night and entered the martial arts tent. "What the hell, Ski?"

"Look, everyone was brought together and told not to interact with you at all. Perception is reality, ya know? 'Female Marines are whores, right?'"

I was open-mouthed at his explanation.

"But I haven't done anything. I've been here two weeks!"

"Yeah, but everyone knows women in a grunt unit are trouble. I guess the major has had some bad experiences and he doesn't want you here. Since he can't get rid of you and we need you to do networking, he doesn't want anyone to be anywhere around you, and he said he would question anyone who was."

"But—"

I had no idea what to say. A combat zone needs camaraderie. Just the idea of a brotherhood is sometimes the only thing that can keep up morale.

"Look, he thinks we are fucking."

I laughed. "That's ridiculous."

"Is it?"

Ski stepped toward me, closing the space between us. He took his hands and grabbed the backs of my arms, pulling me closer.

"Ski, no … I … you're my friend."

I stepped away. The look that passed over his face was one of shock and almost immediate anger. He seemed to grow taller as he spun on his heels and left in a rage. "I knew you were a whore."

Standing in the martial arts tent, with the ground-up rubber under my feet, I had never felt so alone.

9

June 2010, Camp Delaram, Afghanistan

My favorite time of the day is early morning between 0300 and 0400. In America, it is quiet; the roads are empty, the dew begins to form as the moisture in the air chills to its coldest point and settles on the leaves. Everyone is asleep, and I'd be awake with the quiet and my thoughts.

In the summertime desert, that time of day is perfect. It is the coldest that it will be that day, around the high-eighties, and the desert cold is crisp and clear. The air smells faintly of dust, but it's a clean dust, undisturbed by sweat and heat. Hot day dust is damaging, an active swirl of destruction; morning dust is cool and calm.

The Afghan 0300 sky is very different from an American suburb's 0300 sky. In America, it is pitch black and quiet. In Afghanistan, the sky begins to lighten at 0300 in shades of brighter and brighter purples and pinks, fading into oranges and yellows. The sky becomes filled with the sun by 0500 and remains that way, unrelenting in its heat and strength, until 1900 or so.

The horizon was unmarred by any buildings or trees. Only on really clear days could I see rock-covered mountains in one direction far in the distance. Otherwise, the sky was completely open and vulnerable to me at 0300. The colors filled the sky and I'd watch in awe until the sun broke the horizon and I could no longer look for the glare.

On a typical morning, I left my night shift temporarily and headed to breakfast, before the sun rose, so that it gently warmed my back as I walked to the chow hall. By the time I was done with breakfast, the harsh and extremely bright sun was in full force. My first night on night shift, I walked to breakfast alone.

William saw me come into the tent that housed tables and chairs in lunchroom style and waved me over. Glad to not eat alone after my encounter with Ski only hours prior, I walked over and immediately started the conversation. "So, who is Amy's mother?"

"She is someone I was dating and got pregnant. She became crazy once she was pregnant and started doing weird things, like sitting in her car outside of my house and insisting that we were together. The whole thing was a mistake. But Amy is amazing. I only want more children."

"So, she has Amy?"

"My family takes care of Amy when Cynthia doesn't have her."

"Why didn't you stay with Cynthia?"

"My mother doesn't like her, and she honestly acted so crazy. I am trying to get full custody, which is why I'm here in Afghanistan, to get enough money and give Amy a good life. I bought a house in Arizona. It needs a womanly touch."

William gave me a pointed look. I laughed. "Well, I have been told that I make things very homey."

We finished eating together and walked back to the compound. I had a few more hours on my shift, and his shift started soon.

"Hey, grab me before you leave to go to sleep, and I'll walk you back."

I nodded gratefully and left him on the porch as I walked toward my work tent.

I spent the rest of my shift thinking about what would happen when he walked me back to my very isolated tent at the back corner of the camp. Would he kiss me? There was no denying that we were attracted to one another. I could tell by the way he looked at me the night I had arrived and how he reacted when I had leaned into his chest during the mortar attack.

Shaking from the possibility of the unknown, I walked up to his building at the end of my shift and knocked on the door. He popped out and cheerfully asked if I was ready to sleep. "Yeah, I didn't sleep at all yesterday during the four-hour warning I had prior to the abrupt change to night shift."

As we walked to my tent, I filled him in on what had transpired between Ski and me.

"So, you weren't fucking him?"

"No, Jesus, does everyone think that?"

"Don't take the Lord's name in vain. He doesn't like it." He grinned at me.

Not knowing if he was serious, I kept walking. "All of these tents are empty. I think they wanted to make sure the two of us girls were very isolated from the men."

William looked around in surprise. "All of these tents are empty?"

"Yeah."

He went to the closest one and threw the door open. He gestured for me to follow him as he stepped in.

Here it is, this is it. And who cares? If everyone thinks I'm fucking everyone, I might as well do what I'm getting accused of. I'm already getting ostracized.

I walked in and glanced around quickly before the door swung closed, shutting out all light. There were unused bunk beds scattered randomly around the tent. William stood in the middle, watching me.

In silence, he walked toward me, stopping centimeters from me. He was more than a foot taller than me, even when I was wearing my combat boots. I felt like a child next to him. He bent down and kissed me hungrily. I kissed him back, and we exploded in a flurry of touching, exploring each other's bodies. He bent down and picked me up, and I wrapped my legs around him.

"Are you on birth control?"

"No."

As he carried me over to one of the beds, I completely stopped thinking, enjoying it all.

"I'm going to get you pregnant."

I was so caught up in the moment and the feel of him that what he said registered only on a primal level. It turned me on, and I didn't react until seconds later when it was too late. When he came, filling me up, I was horrified.

"William, I'm not on birth control!"

"You said you wanted babies."

"Like, in a year or so, NOT IN THE MIDDLE OF A COMBAT ZONE!"

"I said I was going to get you pregnant. You seemed to like it."

"William."

"I like it when you call me that. A lot of people shorten my name to Will, but you always call me William." He grinned at me.

Shaking, I pulled my pants back up. My boots had never made it off. Tucking in my shirt, I grabbed my rifle from where it had fallen in the midst of the passion.

Without speaking, part murderous, part terrified, and with my body still turned on and breathless, I left the tent, exposed in the harsh sun.

William followed.

10

2017, California, U.S.A.

I found out on Saturday that one of the Marines I'd worked with in Japan had killed himself. He was walking down the stairs during an argument with his wife and blew his brains out all over the stairwell. He had been going through some things in the Marine Corps; he had gotten in trouble and had been demoted. The police suspected his wife, until they discovered a suicide note at his work. This tall, goofy, adventurous, and loved Marine had thought about killing himself so often that he had actually written a note while at work, then he went home and got into an argument with his wife, with suicide already planned as an escape route. It wasn't a spur-of-the-moment decision. He had been suffering inside for so long that he had a plan and the means to execute that plan.

We all get angry when our military friends kill themselves:

Why did he kill himself just because he got in trouble?

Marines have gotten in trouble since the beginning of time.

We were born in a bar and we kill people for a living, for chrissakes!

He is just being a weak pussy. We'd never have allowed hard times in the Corps to cause us to kill ourselves.

Fucking pussy.

But decades ago, getting in trouble didn't end your career like it does now. One slip-up and you lose everything you've worked on for years, including education benefits, the ability to re-enlist, the respect of your peers, and more. There is no more "taking them to the tree line" and beating the shit out of a Marine to teach him a lesson before cracking open a beer and settling the issue. Marine discipline is conducted through paperwork, and paperwork has more lasting effects than a good beating in the woods.

To be faced with the utter destruction of your career and loss of respect, after years of sacrifice, is heart-wrenching for some Marines, when all they wanted was to drink a beer after seeing their buddies blown apart in Iraq and Afghanistan. Instead, they got caught drinking underage, or perhaps sneaking a girl into the barracks to have some much-needed sex.

There is life outside of the Marine Corps.

Well, yeah, of course.

But young Marines don't see life outside of the Marine Corps, because that is all the majority have known in their adult lives. I certainly knew that world-ending feeling, when everything fell apart for me in the Marine Corps. It felt like the slim foundation on which my young life had been built was crumbling under my feet and no matter how fast I scrambled, I couldn't find a firm ground to stand on. How could I survive with nothing to support me?

I'm angry about this Marine killing himself, but I am also not surprised. I am not surprised because at least once a month, someone I know kills themselves. Sometimes they are faces that I've seen and served with, but I don't remember them vividly. Other times, they are really close to me and I try so hard—and yet not hard enough—to keep them alive. The numbers are increasing and not just with combat veterans.

I think the main reason I'm so angry about his death is that I know what he was experiencing because I experience it myself, and yet I haven't given in to it. I'm angry that I continue to suffer, and he isn't suffering anymore. I'm angry that when I get suicidal, it's like my brain is on fire, white hot with rage and disappointment and pain. I feel trapped in my own brain, smashing against the walls of my mind, screaming, and the only thing that calms me down is the thought of killing myself to end it. I'm angry because he gave in, while I just dance around it in my head.

'Til Valhalla, Marine.

11

June 2010, Camp Delaram, Afghanistan

When did I get my period last? Was it April? May? Fuck? I don't remember anything. Is it June already? Yes, it's June. Okay, I got to Delaram like three weeks ago in May, and ... did I have my period on Leatherneck? Maybe? Fuck, I know I got it like twice, but everything runs together like one giant Groundhog Day here. Okay, so we left America March 3rd, landed at Manas on the 4th, and I got here on like the ... 30th? So, the next one was April 25ish and then May ... oh right. I got it here. On Delaram. May 20ish. God dammit, why don't I know when I get my period? Why don't I track this shit? I always hate surprise bloody undies, so WTF ... I need to start tracking this. Shit. So, 16 days ago. I got it 16 days ago. 16. Fucking. Days. Ago. Fuck.

I can't get pregnant. I can't. I have four more months of deployment at least. I'll start showing. Right? Fuck, I don't even know when people start showing! Well, if anything, I know that when a baby comes five months after deployment, I'll be questioned and in some serious shit. But this happened to another girl and no one said anything to her. That baby was only a month "early" and still people talk. She's known as the slut. Fuck, I was even told about her "adventures" as an introduction by other Marines .... What will people say about me? Will I go to the brig? What about William? This fucking jerk who didn't even ASK if he could cum inside of me. Shit!

What about my husband? I mean, fuck him, but I do love him. He'll kill me. He'll straight fucking kill me. So that marriage would be over, even if we wanted to work on it. Eh, I know he's stupid, but I still promised to love him forever. But he won't love me. Not after this. Shit. Shit. Shit. Why the fuck didn't I stay on birth control? Oh right, because I suck at taking pills and Stephanie got pregnant on the pill anyway, and the birth control I was using needs to be refrigerated! WTF! This place is a hot-ass hell hole. What about healthcare? I'm in the middle of a combat zone. They don't have fresh fruits and veggies and they run out of food constantly .... Oh, but I've wanted a baby so badly.

Okay, look, calm down. There's no way I'm going to get pregnant. That just doesn't happen to people like me in a war zone.

12

June 2010, Camp Delaram, Afghanistan

As I walked back to my tent, I was furious and embarrassed. William followed me, completely at ease, almost sauntering.

I reached the door to my tent and started to open it, but William swung out his hand and stopped it from opening. "I'll see you when you wake up."

I glanced at his face; his smile was a mixture of charm and complete confidence in what he was doing.

"Uh, I guess. I have to work."

"I know. I'll be there."

He leaned over and kissed me on the forehead. I walked inside the tent and closed the door.

Throwing my rifle onto the white bunk bed, I sat down, stunned and confused. *What the fuck just happened? He seems* … I glanced at Sandwith's bunk to see if she was around. I hadn't seen her for about a week. *Am I just going to tell her I had sex with some contractor in a combat zone? She doesn't know me. And she's a lance. I bet she'd tell everyone. I can't tell anyone about this. Fuck. Okay, I need to take a shower.*

I unbuttoned my blouse and slid it off my body. The sweaty cammie material didn't cling to the skin on my arms; it simply fell away. The boots were next, with sandy dust falling from the boot laces as I loosened them. Before I could take my pants off, I had to unhook the giant metal boot bands that kept my cammie bottoms tightly against the tops of my boots. We wore boot bands to keep dust and things like giant camel spiders from crawling up our pant legs. Most Marines used soft green fabric boot bands that snapped easily or loosened over time. I had purchased metal boot bands because the return on investment was phenomenal. I never had to buy new bands and the metal ones kept my cammie bottoms tight and looking sharp. The only drawback was the significant dent that the metal left on my shins. Unhooking the bands, I noticed a tingle in my shins as I rubbed the almost inch-wide divot, trying to get blood flowing in the skin and muscle.

My cammie bottoms came off next. Sitting in just my green silky shorts and green skivvy shirt, I collapsed backward onto the white comforter. I stared at the black metal rods that held the empty mattress above me and reached out to lightly touch my rifle.

God, there's almost no airflow in here during the day.

It was 0900. The sun had been out for over four hours and the side of the tent was radiating heat above 110 degrees. The sweat began to dry on my skin. I closed my eyes, almost drifting to sleep when I felt cum slide out of me.

No, seriously, take a shower.

I bolted upright and slid on my flip-flops. Grabbing my small bag of toiletries, I tossed my rifle back over my body and headed for the bathrooms.

Although the area was deserted, the walk to the bathrooms felt like a walk across a stage. I was in shorts and every male who saw me stared unabashed as I walked by. I walked quickly, my rifle smashing into the back of my leg, until I caught it with my hand and slowed its smacks. The walk was a quarter of a mile of hot sand painfully filling my flip-flops.

The showers were the best thing on this small base. They were in white trailers that stood five feet in the air and could only be accessed by a metal ladder. The female shower was always spotless because the only other girl on base was very organized and clean. When I shut the door, I could lock it. This was the only place I had access to on base that could be locked. The top of the door was the kind of glass that you can't see through. Once the door was shut, the place was empty of dust, with the best air conditioning on the base, and as clean as a hospital compared to the swirly, dusty world outside.

As I quickly scrubbed my body of the dust and sweat and grime and cum, I felt how tired I was from only sleeping a few hours the day before. I needed to wake up in seven hours to make it to dinner, before my shift at 1900. Calculating how much sleep I would get, I toweled myself dry with my microfiber towel. What I had saved in space with this purchase, I had lost in moisture absorption. I toweled myself repeatedly, only to remain damp. I grumbled at the dampness and daydreamed for a second about wrapping myself in a giant, dry, fluffy towel while I brushed my teeth of grit and the taste of William's cigarettes.

I combed my wet hair, yanking the tangles out and twisting it into my usual bun with some gel. It was hard for me to make a bun with dry hair so I made my bun with wet hair and would sleep in it. It was uncomfortable to sleep with a bun in but it saved me time and allowed me to just get dressed in the morning. As I opened the door and stepped out onto the ladder of the trailer, a hot gust of wind blew a giant cloud of dust up. My damp skin beckoned the dust and the dust acquiesced.

ARE YOU FUCKING SERIOUS?

I shook my rifle at the mini sandstorm as it swept past me, dirt clinging to my freshly-showered, damp skin.

God. Dammit.

Frustrated, brow furrowed, I stomped the quarter of a mile back to my tent, my rifle furiously smacking my leg.

13

June 2010, Camp Delaram, Afghanistan

SMASH *SMASH* *SMASH*

I jerked awake, delirious. *Where the fuck am I?*

SMASH *SMASH* *SMASH*

"Corporal, wake up!"

SMASH *SMASH* *SMASH*

"Holy fuck, I'm coming ... hold on!"

I sprinted to the door and swung it open, the sun blinding me.

I threw my arm over my eyes and, blinking rapidly, tried to adjust to the brightness. Once my eyes stopped watering, I was able to focus on the person standing in front of me. The Marine stood in front of the door and was awkwardly avoiding looking at my legs and my eyes. I knew his face but had no idea who he was. My eyes weren't focused enough to read his name on his cammies.

"What do you want?"

"Sorry to bother you, Corporal, but you're wanted up on the hill."

"What? By who? What time is it?"

"Staff Sergeant Rambo, Corporal."

He glanced at his watch.

"It's 1300."

I seriously got three hours of sleep?

"What does he want?"

"I dunno. But he said to be quick."

"Of course." I rolled my eyes. "I'll be right up."

I shut the door and went to throw my clothes on. Socks, cammie bottoms, boots, boot bands tight, blouse, cover, rifle. My hair was already done. I walked quickly up the hill.

When I walked into the network tent, there was a Marine standing next to Rambo's desk. He was a lance corporal, who I knew worked in the networking section during the day shift with Ski. It looked like they had been waiting for me.

"Hurry up," barked Rambo.

I quickly shuffled over to the desk.

"Because of the rotations of R&R, we don't have many people to cover the networking work that lies outside of this base. The grunts within the town of Delaram need help with their WPPL [wireless point-to-point link]. Communications went down and it needs to get back up."

R&R was Rest and Relaxation. It was a period of leave that any Marine who had been in-country for over six months was allowed to take to decompress.

The WPPL, pronounced whipple, was a piece of equipment that extended communications from one site to a geographically separate site. From what I could gather, during the ten seconds of this conversation, the grunts inside the town of Delaram were getting communications through a WPPL connection to our site on the base of Delaram. I should've known this, but I had only been exposed to this network for just a few weeks and my brain was jumbled with numbers and locations as it was.

Staff Sergeant Rambo looked at me. "You and Virkler are going to get up comm."

I glanced at the lance corporal. He looked back at me warily.

"Yes, Staff Sergeant."

"Go pack for a few days. You guys get your flak jackets, Kevlar, and all 180 rounds of ammo. The grunts will be here soon."

"Yes, Staff Sergeant."

We turned to leave.

"Cannon, wait."

I turned back. The drop in formality surprised me.

"Look, you aren't supposed to go outside the wire. All females were pulled from the front lines. Congress doesn't want you out there. I could get someone else to cover this for you but—" He shuffled some papers on his desk. "They won't be back for a while, and we need this done. Do you think you—?"

I cut him off.

"I want to go."

He looked at me for a long couple of seconds, perhaps surprised at *my* sudden lack of formality or the eagerness I had in my voice.

"Just don't do anything stupid, okay? You aren't out there, do you understand?"

He gave me a pointed look.

"Yes, Staff Sergeant."

I raced off to get my stuff.

Finally! I get to do real Marine shit!

14

I don't claim to represent the typical female Marine. I am simply one woman who has a story to tell. Plenty of female Marines will not want to be associated with me or my story, and that's fair enough.

As a rule, there are three types of women in the Corps. We hear about them from the day we enter boot camp. There are the dykes, there are the whores, and there are the bitches, and we all fall into one of those categories, even if we are none of those things. We're judged on our appearance, scrutinized when we interact with others. We're openly scorned and marked. I was deemed a whore. I was raised in the South, so I was too nice. My manners, smile, and charm meant I must be fucking every guy who talked to me.

When I joined the Marine Corps, everyone in my hometown of Covington, Georgia, was stunned. I'd been a peace-loving hippie. I wore flowy skirts and a bell anklet that jingled when I stepped. I sang in the church choir, played the flute (and the oboe, and the piccolo) in the marching band. I was in Latin Club and attempted to play soccer. I listened to music and read my heart out.

Despite the outward appearance of normalcy, my childhood was bad. The Marine Corps has a way of attracting people with bad histories and abusive pasts, by promising brotherhood, success, and acceptance. We are an island of misfits—children willing to go to war in hopes of escaping poverty, abuse, and other oppressions of small-town America.

I forged my mother's signature on my enlistment papers when I was 17 and graduated high school early. Everyone said I couldn't be a Marine, that I wasn't strong enough or hard enough. But while everyone in my class was walking across the stage and getting their high school diplomas, I was leading Marines in communications school. And I was great. I was proving everyone wrong.

****

Male Marines aren't very secretive about hating female Marines. In their eyes, we are weak and only get promoted by being on our knees and sucking the dicks (literally and metaphorically) of the higher ranks. We dodge deployments by getting pregnant, and we get out of any shitty working party by batting our eyelashes at the SNCOs.

The problem is that there are very few of us around, so male Marines have only stereotypes, often negative, to shape their perceptions. Virkler would later tell me that Regimental Combat Team 2 had a few females at their parent unit in North Carolina, but the Comm Marines never worked with them, and the females didn't deploy to Afghanistan. In other words, he didn't know any actual female Marines.

Females in the Marine Corps accounted for 8.3 percent (as of June 2017) of overall active duty Marines (officers and enlisted). We are used to being one or two in a platoon of 30 or 40 Marines. As a Data Marine, I was also less likely to serve with another female because computer science is not a field saturated with women. In my entire enlistment of five years, I worked with only three other female Data Marines. If there was a woman in Communications, she was probably Radio or Wire. I served and trained with a few in my unit on Camp Leatherneck and they were pretty cool, but they weren't out on Camp Delaram with me.

Females in the Marine Corps bust their asses to be taken seriously by the males. Of course, there were always a few women who were notoriously weak and fell out of runs consistently, but there are just as many men who fall out of runs. Everyone will call the man who falls out "a weak-ass pussy," but they will look at the woman and say, "Of course she can't keep up." *Of course.* But the majority of female Marines I know are fucking badass women who take on more work, run faster than the men, and try every day to dispel the idea of a "typical female Marine."

Every move we made was scrutinized by the men around us. If we failed at something, it was because we were women and not because we lacked certain skills or weren't trained properly. Our gender was a singularity on which our failures were measured.

In 2015, the Department of Defense lifted all restrictions on the roles women can perform in the military, a decision with which not everyone in the military agreed. I can see both sides, based on my own limited experience in Afghanistan, where I was not welcomed or allowed in certain locations, while being ordered into those locations.

Should gender determine who can be on the front lines? *No.*

Can women do it? *Some. Just like some men.*

Will it be difficult for the women and the men they are in combat with? *Yes.* Unfortunately, female Marines carry the heavy burden of misperception and judgment, as well as sexual harassment, on top of combat itself.

War is hard, no matter what's between your legs.

15

June 2010, somewhere in the desert expanse of Delaram

Everyone had shit going on. Everyone had family issues in the States. Everyone was rounded up onto planes in the middle of all of these issues and sent to the middle of nowhere, with no cell phones, no readily available Internet, no TVs or cable. Lines to the Internet cafe were long and not worth the speeds. River City occurred at random, then all outside communication ceased for weeks. Our community was the sum of the people around us. The States could wait.

Because of the nature of war, you do what you are told no matter what you thought you were there to do. For a lot of people in Communications, our skills were so needed everywhere that we were constantly sent around to fix broken things, regardless of whether we were ever trained on the equipment.

I was taken from the unit I had bonded and trained with in the U.S. and sent to a base far away to live and work with a bunch of strangers in Regimental Combat Team 2. I had been stationed in California and every member of RCT-2 was from a base in North Carolina. I had spent a year training on satellite equipment and the RCT-2 Communications Marines were trained on the equipment they were using. I was sent to Delaram to help the Georgians with their satellite equipment and, because I was a girl, I was forced down a different path with RCT-2. I had to roll with the punches and adjust rapidly. Because I was a Data Marine, it was understood that I was smart and could figure things out. I had no fucking idea what I was doing with this unit, which was not okay for a corporal.

Ski was the only vaguely familiar face. When he dropped me as a friend, I was very alone, until Virkler and I bonded. Twelve-hour shifts and shitty situations will create friendships between the most unlikely of people. Plus,

Virkler is a really awesome person. He didn't trust me at first because of what he had heard about me. He was told that I had fucked Ski and some cyber security sergeant who had decided to favor me by giving me extra access through the network firewall to Facebook. None of this was true, but he didn't know. The rumor mill produces damaging perspectives.

The situation that brought Virkler and me together is a story of stubbornness and two Marines who wanted to get shit done. Almost immediately after Virkler got back from his R&R leave, Staff Sergeant Rambo threw him on nights with me. Everyone was pissed, Virkler most of all. But they knew I couldn't be left on night shift by myself. There was a lot of work, and it was physically impossible for me to do it alone. Enter Virkler.

Delaram was built up in 2010. Everything was mainly in tents and the Navy Seabees were rapidly trying to build enough buildings for the different units. Wire Marines ran fiber lines to the new buildings and the networkers (Staff Sergeant Rambo's team, aka Ski, Virkler, myself, and a few others) scrambled to get Internet into the buildings. However, construction was going on everywhere on base and the units weren't talking to each other to pass along construction plans. Our wire guys laid fiber, and two days later, the Seabees cut through it accidentally, severing the newly installed connections. This happened so often that we devised an emergency WPPL to throw up within an hour to allow services to the severed building, while the wire guys tried to splice, or fix, the fiber.

One particular evening, something had taken out the fiber between the compound and the airfield. Virkler and I were coming onto shift, and we were told to take the emergency WPPL and to get the airfield back up. A WPPL is split into six cases weighing over 1,000 pounds. A set of three of the cases made one end of the WPPL, and the other set of three made the other end. Each end has a radio, a radio tower, a huge power supply, a switch, a router, and a few other items. So, for us to get these services up at the airfield, we would need to transport these cases approximately a quarter of a mile. Simple job, right? Well, all of the vehicles were in use. Every truck, Humvee … everything was being used. And these services needed to get up. We were at a loss.

Overcome by the "good idea fairy" that rarely results in good ideas, I said the unthinkable: "Let's just carry it."

Virkler cocked his head to the side as though reconsidering his take on me and agreed. We could do this. The job had to be done. Problems have solutions, even if they are uncomfortable to implement; you can't ignore the problem just because the solution is hard.

We gathered all of the cases together, each of us grabbing one case by ourselves and holding the last one between our bodies, and we began walking. We dragged the cases through sand, stopping every few feet to readjust or rest. Neither one of us wanted to be the first to admit defeat. But we *were* suffering. About ten minutes into the walk of death, the wind began to pick up. The previously clear sky, full of stars, began to fill with sand.

The sandstorm came quickly and fiercely. We were too far out and much too stubborn to turn around, so we kept going. We pulled our shirts over our mouths and noses, closed our eyes, and walked blindly forward, dragging hundreds of pounds of that stupid equipment. I certainly wasn't about to admit that I was exhausted and miserable to a Marine who already viewed me as a weak link. I proceeded to swallow a beach worth of sand and marched on.

I swore when the case I was dragging rammed into my legs. If I walked faster, it banged harder into my legs, and Virkler had to match my speed or else the case held between us would yank our shoulders out of their sockets. Virkler and I had to watch each other's bodies to see how the other was moving so we could equally match the steps and speed. Every muscle in my body was screaming and a single tear formed into a mud ball at the edge of my eye.

The sandstorm meant we couldn't see where we were going. We stopped constantly to see if we could gain a sense of direction. We could see nothing for a solid 30 minutes. At one point, I was afraid we had walked off the base and were just wandering around in a sandstorm, because we hadn't seen a building for such a long time. I was starting to become scared. I didn't think Delaram had walls all the way around the base; there was an elevated berm of sand, and it wasn't a far shot to think we'd climbed it in the storm and walked off into the night.

Virkler ran ahead, trying to see where we were going to ensure we weren't walking off into the great beyond. Every time he left me with the equipment, I was scared he wouldn't be able to find me again. Whenever I saw him emerge through the sandstorm, I breathed a sigh of relief.

This time, after what felt like seven hours but was probably only half an hour or so, Virkler ran back to me, saying excitedly he could see a light. We had been walking about two degrees too far to the right and we were walking straight past the airfield. We picked up the cases and turned in the direction of the lights, finally reaching the shack that marked the airfield.

We got the WPPL up quickly, building the radio tower in the dark, in the middle of the fucking sandstorm. Virkler and I were cursing and more frustrated than angry, arguing with each other a little while we worked as a stubborn team. We entered the building to set up the other equipment and functioned better as a team with the sand no longer scraping our eyeballs.

The storm had died down as we worked, so the night sky was again clear when we began the trek back to the compound. He and I were laughing and joking around, wiping sand boogers from our eyes, blowing sand out of our noses and flinging the brown snot to the ground. We were covered from head to toe in moon dust, our cammies completely blending into the desert.

Through miserable circumstances, a friendship was born.

Virkler became my rock.

16

June 2010, Camp Delaram, Afghanistan

I grabbed my giant flak jacket from the bottom of my bed. I looked inside the magazine pouches to make sure all of the magazines were there and filled with one hundred and eighty 5.56mm rounds. My IFAK (individual first aid kit) was strapped to the top left side of my chest and my "drop pouch," for throwing any empty magazines during live fire, was on my right hip. I didn't have any cool patches on my flak that had my unit's name and design on them. Would it even be appropriate since I wasn't with my unit?

Jesus, what even was our logo? A giant-ass computer with Call of Duty on the screen?

Looking down at my flak, I thought there was no way it could look more POG-gy. It was so new, freshly pulled out of its package five hours before I deployed and assembled at the last minute. I shook my head. I stuffed some extra shirts, silkie shorts, and a few thongs into my backpack. I threw on the flak jacket and clipped my Kevlar helmet to the front of it. I grabbed my rifle and started to walk out of the can.

Holy fuck, this thing is heavy with a backpack and all this ammo.

I swirled around suddenly to go back to my flight bag. The momentum from all of my added weight caused me to spin a little farther around than I had expected, and I stumbled. Barely recovering, I knelt down awkwardly, with my gear banging into everything. My rifle's sling caught on the drop pouch, causing the rifle to swing forward just as I was kneeling. The tip of the rifle slammed into the ground and the buttstock of the rifle smashed into the bottom of my chin.

"MOTHERFUCKER!"

Eyes watering in pain, I rubbed my chin with one hand, while I searched my flight bag for the bag of Tootsie Pops I had saved from a care package a stranger wishing to support Marines on the front lines sent me when I was on Camp Leatherneck.

If I go on a patrol, I want to give some kids candy. There would be kids, right? That's all they said about Iraq—the kids would be everywhere, wanting candy. This place is a hellhole. They can at least have my suckers.

I stuffed the bag of suckers into my drop pouch, grabbed my camera in a last-minute decision, and awkwardly tried to stand. I had to grab my bed sheets to pull myself up.

Why is everything so awkward with this damn pack on? I'm kinda used to the flak and the rifle feels like an extension of my body. I guess I've never trained with a full combat load on. It feels like 80 pounds.

I did a quick breakdown of the weight:

Flak jacket with SAPI plates to stop bullets—about 30 pounds

Rifle—7.18 pounds

"Lightweight" Kevlar helmet—3 pounds

IFAK—2.5 pounds

180 bullets—roughly 22 pounds

Backpack with various shit—10 pounds?

Roughly 75 pounds. I weighed 125, the last time I weighed myself in America. Starting to sweat profusely, I exited the tent into the hot sun and went to meet the grunts.

17

June 2010, Camp Delaram, Afghanistan

I shuffled back up to the compound to meet up with Virkler before the grunts came to get us. As I entered the compound, I glanced over to see William standing on the porch, cigarette in hand. He looked at me with all of my equipment on and he looked stunned. He waved me over. I glanced around to see if anyone was around to intercept me before I got to the porch. No one was there, so I walked over slowly, unsure if my hesitation had to do with the added weight or with him.

"What are you doing?" He gestured at my complete combat getup.

"Going outside the wire to help the grunts."

"I thought you weren't supposed to leave. Congress pulled all women from the front lines."

I shrugged. "I have to work. They need me."

"You can't go."

"Well, I am, in about five minutes."

"When will you be back?"

"No idea."

"Come find me immediately when you get back."

"Uh, okay?"

"You're mine. Come back. And be safe." He smiled.

I looked back, shocked and perturbed.

Who does he think he is? Does he know nothing about the Marine Corps? I get no say in where I go, when I leave, or how long I'm gone. I am owned by the Marine Corps; he doesn't get to tell me what to do or insist upon anything. I don't need another boss.

Virkler walked out of the network tent and headed in my direction.

"Remember what I said!" William's voice was low and firm.

I waved at William and exited the compound. Virkler and I walked down the hill to the first row of cans that stretched to the left in a straight line. There were four MATVs (mine-resistant all-terrain vehicles), lined two by two, to the right of the row of cans. These vehicles were huge, with V-shaped bottoms to deflect improvised explosive device (IED) explosions, if the IEDs were detonated below the vehicle. Studies showed that the V-shape caused the explosions to travel outward instead of upward, which protected the Marines who rode inside the vehicle, more than the traditional flat bottom.

Marines were milling around the vehicles, some sitting on the ground leaning against the tires and smoking, some sitting inside the MATVs with their legs propped up on the open door and sleeping with their heads lolling about. I counted about ten Marines.

As we approached the vehicles, Virkler strode up confidently while I looked like some kid sister who had stepped inside her dad's combat boots to play dress-up. One Marine walked up to us and, with the most confidence I had ever seen in a man, spoke directly to us.

"Hey, you guys the data dinks?"

"Yeah, that's us."

"I'm Sergeant Poklembo. Call me Sergeant P. We'll be heading out of here soon. Just waiting on some guys to get back. What are your names?"

"Corporal Virkler."

"Corporal Cannon."

"Sweet."

He walked off and started talking to each man in his platoon. One of the guys nearby leaned over and spat out a long stream of dip juice as he looked at us.

"He's in charge, if you can't tell."

"Sure, looks like it."

I watched Sergeant P as he walked around. He moved three times as fast as everyone else, adjusting stuff hanging on the sides of the vehicles. He climbed into the first vehicle and checked the radio communications with the other vehicles. He was a blur of calm direction encased in a well-muscled and tattooed body. Everyone responded to him immediately with respect. I couldn't stop staring at him.

Some guys walked up and threw a giant bag from the small postal exchange into one of the vics (vehicles).

"Hey, Sergeant P, we got the smokes. Owens grabbed the last of the dip cans."

"Hell yeah, let's go! MOUNT UP!"

Sergeant P directed his last words to the mingling men, before heading straight for Virkler and me. The other Marines sprang into action.

"Virkler? It's Virkler, right? You'll be in the second vic. Cannon, you'll be with me."

He had discussed none of this with anyone. He made the decision, and everyone hopped to it. The people in the second vehicle cleared a seat for Virkler and Sergeant P walked me over to the first vehicle. He yanked my backpack from my back and tossed it on the side of the vehicle, deftly strapping it down.

"Get in behind me."

I looked at the door handle of the giant backdoor of the MATV. It loomed above me, what seemed like 8 feet in the air. Having an *Alice in Wonderland* moment, trying to reach the door key that's on the table, I reached up and pulled the handle down. The handle dropped and I pulled on the door. The door did not budge.

I glanced over at Sergeant P, wondering just how hard he was judging me. He reached inside his door to his seat, completely ignoring me. When I yanked the door again, it creaked open about an inch. Sergeant P was still ignoring me, but I was sure he knew exactly what was happening and he was choosing to let me struggle and figure it out. He threw his flak jacket over his head, and that's when I noticed that his flak jacket was *smaller* than mine, less bulky, and well broken in.

I forgot about the giant door and turned to him.

"What the hell is that?"

He followed my gaze squarely to his chest.

"What? This? It's a plate carrier. That shit you're wearing is ridiculous. Do you really think you can move effectively in that thing?"

"Fuck no, look!" I tried to bend down, and I moved about 4 inches.

"Exactly. I'd rather be naked in a firefight than wear that bulky piece of shit designed by someone who has never had to move around while people are shooting at them." Sergeant P was irritated, describing the clear disconnect between men in the field and contractors who designed equipment.

"But how much does it weigh? Where did you get it?"

"I've had it since Iraq. It weighs about 20 pounds." His arms moved freely as he swung into his seat with ease. "What are you waiting on? Get in."

One last time, I yanked on the 200-pound door, and it swung open easily. Crisis averted.

Climbing awkwardly into the back seat, I tried to find a position to place my rifle between my legs. I was stuffed into the seat and when I swung the door closed, it felt like I was being pressed on from all directions. It was suffocating. The vehicle was running, with a little bit of air conditioning circulating, but it didn't make a dent in the sweltering heat of the Afghan sun.

Sergeant P was conducting radio checks with the other vics.

"Vic 1 to all vics, radio check, over."

All vehicles responded in turn. I imagined Virkler sitting in the vehicle behind me and wondered if he was as nervous as I was.

Between radio checks, Sergeant P introduced me to the guys.

"Owens is the gunner."

I suddenly noticed combat boots to the left of my face and craned my eyes up to see a man sitting on a strap and holding a machine gun.

"OWENS! THIS IS CANNON!"

"WHAT?"

Owens ducked his head down so he could hear inside the vehicle.

"Cannon."

"Hey, Cannon, Owens." He waved and then poked his head back up to his machine gun.

Sergeant P introduced the driver. "Dumaw, Cannon; Cannon, Dumaw."

Dumaw turned around and grinned. "Pleased to meet you."

We awkwardly shook hands around Owens' feet.

"Alright, gents, move." Sergeant P was the convoy commander, the one in charge, of course.

As the MATV's engine went from idling to a thunderous rumble, we began to move. I saw the compound grow distant in the window as we drove toward the exit of the base. I had never been in this area of Delaram. We slowed to a crawl and waited in silence for the other vics to catch up. I strained to look over Sergeant P's seat through the windshield. These things were not designed for short people.

Sergeant P took hold of the radio handset. "Vic 1 to all vics, Condition 1."

A sudden seriousness came over everyone.

"Second vic to the left, third to the right. Rear vic face back."

Owens suddenly swung the machine gun around to face forward. The machine gunner mount clicked as he rotated the gun.

Condition 1 is the last condition a rifle can be in before actually firing. In Condition 1, the magazine is loaded into the rifle, there is a bullet in the chamber, and the hammer is cocked. But the safety is on. The safety is always on unless you are shooting someone.

Condition 1.

Of course. We're leaving the wire. This is it. Of course, we would be Condition 1. Why am I surprised by this?

I had never been in Condition 1, unless I was on a firing range with multiple weapons coaches and an ambulance on standby for any accidents. Condition 1 was the dangerous condition.

Condition 1.

I heard Dumaw and Sergeant P rack back their firing handles, sending a bullet into their chambers. In almost slow motion, I saw Owens load his machine gun and I heard the racking back of his giant weapon. My world slowed to a crawl, and I felt my heartbeat directly in my chest.

Thud. Thud. Thud.

I had wasted time understanding what was taking place. Everyone else had their weapons loaded. I reached into my right cargo pocket of my cammie pants and pulled out the full magazine. I sat there and looked at it.

What do I do with this? How do I ...?

I had forgotten how to load my magazine. Dozens upon dozens of times of loading and unloading this weapon, dozens upon dozens of times, and I was frozen.

Turning the magazine in the direction that seemed to make the most sense, I fumbled to insert it. It didn't click and I had to slam the bottom of the mag to seat it completely. My fingers felt fat and swollen as I tried to rack back the weapon to load the bullet into the chamber. My fingers didn't respond very well, and I fumbled further. I was shaking as I realized I was taking much longer than everyone else, and they were waiting for me to finish loading my weapon. They did this dozens of times a day—they were pros.

My weapon was loaded. I breathed a sigh of relief.

Second crisis averted.

Sergeant P talked to a guard at the gate. "PMT heading to the AUP inside the town of Delaram."

Picking up the radio, Sergeant P glanced back at me. "You ready?"

I nodded, frantically.

"Alright, gents, move. Keep an eye out for IEDs."

The four vics weaved back and forth between the staggered concrete barriers at the entrance of Camp Delaram.

18

2017, California, U.S.A.

I could easily write this story more dramatically, changing details to make the situation appear dire and emotional, to make it seem like I have a right to be messed up by what happened, to justify to my readers my nightmares and anxiety. But then it wouldn't be the truth. The reality of war is very different from the movies. The person watching the movie knows that something is coming because the directors make it obvious. My readers know something is coming because otherwise I wouldn't be writing this story. There is a built-up sense of apprehension in the movie or the book. In war movies, during tragic scenes, the camera pans slowly, trying to capture the "fog of war" that each person experiences. There is confusion and destruction everywhere, and the sad music plays while the dust fills the air ....

I think that is what messed up my perception of war, the damn movies with their slow-motion scenes filled with sad instrumental songs. It wasn't until years later that I was able to look back at my tragic experiences and realize: *Oh, that ... right there ... that's when the director would cue a sad song*. Because in the moment, there is no sad music, there is no aerial pan-out of the destruction. There is the moment as it happens, no different than the last moment before the chaos. It is unexpected, with no real built-in apprehension. During the first convoy, of course, I was anxious. I was scared shitless. And nothing happened. So, after enough moments of being scared shitless with no tragedy, you forget to expect tragedy. You have to forget. You can't live for six to 14 months feeling like you're going to die any minute. You'd go crazy. So, you joke around and laugh, you tell stories, you insult each other, you play spades, you chase each other around playing tag, you do everything to reassure your brain that you are not going to die.

When tragedy occurs on deployment, you are both in shock and also not remotely surprised. The moment is happening, you are shocked, but you are living. And there is no end scene. There is the moment of tragedy, and then the next, and the next; every moment flowing together until this is your life and that tragedy is just a thing you experienced.

Perhaps this is why directors tend to end scenes after tragedy happens. They don't know how to capture the emotion of the moment never actually ending. In real life it seems like the tragic moment never ends because there is no black screen—no credits roll. There is the cleanup, and then the shock, and the shock will exist for months or years after the event. After speaking with my friends and Marine buddies, I have come to realize that people who have experienced tragedy become very good at compartmentalization. We have to create our own "end scenes" to properly lock up the experience into a tiny box until we need it again.

19

June 2010, AUP Station in the Town of Delaram, Afghanistan

The MATVs picked up speed as we exited the base. Sergeant P spoke over his shoulder, tossing words at me while he continued to scan the road ahead. His eyes never stopped the back and forth inspection of everything in our path. "We're called PMT, the Police Mentoring Team. We are supposed to 'train the Afghan National Army.'" He tossed his hands up to form sarcastic air quotes.

"Why the air quotes?"

"These men don't know how to fight. They don't want to know how to fight. They want to get paid and have us out of here."

"Well, we are kinda occupying their land."

"Look, this entire area is fucked. This whole country is fucked. The majority of the locals are okay, but the older men see us as the enemy because we are fighting the people who saved them from Russia in the 80s."

"The Taliban?"

"Yeah."

Why did I not know any of this? I didn't even know Russia was at war with anyone in the 80s. I wasn't even ALIVE in the 80s! There was a history between Afghanistan and other countries before this? Shit. I don't know anything. Why didn't we get taught about this?

Sergeant P paused to speak into the radio to his men before continuing. "Gardner, Lewis, get the vics ready for the next convoy when we reach the station."

Grabbing the edge of Sergeant P's seat and pulling myself up a bit, I saw buildings breaking the line of the horizon. We had only been on the road for maybe five minutes.

"Russia invaded Afghanistan, Taliban fought them, now we are fighting the Taliban and the locals are pissed. At the end of the day, I don't give a shit about the intricacies of politics and history. I'm here to do a job and that's to get my men home to their families. Right, Dumaw?"

Sergeant P reached over the center of the vehicle to grab the driver's right shoulder and shake it violently for a few seconds while Dumaw laughed, his whole body moving back and forth from Sergeant P's clasped hand.

"So, you're all grunts from Camp Lejeune?"

"Nah, we are a mix of grunts and military police. Like Dumaw here is an MP. Owens up in the turret is a machine gunner. I'm a grunt. And we are from Lejeune and Cherry Point."

"Have you been here long?"

"Since March."

There was a silence in the vehicle as we got closer to the buildings. The road was small, and the buildings only went up one or two stories high. They were made of plaster or mud and everything I saw seemed to be covered in that dusty desert sand. Sergeant P's voice sounded off-hand when he spoke again. "So, what about you? What's your story?"

"I'm from Pendleton … uh, Data … I'm a … girl?"

I had no idea what else to tell him that was relevant. What matters about an individual in a war zone? My life was my job, which was to support people like him. My voice trailed off as we entered the town and I got distracted by my new surroundings. The streets were empty of cars and people.

"A girl, huh? No shit. I never would have guessed."

Dumaw laughed.

We pulled up next to a high wall that ran alongside the left of the convoy. The wall looked like it formed a very small compound. I saw familiar signs of the American military in the form of Marine Corps sandbags, the same plastic green ones that were stacked on the outside of the concrete bunkers on Delaram. These sandbags were stacked around the one elevated guard post that stood towering over the streets like an Eye of Sauron. As I squinted my eyes against the sun, I could just barely make out two Marines in the tower, pacing the small space that was covered in cammie netting. Their Kevlar helmets could barely be seen over the sides of the tower from where I was watching. They looked like the mushrooms from "Super Mario," pacing back and forth.

Thank God the Eye is on my side. And the mushrooms.

We turned right into the compound, with Sergeant P waving at the solitary Marine in the entryway as we passed. Instead of the concrete barrier entry and exit at Delaram, this compound had giant HESCO barriers filled with sand and dirt that we had to weave through. Dumaw parked the lead vehicle inside what seemed to be a very small staging area and the three other vehicles parked around us. They all shuddered to silence as the engines were turned off. There was faint, painful throbbing in my ears from the sudden lack of sound.

Sergeant P had already leapt out of the vehicle, and I lost sight of him. I struggled briefly with the door, finally leaning against it with my entire body weight until it swung out enough for me to kick it the rest of the way open. Looking at the ground below, I devised a strategy of sliding on my butt down the side of the seat until I could reach the step I had used to clamber into the vehicle. I started to slide down as Sergeant P came around the vehicle, just in time to see me miss the step and topple out.

Striding up to me, he held out a hand and pulled me to my feet. "No one saw, you're good."

"Jesus Christ." *How mortifying! Clearly, I would need to find a different way to deal with these new obstacles, like entering and exiting the fucking vehicle!*

Virkler walked up to us, and Sergeant P waved for us to follow him inside the AUP (Afghan Uniformed Police) Station. All of us pulled off our Kevlar helmets; I clipped mine back onto my flak jacket, as Sergeant P proceeded to give us the grand tour. As we entered the smaller compound, the first thing I noticed was the small rocks. The ground wasn't the typical moon dust that gave way beneath my feet. For the first time in over three months, I had small pebbles of actual stone beneath my boots. The rocks were smooth and flat and varying shades of gray and made a delightful crunch as we walked over them. They were clearly brought here from somewhere else.

"The AUP Station is what used to be the Afghan National Army's general's quarters. When we came in, his house was split into two. They kept half of the house and we have the other half."

"So, you guys share a house?"

"They aren't supposed to be over here, and we aren't supposed to be over there. They don't really like us."

We were walking under a cammie net that partly covered a very small courtyard. The house was directly ahead of us and two large tan tents were to the right of the building. There was a walkway between the tents and the building. Some wooden picnic tables were in the courtyard, and I noticed a small grill that sat next to the building. Next to a picnic table, near the left side of the building, stood a sturdy wooden ladder with large flat steps. The ladder seemed to reach the roof of what appeared to be a two-story building.

Sergeant P led us down the walkway. As we passed the large tents I glanced in to see cots everywhere, some filled with men in various stages of undress, all racked out and asleep. The tent flaps hung limply in the heat.

We reached a door on the right side of the building with an awkwardly designed step.

"Be careful with that step." Sergeant P looked at me with a pointed expression.

"Oh ha, ha." I rolled my eyes, mortified even further.

We entered the house, which was drastically cooler because the walls were rock. There was a room to the immediate right that held two cots. I saw a Marine sitting on one.

"Hey LT, we're back. Here are the two data dinks that are gonna fix comm."

The lieutenant was skinny and when he stood up, I saw that he was very tall, and very young. He had an air of newness and excitement, with the smallest bit of fear and apprehension, and it seemed like he was trying to hide behind the veil of authority.

This is the officer? He's so young. He's so ... proper. Hah. Aren't we all really young? Just a bunch of kids fighting the wars.

I glanced over at Sergeant P as he pulled out a tin of chewing tobacco and shoved a wad between his lower teeth and lip.

As we stood in the hallway, Marines squeezed past us. Sergeant P spoke to each one as they went by, asking about their shifts and their sleep, or if anyone had unloaded the food. The LT ignored them as he shooed us down the hall.

Two very different people. Sergeant P is in charge, he knows his Marines and he cares about them. This kid is in charge on paper. How frustrating it must be for Sergeant P to take orders from a child. Sergeant P is 27, 28? He's already been to Iraq as a grunt at least once. And this kid looks like he's still doing keg-stands with the other frat boys.

Virkler and I were herded into the next room. As we entered the room, there was a long table on the left wall full of radios, a few Toughbook laptops, and one particularly large screen with a joystick below it.

"How long will it take you guys to fix it?"

The LT was looking at us expectantly.

"Uh, well, we need to take a look and see what's wrong first."

Virkler and I avoided each other's eyes because we wouldn't be able to keep from rolling them. We were used to "customers" needing immediate assistance, of course. And this was an extremely important connection. Their Internet was completely down, which wasn't life-threatening, as they had radio communication, but their mission was severely affected by the lack of quick chat with the Combat Operations Center on Delaram. There was no way we could predict how long it would take when we had no idea what was wrong.

Sergeant P walked into the room. "Hey, do y'all need anything?"

"Nah, I think we're good."

"Alright, well, take all your shit off. We are relatively safe here."

Virkler and I threw our packs into a corner and removed our flak jackets. I had to peel my top from my skin; the sweat caused it to stick tightly to me. We were wearing flame resistant organizational gear (FROG) suits, which are designed to not melt to our bodies when we catch fire or explode from an IED. *Too bad the sweat makes it melt to my body anyway.*

FROG suits are super comfortable. The bottoms look a little darker than normal cammie bottoms, but the tops are completely different from our typical cammie top.

The LT stood over us as we began to troubleshoot. Virkler pulled out his Toughbook from his pack and we started verifying connections and settings of the wireless point to point link. I hate nothing more than to have people watch over my shoulder as I troubleshoot. Virkler and I studied the equipment while the LT tapped his foot with impatience.

"Hey LT, can I talk to you for a second?"

Sergeant P motioned the LT over to another side of the room and started talking to him over a map. I caught Sergeant P's eye and mouthed THANK YOU. Sergeant P nodded and kept talking to the LT.

We got the WPPL up within 15 minutes. Virkler and I had climbed onto the roof and verified the direction of the radio shot to Delaram. The station had lost power a few days ago and a few settings of the radio were incorrect when the power came back on.

The LT shot us a quick thanks as he hopped onto the computer and started typing away.

Sergeant P looked at us.

"So, what do we do now?"

Both Virkler and I had hoped he wasn't going to make us go back to Delaram immediately.

"Well, we can't get you two back for a few days so just hang out. Stay out of the way."

All responsibility dropped from my shoulders. Sergeant P turned away and missed the two of us grinning at each other.

20

June 2010, AUP Station in the Town of Delaram, Afghanistan

Virkler and I hung out for a bit and watched the grunts move around. They were switching post duties, eating, and sleeping. Sergeant P mentioned that it was time to conduct their evening patrol through the city. The Marines started to wake each other up and gather their equipment. They looked exhausted and dirty. Virkler and I were relatively well-rested and clean. The men were arguing about who had the least amount of sleep this week so they could avoid the patrol. I immediately felt guilty at the state of my physical well-being and double-checked with Virkler before walking up to Sergeant P.

"Hey, Sergeant P, can we go?"

He looked intensely at me, taking in my thinly veiled excitement. Virkler stood slightly behind me, just as excited. Everyone was looking at each other, until I spoke again. "Every Marine a rifleman, right? And you need Marines." My heart was beating quickly at this chance I was told would never happen.

Sergeant P looked around at his exhausted men. "Decker, Red, go back to sleep."

"Hell yeah!" One of the men fell face first back onto his cot, boots still on, snoring before his head hit the jacket he was using as a pillow. Sergeant P immediately set about getting us ready.

One of the other grunts came up to me carrying a large green box.

"You're Comm, right?"

"Yeah."

"Cool, can you take the radio?"

I mean, I could, yes. But that thing has to weigh a ton and I'm already carrying over 75 pounds. But I can't tell him "no" because I'm "feeling a little overwhelmed with the weight." That will only perpetuate the image of female Marines not being able to keep up with male Marines. Plus, communication IS MY JOB! If I can't communicate on a patrol, what the fuck am I worth? Am I being tested right now?

I was panicking.

"Yeah, of course."

Immediately, I was handed the giant radio to carry. When I felt the weight of the radio in my hands, my heart sank. It weighed about 25 pounds. Suddenly, very grim-faced, I asked Sergeant P how far the patrols were.

"It's just around the town. Three miles? Maybe five, depending on what route we decide to take or if something pops off."

He was running around, making sure everyone's equipment was ready and that everyone had what they needed. The sun was starting to lower in the sky as we moved into the staging area. I shoved the radio into my backpack, did a few radio checks, and sat the pack on the ground while I waited for everyone to be ready.

Sergeant P reached me waiting in line and started adjusting my flak jacket around me. "Damn, this thing is huge on you. Can you even fire a weapon with it on?"

"It's not easy."

"Put up your rifle."

I grabbed my M16, placed the buttstock into my shoulder and drew it up to aim at the HESCO barriers surrounding the compound. The flak jacket was so large and thick that the rifle sat a good inch and a half away from my shoulder. It was awkward. I kept my finger pointed straight and off the trigger.

"Put your finger on the trigger."

The tip of my right trigger finger just barely touched the trigger. My arm was too short.

"What the FUCK! Who gave you an M16 instead of an M4?! You can't reach the goddamn trigger in a combat zone. Hold on."

He left. I fiddled with my rifle, pulling the buttstock out of my shoulder and aiming with the scope much closer to my right eye. I could reach the trigger easily then. If I fired, I knew I would have a black eye from the scope hitting me during the kickback of the rifle. I knew this from when I qualified on the range. A flak jacket and an M16 are not conducive for a short-limbed person to fire effectively. M4s have collapsible buttstocks to be adjustable. I wasn't issued an M4 because I wasn't supposed to be exactly where I was. I didn't rate.

"Ever used a shotgun?"

I wheeled around to see Sergeant P holding a large black shotgun.

"What the heck? No. I've never even seen a Marine with a shotgun."

He loaded the shotgun and handed it to me.

"Aim at whatever you want dead and pull the trigger. Hold it at your hip and watch for the kickback."

I was placed in a squad with Dumaw and two other Marines near the end of the patrol and on the right-hand side. I was carrying my flak, Kevlar, the backpack with the radio, 180 rounds of ammunition, my M16, and a loaded shotgun; roughly 110 pounds in all. It was 120 degrees and the sun was still blazing. Sergeant P glanced around at his Marines.

"Condition 1."

21

June 2010, Town of Delaram, Afghanistan

Sergeant P went over the rules of engagement as everyone placed their rifles in Condition 1. "Remember: Do not engage, even if we are fired upon. Evade fire and wait for further orders."

"We can't fire back?" I was incredulous.

"Nope, we are here to train and protect, not to kill, unless we are in danger."

"Well, that's a load of shit. If I'm being shot at, I would assume I am in danger. Fucking bullshit."

"Keep your eyes open and report anything suspicious to your fire team leader."

The fire teams were four men deep. Sergeant P led the way in the first fire team. As I watched him leave, all I wanted was to be in his group. I waited to hear what my fire team leader would say while we lined up to exit the compound. We were at a different, smaller entryway from the one we'd first entered in the MATV. Marines left two at a time, one on each side of the road. The rest of the platoon filed out and my fire team was the last to go. Dumaw, my fire team leader and the only one with a handheld radio (PRC-153), placed me on the right side of the road; I was staggered across the road and behind him. Owens was behind me and across the road.

As we began to walk through the village, I was already in pain. Marines are supposed to be physically fit. There is a reason grunts train in tough physical conditions with a lot of equipment. That is their job, to be fit killers. POGs don't physically train (PT) like that. If we go on hikes, it is with maybe 25 pounds of equipment and it's for a five-mile stroll in 70-degree weather. Personally, I hadn't PT'ed more than sporadically while I was in the fleet. Our leadership was too concerned with training our brains by sending us to classes. While the classes were necessary to perform our jobs, we had completely neglected the physical portion of our training. In fact, we had exactly one hard physical training session in 2009. A gunnery sergeant took us on a nine-mile run up the coast of California. We had to swim a portion of it and I eventually took off my shoes and just ran barefoot. When we got back to base (with me sans shoes), the command told the gunnery sergeant never to do that to us again. We had hated it and we had loved it ... and it was probably necessary for us to not be weak.

So, there I was, when physical training was necessary, and I was trained on all of the wrong stuff. I had to remember a lot of what I had learned in Marine Combat Training (MCT), from April 2008, and Rear Area Security (RAS) training in December 2009. It was a total of five weeks of combat training that spanned over two years. The technical terms came back quickly enough. I could follow Dumaw's orders and properly scan the area, spinning slowly left and then right with the shotgun in my hands. But physically, I was in a rough spot. Nothing prepares you for that heat. Even the heat of the Mojave Desert, where the Marines train in the U.S., does not equate to the heat of Afghanistan. I took constant sips of water from my CamelBak mule pouch in my backpack.

We walked through the village, mainly alongside walled compounds that had their monotonously sandy mud walls broken by an occasional gate. As we passed one metal and rusted gate, immediately on my right, it creaked open. Three girls—maybe ages five, 11, and 15—gazed wide-eyed at the patrol. They looked at all the men and when their eyes fell on me, they broke into huge smiles and walked out to me. They were barefoot and dressed in long, brightly colored robes that covered every inch of their body. Khamir headscarves fell loosely around their faces. Dark blue, red, and purple—these colors were brighter than anything my eyes had seen in months. They were a stark contrast to their surroundings.

The girls walked up to me quickly and began speaking to me in a language I couldn't speak. Our Afghan interpreter, Stone, was up with Sergeant P. I looked wildly around to see if anyone could translate. The girls touched my skin and my hair, speaking to me the entire time.

"I'm sorry, I don't know what you're saying."

The older one kept gesturing up and down at me and then to the male Marines. Stone walked up to us.

"They have never seen an American woman with blonde hair. Certainly not one who fights like the American men."

The reality of who I was and where I was came crashing down on me. I was representing America, and more importantly, American women. We were women of different cultures, the invading and the invaded, meeting on the side of the road in a war zone. What choices, of ours and of others, led us to this place? What would they think of America after meeting me? What did they endure that I would never understand? What makes them happy? What makes them cry?

More smiles and gestures. The youngest one touched my cheek. Her eyes were bright and kind. I reached into my dump pouch and grabbed three suckers and handed them over. They made thankful noises and touched my arms in thanks.

I looked up and noticed that the patrol had continued to move and Dumaw was stalling for me to catch up.

"Thank you for this. And I'm sorry we are here. I'm so sorry." With that, I turned and ran to catch up with the patrol. The girls stood watching me. I looked back and waved. They smiled and waved back.

I was winded when I got to the guys. I had only fallen behind a few dozen feet but that 110 pounds didn't sprint well. I couldn't catch my breath. As we rounded a street, filled with trash, my body went into the hurt locker.

Fuck, fuck, fuck. My hips. My spine feels compressed. My hips. Fuck.

Suddenly, we were in the marketplace. There were people around, watching us walk past them while they were selling their wares.

The sun had begun to set, and people were moving about in the sudden shade. The smells of the marketplace were both disgusting and aromatic. There were puddles of liquid on the ground and—with no running water—heaven only knows what the liquids were. We were glared at by everyone as we walked by. I noticed Stone speaking to some of the locals.

There was yelling when the townspeople noticed that I was a girl. I was suddenly surrounded by children and, at first, I was pleased. I handed out a few suckers, which was a mistake.

Don't let them take your pen. They can use it to make a bomb. Shit, don't they also swarm people to separate them from their patrols before killing them?

Dumaw shouted at me. "Hey, get away from them! They can kill you! They probably won't, but still, get away!"

Stories from Iraq that I had heard throughout the years swelled in my mind. The kids were as young as two and the oldest around 15 and much taller than me. They were all laughing, but suddenly they started to grab at me, pulling on my equipment and my radio and yanking all of the suckers out of my pouch and dumping them on the ground. Terrified, I looked in panic at Dumaw.

"Get out!"

"I'm trying!"

I was trying to walk out of the crowd, but I was stepping on little feet and the crowd of kids kept growing. I slapped the hands of a few children who were grabbing at my loaded rifle dangling down, since my hands were filled with the shotgun.

They are going to use my own weapon on me!

The rest of the patrol heard the ruckus behind them. Sergeant P started running toward me. Before he was halfway back to me, Dumaw and Owens ran up to me, smacking the kids and yelling at them to go away. The kids scattered.

We started again, but the kids kept coming back to me. If they got too close, I raised the shotgun in their direction and yelled for them to go away. My finger slid onto the trigger.

I'm aiming a gun at children. I am a woman aiming a gun at children.

Suddenly gunshots rang out. Sergeant P yelled for us to change direction. We immediately sprinted down a few streets to where the gunshots originated.

I heard the crunch of the rocky sand underneath my feet as I ran, my flak jacket bounced up and down on my hips, and I stopped paying attention to my surroundings. I went completely internal to try not to collapse. My lungs could barely expand as I ran. The protective equipment pressed on me so heavily that I could only feel the pain and not the terror that we were actually running toward gunfire. We stopped running and Dumaw made us crouch down and provide cover while Sergeant P went to talk to the Afghan National Army who were there.

I felt a single tear leak out from my eyes as I crouched. I was unsure if I would be able to stand again. We were three and a half miles into the patrol.

We sat in this position for over ten minutes. The sun sank lower in the sky.

"Psst." Dumaw was trying to catch my attention from across the road. I nodded that I was listening.

"How are you doing?"

"I'm good."

"You sure?"

I thought long and hard about my answer and didn't respond. Silence was better than accepting defeat …. *Fuck.*

Sergeant P walked up to Dumaw and after talking for a few seconds, came back to me. "Give me the radio."

"Nah, I'm good."

I'm not good.

"You don't look like you're good. We still have to get back. Give me the radio."

Embarrassed, I slid my backpack from my back and handed over the radio. It was given to Virkler, a few fire teams ahead of me. I felt a thousand pounds lighter (aside from the added guilt of failure), and I could walk without too much trouble. Without knowing what the gunshots were for, we walked a few more miles back to our compound and entered safely in almost complete darkness. The men scattered to get water and food.

I pulled off my equipment and threw it onto a cot. Virkler snapped a blurry picture of me in all of my sweaty glory—the glory of surviving my first patrol.

"Hell yeah! We survived!"

Virkler and I high-fived.

"DEBRIEF IN FIVE!"

22

June 2010, AUP Station in the Town of Delaram, Afghanistan

I pulled my FROG top out of my pants to let my body breathe. My entire outfit was soaked and dark with sweat. Feeling pain when the material was pulled from my hips, I unbuttoned my cammie bottoms and shimmied them down around my thighs. I gently pulled my green skivvies away from my hips and glanced down, unwilling to look at what I might find. My skin was completely black and blue, broken open in areas and bloody.

"What's up?" Virkler walked up as I gingerly replaced the skivvy waistband and pulled my pants back up.

"Nothing."

Virkler studied me before attempting to get me to admit the truth. "That fucking flak jacket hurts, doesn't it?"

"Yeah, so should we go to the debrief?"

"Well, yeah, we *were* on the patrol, Cannon."

"Hey, smart ass, thanks for taking the radio."

"Sure thing. Was it too heavy?"

"I was suffering after those sprints. I'm sorry."

"It's cool, don't worry about it. It certainly wasn't light."

We walked over to where the Marines were gathering in front of Sergeant P.

"Alright, gents, the gunfire was over by the blue building to the west. It's probably just someone celebrating. The ANA won't tell us much, so we will patrol later tonight and see if we can get more informat—"

There was shouting from the Marines at the Entry Control Point (ECP). "Hey, we got a situation!"

Sergeant P strode over to the ECP and everyone followed. Confusion began to take over as Marines ran around and began grabbing their equipment.

"They are dead!"

"Who?"

No one would answer us, so we grabbed our shit, threw it back on, and headed out. Just outside the ECP, one of ANA's green pickup trucks was parked facing the entryway. Sergeant P was yelling at people to spread out and provide cover. We were just outside the compound, milling around—a complete cluster fuck of Marines yelling and confused. It was pitch black outside and the only light came from Marines' flashlights.

I walked to the back of the truck and as I circled it, I noticed that the tailgate was down and everyone was looking inside. Sergeant P, the interpreter, and two ANA members were talking among themselves and occasionally glancing at the truck. As I rounded the tailgate, a stream of light crossed over the back and I saw a brown foot. It was dirty, the bottom whiter than the top; the toenails were dark and hadn't been cut in a while. The foot was hanging to the right, like the man was just lying down and relaxed.

My stomach lurched. I had to see more.

Stone was rapidly translating to Sergeant P and as I got closer, he began translating to me.

"They were on a bus going from Iran to Pakistan. They were fleeing. The Taliban stopped the bus, put a gun to the driver's head, and forced these men off. They lined them on the side of the road and—"

His voice trailed off as he gestured to the bodies. The three men were awkwardly stacked in the back of the truck. They were dressed in white and gray, and the blood was seeping from four distinct points on their bodies.

My voice shook as I asked what happened next.

"They just shot them?"

Stone spoke to the ANA and then back to us. "They made them kneel, then shot them in the knees, one by one. The men were screaming and didn't speak the language of the men claiming to be the Taliban. They couldn't answer them so they were shot more."

His eyes followed mine. The men's arms were awkwardly bent. He spoke softly. "They made the men hold out their arms and they smashed their arms in at the elbows before shooting them in the head. They suffered a lot."

My eyes welled up and bile rose in my throat.

Sergeant P kept asking questions: "How did you get them?"

"They pulled over the first car that drove by, it was a taxi, and told the driver to drop the bodies at the closest American base as a warning. The driver was scared shitless. They threatened to kill his entire family if he didn't deliver."

I forced myself to look at the men. They looked so broken, all humanity stripped from them as they lay stacked in the back of a fucking pickup truck. Blood dripped from one of the bodies and pooled at the bottom of the truck. They were young, probably in their twenties, with full beards. They were tan and looked clean, besides their feet and the obvious blood.

They were just riding on a bus and were randomly picked off and tortured? What the fuck? How fucking terrible must the Taliban be to senselessly torture and murder completely innocent people? The Taliban aren't protecting their people at all. They are fucking murderers and deserve to be killed. I'm not surprised it's easier for the grunts to kill. This is madness. These men did nothing.

My nose began to drip from my attempt to hold back the tears of anger and frustration and sadness. I furiously wiped the snot away with my sleeve and sniffed.

"You okay?" Sergeant P looked at me carefully.

"Yeah, I'm good. What do we do now?"

What do we do? Keep moving. What's next? Blank everything out. Just focus on what's next.

"We will take them and see if we can identify them. We report it and try to find their families."

"Alright, then let's get them out."

Two Marines hopped into the back of the truck. As they reached for the first man, the ANA members began yelling and hitting the Marines.

"Ow, what the fuck!"

The terp spoke quickly. "No man who is not Muslim can touch a Muslim body. Only women and Muslims."

He gestured to me.

Uh, excuse me? What the hell kind of a rule is this? I have to do this?

Marines were all around us, still in a confused state.

"Hey, what the fuck, guys, everyone get back inside." Sergeant P scolded everyone who was walking around in a mass gaggle of disorder, trying to catch a glimpse of the bodies.

I caught Virkler's eye as he was told to go back inside. He looked pissed. Sergeant P and I looked at each other. My face must have had a look of horror. I climbed up into the back of the truck with one of the ANA, while struggling with all my equipment and flinging my rifle behind me.

As I climbed up, a Marine walked up. I think he was a Radio staff sergeant who had joined Virkler and me from RCT-2. When he saw the bodies, he became very excited and pulled something from his pocket. "Hey, man, shine the light at their faces; I want to get a pic of all of that blood." He was excitedly snapping pictures of these men in the most vulnerable positions, with their arms bent backward, their eyes wide open in horror and their mouths in strange grimaces of pain. "The guys back home are going to love these."

He sounded so elated. I was furious and didn't give a shit if he was a staff sergeant.

"Hey, knock it the fuck off, they are dead! Do you have no respect? What the fuck is wrong with you?"

"But this is so cool!"

I knocked his arm to stop him from taking more photos. The last picture I saw him capture was one of the men's waists, the front stained yellow. *He pissed himself, he was so scared.*

"Knock it the fuck off!" My anger transferred from the Taliban, who had murdered these men, to the American man in front of me, who was laughing and grabbing souvenirs. I shoved him hard away from the truck, swinging a kick at him and missing. I almost fell onto the dead men from where I was standing on the tailgate. Sergeant P glanced over and told the staff sergeant to go inside, before turning to talk to Stone.

I wanted to take my rifle and smash it in the staff sergeant's face.

I grabbed the first man's ankles and pulled hard. The body was stiffening and getting him off of the other two men was difficult. His body kept catching on theirs. The ANA member was holding the shoulders, arms underneath the armpits. I jumped down and kept pulling. When the weight of the man was mostly on me, the ANA guy swung to the side, jumped down, and we slid the body off the tailgate. Awkwardly struggling with the weight, I felt my flak dig into the bruises on my hips. We carried him to a body bag that had been placed along the wall. One by one, we got the men out of the truck. One by one, they were placed into body bags. One by one, I searched their bodies for IDs, feeling invasive as I patted them down. Only one had anything on him. I handed the small flat wallet to Sergeant P, who studied it with Stone.

I walked up to the bodies and, one by one, forced their eyelids closed. I tried forcing the jaw closed, of the one screaming in horror, but rigor mortis had set in. He remained screaming.

I zipped up the bags and walked back inside the AUP station without saying a word to anyone.

23

June 2010, AUP Station in the Town of Delaram, Afghanistan

My heart changed after I saw those men and the torture they had experienced in the name of war? Oil? Family? Religion? Unbridled hate? Mental illness? It made no sense to me.

In Afghanistan, less than two years after my high school graduation, I was seeing the ruins of men who had probably never driven a five-speed recklessly through the countryside, who had never gone streaking on their high school football field, who had never picked honeysuckle from the vine and sucked its sweet juices from the flower. I didn't know what it was like to grow up in a land of sand and stale sweat. I knew nothing of them but what the insides of their elbows looked like. But I knew they felt the same fear that I did. I knew they felt pain. And I knew that my disgust with the human race, including myself, would only grow.

I'm not sure what happened when I walked back inside the compound. I probably wandered back to the cot that held my pack and unhooked my flak. I'm sure I grabbed water and maybe some food, since I hadn't eaten since breakfast. Maybe I talked to Virkler about the men. I don't know. I was so inside my own head, seeing the men's screaming eyes and broken bodies; I was just going through the motions. I was trying to contemplate the circumstances of death and … why. This was no longer training. It was no longer something I heard about as tales from seasoned Marines. The war was real now.

I wanted to throw up. I wanted to run. I wanted to be held. I wanted to cry and hold their broken bodies.

And I wanted to kill. I wanted to use my thumbs to poke into the eye sockets of the men who murdered the innocent civilians. I wanted to see their eyes ripped out of their sockets while they screamed and to know that I did it and that they felt pain for what they did. An eye for an eye makes the world blind? I didn't fucking care. I was reduced to the same primal hate that caused those murderers to kill.

When Sergeant P said we were going to conduct a night patrol within an hour, I was ready.

24

June 2010, AUP Station in the Town of Delaram, Afghanistan

"You're staying here."

I looked around at the other Marines. They all shook their heads and averted their gaze. Sergeant P was firm as I pleaded with him to go. "This is bullshit. Just let me use someone else's NVGs."

"You don't have NVGs, you don't go."

Night vision goggles. NVGs. Yet another piece of equipment I hadn't been issued to deploy to Afghanistan. My equipment was too large, too inhibiting, or non-existent. I looked over at Virkler. He looked at me with a bit of pity and smugness. "You weren't given NVGs?"

"I was originally part of a logistics group. Why would they waste NVGs on a bunch of fobbits?" A fobbit was a derogatory term for someone who never left the FOB (Forward Operating Base) and just got fat from the chow hall food safe inside the wire.

"Sucks for you!" Virkler was giddy. I was upset. Sergeant P was firm.

"Come on, Sergeant P, this is bullshit. You guys get to have all the fun."

"You can stay here, at the ECP, and provide cover while we move out."

Brow furrowed, I accepted my fate for my lack of bullshit equipment. *Who needs NVGs anyway? We have flashlights. Just shine a light on those motherfuckers.* I'm pretty sure I kicked rocks in frustration as I grabbed my flak and Kevlar.

When I met back up with the Marines who were going on the patrol, I felt distant from them. They were arranging their fire teams, conducting gear checks, and smoking. As Sergeant P reminded us of the rules of engagement, I was surly.

"Cannon, come here." Sergeant P beckoned me to the front of the line to join him and a Marine whose name I didn't catch.

"Lights off. Condition 1."

Suddenly pitched into darkness, we exited the compound and passed the staggered HESCO barriers. We walked to the wall that lined the street. The wall's opening was big enough for our vehicles to enter and exit, but with less than a foot of room on each side of the vehicle. I tripped on the slight hill down to the wall, but I covered the sounds of my trip with a quick cough. Sergeant P placed me on the right of the wall opening and the other Marine on the left.

"Look down the road to the left. He will look down the road to the right. If you see anything suspicious, yell. Watch out for cars that might roll up with their lights off. They will blind you when they flick the lights on and ambush you. Stay behind the wall. Be safe. We will be back around occasionally."

The other Marines filed out in twos, disappearing down the road into pitch black. The other Marine and I stood in silence, just behind the wall that was 62 inches tall. Exactly 62 inches.

Ho-ly. Shit. I can't see anything.

"Hey! Hey!" I harsh-whispered to the Marine across the eight-foot opening in the wall.

"What?"

"Can you see anything?"

"Yeah, I have NVGs. Don't you remember how to see in the dark? Didn't they teach you that?"

Marines are taught how to see effectively in the dark without the use of NVGs. I remembered the four-minute period of instruction from two years prior. "Since everyone is issued NVGs, this doesn't really matter anymore, but maybe you'll need to know this if your batteries fail." *Fantastic.* I struggled to remember what I was taught.

Completely immerse yourself in darkness. Cover one of your eyes and slightly close the other. Let the slightly open eye focus on an object that you know exists. Gradually open that eye, and then repeat with your second eye.

I felt my pupils dilate painfully as I strained to see. If someone shined a flashlight in my eyes, or flicked on headlights, I would be blinded. Hell, the other Marine would be blinded worse. NVGs collect and expand limited light, so full light could burn the eyeballs of anyone wearing them.

The moon was small and distant, but it allowed me to see some stuff. I began to notice the edges of the buildings around us. There was a rooftop across the street and directly in front of me. I could see the rooftop over the wall that I was behind.

There was a noise down the street and the other Marine and I swung our rifles up and faced the noise. I couldn't see anything.

"It's someone running between the buildings. Probably kids fucking with us."

We waited with our rifles engaged for a few minutes before I swung back to "look" down my side of the street. I gazed into darkness.

When was the last time I peed? I haven't peed since .... I did some calculations. Holy shit it's been almost 24 hours. I'm dehydrated.

I picked up my CamelBak nozzle and guzzled some water.

Too much. That was too much.

The sound of someone running toward us washed over us. I wasn't scared. I knew that run. It was Sergeant P running through the streets of this town in darkness, by himself. His run wasn't frantic, it was steady and full of purpose.

He just ran away from the patrol, by himself. What a crazy motherfucker. He must know these streets like the back of his hand.

"Hey, y'all doing okay here?"

"Yeah, we are good, it's decently qui—"

Gunshots rang out.

"GET DOWN, GET DOWN, DOWN DOWN DOWN!"

I felt 260 pounds slam into my body and shove me to the ground, landing on me. The water in my stomach sloshed and my head cracked against the wall. Sergeant P leapt back up with his rifle pointed at the rooftop across the street. I looked up just in time to see a flash of white fleeing.

"GET THE FUCK BACK HERE, YOU COWARDLY MOTHERFUCKER!"

Sergeant P was livid. I couldn't breathe. Two hundred and sixty pounds is a lot to take at a full tackle. I got to my feet shaken and engaged my rifle toward anything I could see. If red is the color of anger, and blue is the color of calmness, white is the color of fear. I could suddenly see everything sharpened and clear and bright, like a floodlight had been cast over the scene.

Catching my breath, I choked on the air and my words. "What the fuck was that?"

Sergeant P was yelling into his radio. "Target headed toward the west edge, fleeing the rooftop across from the compound. Move in that direction and watch yourselves."

He yelled at me as he ran away. "Stay the FUCK DOWN."

The other Marine was stunned: "He was aiming at your head."

That wall was 62 inches tall. With my boots and Kevlar on, I was 64 inches.

25

June 2010, AUP Station in the Town of Delaram, Afghanistan

Were the gunshots aimed at my head? I don't know. I don't think so. I didn't hear anything whiz past me, like in the movies. All I saw was a flash of white fabric. I couldn't see a rifle; I couldn't see his face. My lack of NVGs could've meant that I would have never seen the person who killed me. The Taliban are known for being really bad at shooting. They are cowards. They don't aim at their targets; they are seen hiding behind cover and wildly firing into the air or in the general direction of their target. So, was I in any danger? I don't know.

The gunshots could have been on the other side of the building, towards where Sergeant P ran. Regathering my breath, I crouched down behind the wall and looked up the street. The other Marine, also crouched down, looked in the opposite direction. We were both silent.

I wonder if the guy aiming at me saw my head barely over the wall. I wonder if he knew I was a girl. I wonder if he was trying to kill me or if he was just trying to scare an American. I wonder if he was one of the kids from the street. I wonder if he was angry and filled with hate.

In the years since this happened, I have put myself in his shoes, looking down at me and aiming. Maybe I looked like a mushroom to him, or just an easy target. I was angry with myself for allowing the top of my head to be silhouetted over the wall. That's the easiest way to be targeted. If I had been hit, it would've been my fault.

I wonder if the bullet would have connected with my head. I wonder if my Kevlar would have held up to the gunshot. I wonder if I'd have headaches from the Kevlar cracking open my skull from the impact of the gunshot, if I survived. I wonder if my husband would be upset when he heard. I wonder if Staff Sergeant Rambo would be pissed at me. I wonder if they would cover it up to prevent backlash from me being out there. What if Sergeant P hadn't been there?

My mind was numb and racing. After a time, the patrol came back. They were excited. I walked back inside the compound and went off to be alone. When the debriefing happened, I wasn't present, and no one came to get me.

It was about 0100 when the night patrol wrapped up. With the sun down, it was a brisk 110 degrees. The tent that held the cot I had claimed was stuffy. When I finally walked into it after the patrol, Virkler was setting up his cot to sleep. The sadistic staff sergeant who laughed while taking pictures of the dead was on the cot next to mine.

Fuck this. I don't want to be in here.

The tent smelled of dirty sweat and I couldn't breathe. Walking outside, I found Sergeant P. "Hey, is there anywhere else I can sleep? Literally anywhere away from that fuck."

"Not really, all of the Marines are crammed in the other tent and they live like animals. Me and a few others have our own tent, but it's also crowded."

I looked around. I would sleep anywhere, even on the picnic table if I could. "What about the roof?"

"You wanna sleep on the roof? Alone?"

"Virkler will probably come too. It smells like ass in that tent."

"I mean, sure. No one goes up there anyway."

"Thanks."

He watched me walk off. I wanted to sleep next to him, but it wasn't proper, and people would talk. I doubted I would ever feel safe again if he wasn't around. I grabbed my stuff and told Virkler I was going to the roof, and he could come if he wanted to.

"Yes!"

We climbed the ladder to the roof and laid out our sleeping bags next to each other on the dirt. The roof wasn't flat—there were large mounds and valleys of dirt. When we laid down, our feet and heads were elevated, and our butts were at the bottom in the rut. We sat awake for a little while and talked. I took another picture of him.

When the flash from the camera went off, I panicked. "Shit, that probably wasn't the best idea, huh?"

"Uh, no, now everyone knows we are up here."

"Oh god, that flash of light."

I collapsed into a fit of laughter, almost delirious. Virkler started to laugh, and we fell asleep laughing and looking up at the stars.

26

June 2010, AUP Station in the Town of Delaram, Afghanistan

I woke up with a jolt.

The sun hadn't broken the horizon, but the sky was bright pink and blue. I glanced at my watch and saw that it was 0445. I reached up with my hands and scraped the giant clots of sand from the corners of my eyes. It was painful to grab the sand that had turned into a binding mud on my eyelashes. Throughout the night, dust and sand had settled over us, coating us in a layer of dirt. This dirt collected inside of our ears, noses, eyes, and mouths as we slept. The first thing we had to do upon waking up was clear our eyes, lick the grit from our teeth, and wipe the goobie mess on our cammies. It didn't matter if you slept inside a tent or on a roof, that fine sand was inescapable.

I sat up aching, my hips on fire. I did a quick assessment of my injuries and noted that the bleeding had stopped on my hips, but my cammies were welded to them from the blood. I started to peel the material away and then stopped. No need to rouse an infection. Virkler was still asleep but as I started to stir, he woke up and stared at me rustling around.

I asked him, "Did you sleep well?"

"Best three hours of sleep in my life."

"Yeah, I love these sand boogers." I was digging into my right eye.

"Right."

"No, really, it's satisfying to clean them out."

"Yeah, I can see that."

As we packed up the sleeping bags that we had laid on, I glanced over the edge of the building. Marines were milling about already below us. I could see the Afghan boys' school behind the compound. The girls' school didn't exist.

Climbing back down the ladder, we entered the radio room looking for Sergeant P. Two Marines were on radio watch. They glanced up as we walked in.

"Hey, seen Sergeant P yet?"

"Yeah, he's around. Dude never sleeps."

The giant video game-looking console with the joystick no longer had a black screen. When I glanced at it, one of the Marines scrambled to move the joystick.

"You ... you were watching us sleep?"

"We were watching the village."

"Uh, that thing was pointed directly to where we were sleeping. You were spying on us?"

"Come on, you guys slept on the roof. A girl, a guy, sleeping together .... What else were we going to do?"

"Uh, I dunno, watch the goddamn war zone instead of two fellow Marines?!"

The second Marine interrupted us. "Hey, should we show her?"

"Nah." They both hesitated and trailed off awkwardly.

"Oh, hell no. You're showing me. You watched me sleep all night. You owe me. And what the hell is this thing?"

"It's a GBOSS. Ground based operational surveillance system. The tower is on the roof. You control the 360 camera with the joystick. You can also take videos of activity."

"Oh, that's cool." *Did they get a video of me sleeping? Creepy.* I started moving the joystick around.

"Hey, Virkler, look, you can see Camp Delaram from here! I think I can see our compound!"

The guys on radio watch were relieved that I had apparently forgotten what they were going to not show me. Without my eyes leaving the screen, I spoke again. "So, what were you going to show me?"

"Uh—"

"Think I can't handle it?" I laughed. The thought of me not being able to handle something after the previous night was laughable.

"Fine, just don't tell anyone we showed you."

The Marine pulled out a laptop and navigated to a folder of GBOSS videos. As it began to play, my eyes had to adjust to the night camera lighting.

The camera zoomed in on a man standing behind a large animal near what seemed to be a housing building. He was grasping the flanks of an ox/bull/bison/cow. As his hips pumped away, my brain registered what my eyes were seeing, and I was disgusted. I couldn't look away.

"See? We call them goat fuckers for a reason."

"But … why isn't the animal fighting back? How is he not being bucked or kicked off? Isn't the cow in pain?"

"It probably likes it."

The other Marine butted in. "Yeah, because animals like being fucked in the ass just like you, man."

Everyone laughed. Sergeant P walked in. "Put that shit up."

"Yes, Sergeant."

"Cannon, we are taking you and the others back to Delaram. We leave in 30."

"Aw, man." I was seriously bummed. This was the first place I wasn't treated differently. The grunts treated me almost like a sister.

Oh well, back to Delaram, where I am a leper.

The convoy back to Delaram was uneventful. I felt extremely safe behind the bulletproof doors I could now swing shut with ease. I felt cocooned and comfortable with the weight of the doors, with Owens in the turret, with Sergeant P in front of me. Unless someone hit us with an IED, I was the safest I had been since leaving Camp Leatherneck. I wouldn't even have minded an IED. The bottom of the MATV could sustain a blast. My Kevlar probably would've shattered to bits with that gunshot.

I allowed my mind to wander on the drive. As we bounced through the sand, a realization came to me slowly. Panicking, I tried not to think about it, but the thought forced itself to the surface and made itself known.

My period is late.

27

2017, California, U.S.A.

This morning, on my way to work, I was jamming out to some 80s rock while at a stoplight, waiting to take a left turn. A really old RV, with the usual yellow, tan, and orange stripes so typical of RVs from the 80s, pulled up next to me. The driver was a scraggly old man with long white hair who looked stoned out of his gourd, which was impressive before six in the morning, but probably not so impressive for the part of town I lived in. As the RV shuddered to a stop, it backfired with a loud pop.

My heart rate instantly spiked, and I felt a sparkly pain travel from my stomach to the bottoms of my feet and fingertips. The pain lasted for about 30 seconds as I calmed myself.

It's just a vehicle that backfired, calm down, breathe, calm down.

After the initial panic, I had to work to rid my body of the intense pain radiating through it. The "fight or flight" response to danger is talked about often, but I never hear anyone discuss how PAINFUL it is to resist the flow of adrenaline as it courses through your body.

It took me a long time to realize that I had post-traumatic stress disorder from Afghanistan. Of course, my anxiety and depression had increased after I came back, but I just chalked it up to how shitty my personal life was while ignoring the other signs of PTSD. I tried to rationalize my behavior and made excuses like: "Well, I wasn't shot at every day." Well, yeah, not every day, but there were days. And we were mortared constantly. In fact, the Navy Seabees were building an airstrip to replace the giant rock the Osprey had landed on when I was originally dropped at Delaram. The explosions from their dynamite were so frequent and so close that we became accustomed to the explosions and eventually stopped taking cover when we were mortared because we couldn't tell the difference.

After a while, you become numb to the danger you are in. Your guard is constantly up, but it eventually goes down because your body can't live in a constant state of "fight or flight." Multiple studies have shown how constant stress harms the hippocampus by disabling its ability to remodel or properly react to dangerous situations.[1]

I am not a scientist, but after reading about the constant stress that combat veterans experience, it is clear why they might become robotic in dangerous situations. Our hippocampi are damaged for years, sometimes for life, and we can't react "properly" to dangerous situations. Sometimes we laugh, sometimes we shut down and go completely internal, and sometimes we "fight or flight."

Veterans must work to regain a sense of normalcy with their damaged brains when they re-enter civilian life back in the U.S. We are no longer "in danger," but our brains don't know that, and we might overreact to regular events such as a slammed door, or a vehicle backfiring, or a dropped book, or any noise that we aren't prepared for.

About three months after I got back from Afghanistan, I was driving down a highway in California when I heard a mortar. There was a long whistle that got louder and louder and louder, and I freaked the fuck out, almost losing complete control of the car I was driving at 60 miles an hour. In the seconds that I heard the whistle, in the seconds my body had to react, I remember thinking: "What the FUCK, this is impossible, I'm in the U.S. Where the fuck is it going to hit … Slam on the brakes, *get away!*"

When the explosion occurred and the car salesman's voice came over the radio exclaiming how "explosive" their savings were this Veterans Day weekend, I pulled over and bawled. My hands had gripped the steering wheel so hard they were sore for a week.

I will always doubt I have a right to be damaged from my experiences in Afghanistan. However, even if other people had it worse, which they did, and even if I wasn't having to dodge bullets daily, I need to learn that my body has reacted and adapted to the dangerous situations I was in. And if my body feels that way, I can't ignore it because "someone else has it worse." I am living with a damaged brain.

---

[1] What Is the Functional Significance of Chronic Stress-Induced CA3 Dendritic Retraction Within the Hippocampus? *Behavioral Cognitive Neuroscience Review,* Author manuscript; available in PMC 2006, Jul 18. Published in final edited form as: *Behavioral Cognitive Neuroscience Review,* 2006 Mar; 5(1): 41–60. doi: 10.1177/1534582306289043.

28

June 2010, Camp Delaram, Afghanistan

I waved to Sergeant P as he climbed back into the MATV to leave Delaram. "We make trash runs here occasionally and drop by to get food or water. I'm sure I'll see you around." He grinned at me, and I smiled back at him.

Seeing those MATVs leave, I felt like I was watching my family drive off after they'd dropped me on the side of the road. I felt closer to them than any stuck-up Marines from RCT-2. Virkler and I were becoming fast friends, of course, but his friendship with Ski made me wary. Sergeant P and the guys had no connections to anyone else I knew. They were not from my past or my present. The grunts were like an oasis from the shitty deployment I had experienced thus far. I couldn't wait to see them again.

As Virkler and I walked up to the compound to report back in to Staff Sergeant Rambo, I became tense. William would be around, I was sure, smoking his cigarettes and grinning at me as I walked up. Of course, he was. He was always around. As we walked past, he motioned for me to come over.

"I have to check in!" I yelled and kept walking, looking at the ground as I passed him.

It's nice someone's looking for me, after months of everyone avoiding me. William actively keeps an eye out for me. He cares.

When Virkler and I entered the tent, things looked as usual, with Marines sitting around fiddling with equipment. Everyone ran to Virkler and asked him about the quick four-day trip, ignoring me. As the Marines all smacked Virkler on the arm and bugged him for all the details from the patrols, he was reaccepted into their fold, and I went to speak to Rambo. "Checking in, Staff Sergeant."

"How did it go out there? Everything good?"

"Yeah, it went great."

"Good, it seemed like an easy fix for you guys."

"Yeah."

"How were the grunts? I didn't want to send you out there."

"Oh, they were great. Seriously. I loved it."

"Did you do anything dangerous?"

"No, Staff Sergeant."

"Good. No sense in putting yourself in danger out there."

"Don't be afraid to send me back out, Staff Sergeant. I'm a Marine."

"You'll probably be needed. If that went well, then I could use you on a few more things coming up. But no promises. You're still not supposed to be outside the wire."

"Yes, Staff Sergeant, thank you."

"You're back on night shift tonight with Virkler. Go grab some sleep."

I passed the word along to Virkler before heading out. He stayed to talk to the other guys. I, however, was bone tired and dreaded the conversation I needed to have with William.

"Hey, how did it go?"

"Great. It was great."

"Good. Knew it would be simple for you."

No sense in telling anyone about the near-death experiences and horrific scenes of torture, right? Just push everything down.

"I've missed my period."

William's face lit up with excitement as he grabbed my arms.

"Are you serious? This is fantastic! Plus, I knew it. I'm great at making babies."

"What? No, it's not fantastic. I could be pregnant. I have three and a half more months out here ... you know, in a combat zone."

"You'll just go home immediately."

I was stunned. The quickness and simplicity with which he answered shocked me. I couldn't believe he was so blasé about this huge, life-changing thing. He was someone I had known for a month, and he was treating my possible pregnancy almost like a planned event.

"William, I don't know what I'm supposed to do. This isn't okay. Me going home isn't okay. I won't even have a home."

"Look, I'll order some tests. We'll know for sure soon."

"You'll order them? That won't look suspicious? A male contractor ordering pregnancy tests?"

"They don't check our mail, sweetheart."

He was so smug.

When I got to my can, I grabbed my shower stuff, made the trek to the spotless showers, and scrubbed down quickly, avoiding the wounds on my hips. I felt a billion pounds lighter only carrying my rifle and shampoo. No flak and Kevlar. No ammunition. No patrols.

I was asleep before my head hit the pillow. I had no dreams, but there was a vague sensation of how I felt when Sergeant P smiled at me before he left.

When I woke up, I went to work in the stark reality of what my life had become. My concern about being pregnant was going to be delayed for a few weeks at the earliest. Mail was ridiculously slow in Afghanistan. I hadn't received any mail in the two months I had been on Delaram. Either people weren't sending me anything, or the mail was being held at Camp Leatherneck. Either way, I knew that packages I had ordered while on Camp Leatherneck, a major Marine base, had taken 4–6 weeks to arrive. So, I went to work thinking through all the possible logistics of being pregnant, but only hypothetically, because there was no proof—just dread. I was forced to be patient.

Imagine my surprise when William approached me with a small brown package less than a week later.

"How the heck did it get here so quickly?"

"It was just fast."

This is impossible. Did he order them from Leatherneck? The British are at Camp Bastion right next to Leatherneck. Maybe they have a different view of pregnancy than the American military and keep these things handy. The British hospital IS there. That's probably it. That has to be it. But how did he get someone to send them?

Tons of red flags began to form but I ignored them. I had the answer to my dreaded question in the small brown box in my hands. All I had to do was find out for certain what I already sensed was true.

"I got a few different types. Sometimes they don't always come up positive on the first go."

"Then I guess I'll go find out."

"Have to pee already? You should probably wait until you first wake up. The hormones are more concentrated in your urine then."

"I'm going now."

We walked off to the first bathroom I could find. It was a tent with two rows of toilets in the center. Each toilet was elevated over a foot in the air on a weird wooden platform and separated by canvas flaps. There were no doors to the "stalls."

I climbed up onto the platform and sat on the toilet. I felt like I was on a giant throne. I opened the package and pulled out the first pregnancy test I could see. There were four tests and two bottles of prenatal vitamins.

My hands shook as I opened the test. As I peed, I looked down at the test in my trembling hand. The plus sign appeared within three seconds.

Emotions collided.

I'm pregnant! I'm having a baby! This is all I ever wanted! Oh god, a squishy baby with rolls like Amy has. A baby to love and raise and … I'm married. To someone who doesn't want to raise another man's child. And I'm in a fucking combat zone for three more months! How do I hide this, so I'm not charged and arrested? How do I protect this baby? What if I'm shot at again? Well, hell, she made it through a few other shitty times. She's already a badass! She has to be a she. Amy would want a sister. How the hell am I going to do this?

I scrambled to get everything together before dashing out to William.

"It's positive!"

He grabbed me in a giant hug and swung me around. "This is great! I knew it. Just you wait. I make awesome babies. This is so … amazing. Isn't it?" He was smiling down at me, holding me close and squeezing me.

"Yeah, completely."

The thought of life filling my womb was exciting, overwhelming … it was everything I had ever wanted.

"Well, you have to start taking those vitamins immediately. And eat healthy. And drink lots of water. And sleep."

And not be in a combat zone.

I fell asleep grinning.

Push it down. Push everything bad down.

The vice grip on my life tightened.

29

June 2010, Camp Delaram, Afghanistan

Boots dangling off of the black metal footboard of my bed, I propped the pillows I had stolen from empty cans behind my head and pulled my laptop onto my stomach. I couldn't put my boots on the white comforter. Putting my feet on the bed would get the place where I slept all sandy, and all I wanted was to be far from the sand that permeated everything.

Opening a Word document, my hands hovered over the keyboard, waiting to form what I wanted to say, the words that ached in my heart:

> Dearest Baby of Mine,
>
> Welcome to the world! You are so loved and wanted by your mother and your father. I'm already so amazed at what you have been through. You are definitely going to be tough! I can't wait to hold you in my arms and kiss your sweet cheeks. You are currently about five weeks along and your due date is March 9th, 2011. I can't wait for you to meet your sister, Amy. I bet your thighs will be just as chunky as hers are. You'll be a year and three months younger than she is. I bet you'll be fast friends.
>
> Baby, you are so loved. We would do anything for you.
>
> I love you and I'll see you soon.
>
> Love,
> Your Mom

I saved the document as "To My Baby" on my external hard drive. I closed the laptop and placed it on the floor next to the bed.

I'll just close my eyes for a minute.

I fell asleep with my boots still on and dangling in sandy space.

30

June 2010, Camp Delaram, Afghanistan

"Cannon, you and Virkler are going back to the AUP station."

"Yes, Staff Sergeant." I could barely contain my grin.

"They need CENTRIXS installed. Bear will join you guys with the crypto."

There are multiple networks that the Marine Corps uses in Afghanistan. NIPR is the unclassified network, where you can access Facebook and Gmail and other such sites. SIPR is the secret network, where secret communications are held. CENTRIXS is the NATO network for secret communications between NATO countries. All NATO countries were supposed to support CENTRIXS at their locations. Now, no one actually used CENTRIXS to communicate, but hey, we were supposed to support the requirements. I picked up the layer 3 switch and the encryption device. I could fit the encryption device in my backpack, but I had to carry the giant switch.

Boots, flak, Kevlar, ammo, CamelBak, backpack, FROG suit, dump pouch, IFAK, rifle, switch. Zero suckers.

Never giving suckers out ever again.

Ninety-five pounds this time.

As I left the compound, I practically skipped down the hill to the grunts' vehicles, excited to be back with the grunts who liked me, excited to be around Sergeant P's assuredness. I had known that I was pregnant for a total of 17 hours. I had mentioned leaving the wire again to William and he was angry at me for putting myself in danger. However, I was following orders … just not his. If I said no, I would be in trouble.

When I reached the vehicles, I went to find Sergeant P. "Hey!"

We grinned at each other. He looked tired but clean. They appeared to have had a few hours before we met them to grab showers and maybe some hot food. As everyone started loading up into the vehicles, I shifted the switch from one side of my body to the other side. My hips still hadn't healed from the last time out. Sergeant P went to grab my backpack, but I stopped him. "It has to be in the vehicle. Comm stuff."

"Alright."

He shifted the contents of the empty back left seat to provide some room for my pack. I threw the pack in and continued to hold the switch. It wouldn't fit in the seat and I couldn't simply toss it on top of my bag. If the bag shifted and the switch fell, it could be severely damaged and not work, which would be a waste of time and resources.

Hey, on second thought, maybe an excuse for another trip out to the station would be worth the ass-chewing.

As I climbed into my usual seat in the back behind Sergeant P, I said hey to Owens and Dumaw. We waited for Sergeant P to finish outside, and I asked some questions to fill the time. "Dumaw, is this thing hard to drive?"

"Nah, it's just really hard to steer around the barriers at the ECPs."

Sergeant P climbed up just in time to hear the exchange between us. "Cannon, you wanna drive it?"

"Whaaaaaat?"

"You have a Humvee license, right?"

"Well, no. Never went to the course."

"Eh, who gives a shit? You can drive a car, right?"

Owens poked his head down from the turret. "P, did you just ask a girl if she could drive?"

I laughed and told Owens to suck my dick. "Yeah, I can drive."

"Well, let's go. Switch with Dumaw."

I leapt down and walked around the MATV to the driver's side. Dumaw swung out of the driver's seat and jumped into the sand. I handed him the switch. "Please be careful with this."

"Please be careful with this!" He motioned to the giant vehicle.

"I promise I'll only run over a few IEDs."

"Just make sure you hit them good so we can go home."

Morbid humor. My favorite.

I climbed into the driver's seat and sat down. I had to sit completely straight up to see over the steering wheel and I couldn't reach the pedals. Sergeant P had to run around to my side to slam the seat as far forward as it could go. They had never adjusted the seat forward before, and the seat adjustment tracks were slightly eroded and filled with sand. Even with the seat forward, my tippy toes were barely touching the accelerator. The vehicle was already rumbling when I switched with Dumaw, so I didn't need to struggle to turn it on.

I looked back at Dumaw in my seat. "Seriously, please be careful with that switch."

"Whoa, man, how dumb do you think we are? Think I can't hold onto a box for a drive?"

"Look, all I know is that grunts eat crayons and glue and talk about how badass they are while they scratch their balls."

We grinned at each other.

"You sure got lippy since last time I saw you. Guess you're turning into a real Marine, thinking you can talk shit to grunts."

"We all know you're a bunch of soft pansies anyway, whining about your sleep and food and how you never get any of either."

"Hey, did you enjoy your shower last night? And the night before that? And your AC? Yeah? Yeah? Yeah?"

I kept trying to interrupt and fight back before laughing and giving up.

"Haha, alright, alright. Don't get angry at me because you were too stupid to get a good job. Plus, you're not even a grunt. You're an MP. I bet you give out traffic tickets in America."

"Fuck no. There are two types of MPs. We call those guys buddy fuckers. They strut around and screw their buddies over by arresting them and shit. I'm a field military police officer."

Rolling my eyes, I made a "blah-blah" motion with my hand, mocking him.

"Ha, ha, shut up and drive, boot."

"Boot?! How dare you! Your mom is a boot."

My mock anger made everyone laugh as I turned ahead. Sergeant P joined in the conversation with a thick layer of sarcasm.

"His mother is a nice lady. How dare you insult her? Just drive, boot."

Fuck. I'm definitely a boot.

I accelerated the vehicle once the radio checks were conducted. I was the lead vehicle. When we got to the exit of the base, the same stuff happened as last time. The machine guns were rotated around to various positions. The weapons were loaded. Seriousness washed over the convoy.

Dumaw was right about navigating through the barriers. The vehicle was huge.

"Think you can handle this?"

"Yeah, I've been known to handle large things well."

I winked at P and laughed. His expression was one of amusement and slight shock. I was feeling untouchable and a little feisty.

"Oh really?"

I stuck my tongue out at Sergeant P.

"Hey now, keep it PG, you two." Dumaw was smiling at us from the backseat.

I felt giddy. That behavior was definitely not acceptable. But what were they going to do? Shave my head and send me to the desert? An ex of mine used to say that phrase constantly when faced with adversity. "What's the worst they can do? Shave my head and send me to Iraq?" He said it with conviction. I didn't understand until I was in a combat zone. What's the worst that could happen?

Passing through the barriers, I took to the road. P told me to turn off the road and hit the wadi, the dried-up riverbed that was relatively flat. "We wanna avoid the roads. Too many IEDs."

The thought that every motion of my hands and feet could steer us directly onto a bomb at any second was thrilling. As I turned off the road, the stability beneath the wheels of the MATV disappeared. I had to accelerate a little more and grip the steering wheel a little harder as I leaned over it and drove through the sand.

"It's safer out here? Seriously?"

"What are they going to do? Plant random bombs in the middle of the desert? Then what happens when they walk over them later because they forgot they were there? Their kids play out here. Speaking of, watch for kids." Sergeant P kept his gaze on the desert ahead as he spoke.

Fuck. My brain was already scanning the horizon for every possible sign of an IED. All four of us were keeping an eye out.

As I climbed the side of the wadi, the front wheel caught on something, and the vehicle jerked. Owens was tossed around in the turret. "SEE?! TOLD YA SHE COULDN'T DRIVE!"

"Shut UP, OWENS!" Sergeant P looked over at me, while yelling at Owens. "Gun it."

"Really?"

"Yes."

I slammed the gas pedal to the floor with my tippy toes. The MATV launched up the wall of the wadi and into the air, onto the other side. When we landed roughly, Owens was tossed back and forth in his seat, his sides smashing into the rounded edge of the circular turret. Dumaw, P, and I cracked up while Owens cursed our names and our mothers' names and our first-born children's grade school teachers' names.

I wiggled the steering wheel back and forth for good measure, the MATV swinging around.

"Alright, alright, that's enough."

Feeling chastised by Sergeant P, I stopped and became serious. The radio beeped and Vehicle 2 checked to see if we were okay.

"We're good. Just teaching someone a lesson."

We entered the town of Delaram and the compound with ease.

31

June 2010, AUP Station in the Town of Delaram, Afghanistan

This time when we entered the grunts' compound Virkler and I acted like we owned the place. We strode in with the guys from the convoy and immediately headed to the radio room. Waving to some of the guys I remembered from last time as we walked in, I felt at home and completely safe. The boot lieutenant was standing in the middle of the radio room when we entered. He was speaking to a large Afghan man wearing a blue ANA uniform. The presence of the Afghan put me on immediate alert.

This is an American compound, meant for Americans to be safe. And didn't P say they weren't supposed to be over on our side?

The LT looked over the man's shoulder as I entered the room. His face was one of sudden concern. "Ah, Corporal Cannon, you guys made it."

"Yes, sir."

"This is Major Farid Barakzai, commander of the 2nd Brigade of the Afghan National Army."

The major turned to me and sized me up and down with his eyes. I reached out to shake his hand. He glanced down at my extended hand with a calculating look, before extending his own and grabbing my hand in a firm grip. I quickly tried to remember what I had been told to say in the briefs the Marine Corps gave everyone before we deployed to Afghanistan.

"As-salaam Alaikum." *"Peace be unto you."*

The major seemed surprised that I knew the proper greeting. As he spoke back to me, he didn't release his grip on my hand. Instead, he squeezed harder.

"Alaikum salaam." *"Unto you peace."*

I knew what I was meant to say next. It was something along the lines of "Sin gay ye"—*how are you?* Then he was supposed to say "Haik"—*fine*—with a throaty finish. But I couldn't speak. The major's grip on my hand was getting tighter and tighter. He looked down on me and we locked eyes as he crushed my fingers together, the bones cracking as they slid past each other and crumpled.

Do not show pain. Do not grimace. Keep your face calm. Smile.

I smiled at the Afghan as he slowly gripped my right hand tighter. My eyes were wider than normal, and I struggled to breathe from the pain.

Don't pull away. This is the major of a country we are at war with. If I pull away, it will show that America is weak. This is a test, simply a test. Don't give in. It has to end soon.

What was occurring between the major and me seemed to be just that, between the two of us. The people looking on couldn't see a change in either of our behaviors. The major knew what he was doing to me, and I refused to show weakness by pulling away. It was a battle of wills between friend and foe, old and young, man and woman, officer and enlisted. In that moment, I stood for everything this man hated, and he stood for every man who had ever tried to say I was weak. I refused to be weak, I refused to break, and I refused to let him see me give in.

After what seemed like eternity, the major appeared satisfied with my lack of response to the pain. He released my hand, said a few words to the LT, and walked briskly out of the radio room.

I waited until he was gone to look down at my hand. It was still white from the lack of blood flow. My entire body was shaking from the adrenaline that had rushed through it and prevented me from screaming during the exchange. I couldn't flex or extend my fingers. Using my left hand to break apart the fingers, I gingerly bent them, one by one. My heart rate spiked with every bend. After I ensured that no bones were broken, I rubbed my hand. As the blood re-entered my fingers, the sensation of a thousand needle pricks coursed through my veins and everything in my field of vision started to go white.

I swayed back and forth until I fell backward into a chair that was luckily right behind me. I tried to downplay it and started pulling off my equipment using only my left hand, while my right hand dangled uselessly at my side.

32

June 2010, AUP Station in the Town of Delaram, Afghanistan

Once the major had left, the atmosphere around the compound was much more relaxed. Virkler and I got to work installing CENTRIXS inside the radio room. We pulled out the equipment and started the process of connecting the new switch and encryptor.

Networking is best done in pairs. There is one person to "drive" on the keyboard and one person looking on, suggesting ways to fix issues or advance through the configuration steps. These pairs of workers must be respectful to each other, and most importantly, understand how the other troubleshoots and thinks, to properly follow the logic. A perfect match will contain two people skilled in various different aspects of the technology and intelligent enough to follow what the other person suggests. It is a balance of teaching and learning between two professionals who have the same goal—to get the network working. To an observer with no background in satellite communications, network design, or computer science, the things said between networkers make little sense. But as networkers, we are exposing our logic, our intelligence, and our lack of intelligence with every phrase. Setting up a network with another person will earn you either respect or ridicule from your teammate.

Virkler and I were hunched over his Toughbook laptop and murmuring to each other while the grunts moved around us. Virkler was typing ("driving"), and I was making suggestions as he worked. "Put it on 1/1."

"The trunk?"

"Yeah."

"Nah, I'll put it on 1/24."

"That's dumb. Put it on 1/1."

"It doesn't matter."

"No, it doesn't, but 1/1 is closer to the encryptor. Saves cable."

"Just move the encryptor."

"Just make a longer cable."

"You just make a longer cable."

The logic for every step is argued, but in a friendly manner. Learning to concede to a better idea is one of the best adaptive skills a networker can have. Listen to the team, argue your points, but always be willing to change the plan for a better one.

Sitting side by side, legs touching, the compound faded away around the two of us. My brain was focused on the screen, traveling along the wires that I could see in my mind, with streams of light that reflected the ones and zeros as information traveled across the wire. I was inside the switch in my mind, making connections, forcing the logic to work on the devices as Virkler typed and I predicted what needed to be done next. Absent-mindedly, I reached into my backpack and grabbed the small package of six Oreo cookies I had taken from the chow hall on Camp Delaram. I shoved one into my mouth and continued to troubleshoot, occasionally speaking through crumbly chews.

Virkler glanced up at me as I talked with my mouth full, his expression full of judgment. "Where did you get those?"

"Chow hall."

"When?"

"Is this the Spanish Inquisition? I dunno, a few days ago."

"Gimme one."

"No, get your own."

"Just one."

"No, my cookies."

With a sarcastic glare, he turned back to the Toughbook. "Time to make the tunnel. What should we name it?"

"Staff Sergeant Rambo didn't tell you what number to use?"

"Did he tell you?"

"No."

"Well, we can't just use anything; what if the number is already in use?"

"Does it matter?"

Virkler shrugged his shoulders in answer to my question. We looked at each other, thinking silently of the ramifications of using a random number that could cause the entire network to collapse. Suddenly, Virkler grabbed the package of Oreos from my lap. Unprepared for this because of the slight sugar coma I was entering, I lurched after him. "WHAT ARE YOU DOING? MY COOKIES!"

"Calm down, fatty."

He grinned at me before inspecting the package of Oreos. Seeing that they were safe from harm for the moment, I watched him warily. "Are you trying to see how fat I'm getting by eating a few cookies?"

"We'll use 70."

"Huh?"

"For the tunnel. 70. It's how many calories you're shoving into your mouth."

"Oh, haha, okay, sure. It's only 70? Man, I need to find more of those."

He handed the package back to me unharmed and started typing again.

One left. I should give it to him. Psh, why? Why should I share? They are my Oreos, and they are so delicious. If he wants one, he can get his own. Right? Oh, yes, right. Oreos never show up at Delaram and this was the last package. But I had five and this is just one. I can give up one.

I shoved the last Oreo into my mouth and focused on the screen.

After a little while, the tunnel was set up and traffic was flowing. We ran cables within the radio room and then to a building out behind the main house for a solitary computer that someone would use. The work was quick, and we were done within 30 minutes. The sun was at its highest point as we finished. Glancing around, I found Sergeant P and asked if they needed anything else done while we were there.

"Yeah, some of the guys' personal computers are slow as fuck. Can you fix that?"

"We can take a look."

He went around and asked who needed their computer looked at. As people brought us their laptops for quick maintenance, Sergeant P suddenly spun to us. "I almost forgot. We have a NIPR computer out back that we use to contact family occasionally. It refuses to connect and it's also slow as fuck."

He led me around the corner to a secluded area that held a lone computer. I booted it up and indeed, it was extremely slow. "When was the last time it worked?"

"It's been awhile. A month?"

I set about fixing the hunk of junk. Besides needing a quick defragmentation and deletion of a few files, I noticed that the cable connecting the computer was frayed. I needed to make a new one. I grabbed some cable and a pair of cable crimpers and started making it.

White orange, orange, white green, blue, white blue, green, white brown, brown ....

I repeated the sequence in my head as I lined up the small lines of colored copper held within the category-5 Ethernet cable. Sergeant P watched as I worked. "It's awesome that you can do this stuff."

"What do you mean?"

"Just fix things. You're really smart."

"Nah, I've just been trained. Same as you. But I learned how to slay cables instead of people."

"No, you're smart. I heard you and Virkler talking, setting up whatever it is you're setting up, and I understood none of it."

"Two years ago, I didn't understand any of it either. Hell, I still don't understand it. I bet you missed the moment in there where I needed to do something, and I had no idea what I had to do to get it to work. Not knowing what to do is the worst. I feel so helpless."

"But you got it."

"Not without lots of question marks."

P looked at me like I'd grown two heads. I explained, "If you don't know what to type, you can simply type in a question mark, and it will give you options. You can guess from there."

"Still, you figured it out. That's really cool. You saw our laptops. We don't do this stuff. We just use them."

"Me too." I laughed and shook my head.

"I worry that someday I'm really going to screw up something badly," Sergeant P admitted.

"I think we all fear that."

The weight of what he'd just said hit me and I was silent. If I screwed up, people wouldn't get email. If he screwed up, people would die.

How can I be freaked out about screwing up? This man has literal lives in his hands every day, even right now.

Sergeant P continued: "Even if you do mess up, you're smart and you'll figure it out."

"Thanks, I'm glad you have more faith in me than I do."

Even with the great disparity between our responsibilities, he comforts me.

I finished the cable, crimping the wires down tightly with the cable crimpers, and plugged the computer back into the network. Praying the connection would work, I navigated to Facebook. "There you go."

"Sweet." He immediately sat down and logged in. "I need to tell my family that I'm okay."

"Yeah, I totally understand. It's like family doesn't understand we have jobs to do out here. I'll let everyone else know it's working."

I walked back to the main building, feet crunching on the smooth rocks, and told the others that the "recreational" computer was working. Everyone sprang to their feet and sprinted to where Sergeant P sat, practically knocking me down in the rush.

"Geesh, guys, calm down."

Dumaw glanced back at me as he swung his long legs around to sit on the tiny stool in front of the computer. "Dude, we never get to talk to our families. We have a single satellite phone and the service is shit."

"I'm sorry."

"Not your fault. You just hooked us up. Thank you."

Sergeant P looked very seriously at me. "Morale is important here. You seriously helped us out."

"Hey, it was just a cable. But you're welcome. I'm glad I could help."

"Just a cable that we didn't know how to fix and couldn't have fixed if we tried."

A sense of pride and accomplishment flowed through me as I watched Dumaw log in next. CENTRIXS was important to the people in charge. The ability to send a simple Facebook message to family was important to the people in front of me, the people who mattered. I did that.

33

June 2010, AUP Station in the Town of Delaram, Afghanistan

Stuffing the crimpers back into my backpack, I saw the blue Gatorade that I had brought along from Delaram. I had hit the jackpot with the Oreos and small Gatorade. Whenever I went to the chow hall, all of the goodies were always gone. I had managed to arrive in time one morning to get the last Oreos and one of the last Gatorades. Generally, we ran out of food before everyone on the base was fed. If the Georgian battalion was around, Marines went hungry. It wasn't malicious behavior on the Georgians' part. The logistics of providing food to an outlying base were difficult. Convoys of food supplies were rumored to be attacked and resupply planes couldn't land because the airstrip wasn't completed yet. Only helicopters could land, and helicopters can only hold so much. Delaram, as a base, was expanding more rapidly than the logistics could handle. Supply was less than demand, and we were hungry.

Oreos and Gatorade. It was like manna from heaven. I'll save the Gatorade until I really need a pick-me-up.

Gazing longingly at the Gatorade, knowing that it would be delicious when I finally cracked it open, I imagined the sweetness filling my mouth. It would be warm. Everything was warm here. But it would be warm sweetness that would stain my mouth blue. I was testing myself by not drinking it. Put off a reward long enough and it will taste three times as sweet once it is finally consumed.

I was wiping the drool from the edge of my mouth when a Marine walked up to Sergeant P.

"Hey, there was some sort of accident and a bus of locals flipped up the road."

P wasn't even fazed. "Alright, bring them in."

He looked at me and responded to my shocked face: "We have the most medical help in the area. We treat locals when we can."

The Navy corpsman, who was embedded in the platoon, had been woken up and was walking toward us on the way to the "medical bay." The medical bay was a tiny building behind the main building and to the left of where Virkler and I had set up the lone computer. As the long-haired Navy guy passed us, I chased after him. "Hey, Doc! Need help?"

"Uh, sure. I could always use a hand."

I followed him into the small one-room building that was his domain. Docs in the Navy are not doctors; they are enlisted sailors, or corpsmen, who have been trained in combat medicine. They deploy with the grunts as the first line of medical help. A corpsman's job is to slow down a Marine's death until the Marine can be medically evacuated and treated by real doctors. All corpsmen are dubbed "Doc" by their Marines. It is a friendly term synonymous with the boys in blue.

Doc picked up a giant black bag from the ground and threw it onto the table in the center of the room.

"Holy crap, that thing is huge."

"Yeah, it's my bag of med stuff."

He unzipped the bag and unfolded it, displaying medical supplies that were organized and well-stocked.

"You have actual real medical stuff?"

"Well, yeah, how else do you think I'd save people?"

"I dunno, throw them some Motrin and a pair of socks?"

"And if someone steps on an IED and doesn't have any feet for the socks?"

"Knowing the Navy, you'd probably still throw them the socks."

Navy medical care is known for ignoring serious issues and proclaiming that the Marine simply put on a fresh pair of socks and take some Motrin to relieve their pain. This jab at medical treatment stems from World War I, when Marines got trench foot from having damp feet by standing and sleeping in the trenches for months. Trench foot required amputation of the feet, and sometimes the legs of Marines, by the medics in World War I. Only a person with the military's dark sense of humor could laugh at the idea of socks preventing amputation.

The doc rolled his eyes.

Rolls of bandages and needles and tourniquets and bags of IV solutions spilled out as he unzipped smaller pockets within the bag. I saw bags of QuikClot, the powder that is poured into bullet wounds to prevent bleeding out. There were splints, and Band-Aids, and, yes, even Motrin.

"Whoa, you have everything. Have you had to use any of it?"

"Someone rolled their ankle once. We've been lucky, no serious injuries."

"That's good."

"Yeah, of course."

"So, what do you want me to do?"

"Let's see what they bring us." Doc was nonchalant about the prospect of what could be coming through the door.

We turned to the doorway and waited. The hustle of the compound grew as locals began to trickle in. They were physically patted down by the Marines as they entered the compound. Locals were supposed to be non-combatants, but we knew the line between friend and foe was blurry, so everyone was subject to a thorough search. Some were limping, some were slightly bloody, but no one was seriously injured. There were maybe five men and one child.

The little boy looked about four or five years old. He was limping, walking ahead of an older man, left arm reaching back to hold the older man's hand. He seemed to be leading the man. The doc and I walked toward the boy, meeting him on a flat concrete surface on the outside of the main building. Stone walked toward the four of us. When we approached the pair, Doc and I could see why the boy was leading the man. The older man's eyes were a milky white and he looked vaguely in our general direction as we spoke.

Doc began asking questions and the interpreter translated to the man. According to the translations, the boy's foot had been injured in the crash. When Doc tried to speak to the boy, he mumbled a response and wouldn't look us in the eye. The man refused to speak.

Maybe he is also deaf and mute? Or he just hates us.

I looked at the boy's foot. It was cracked open and bloody on the side. I urged him to sit down, gesturing to the concrete behind him.

"Cannon, get some gauze and antiseptic."

I ran to the medical bay. I stuffed gauze and a bottle of antiseptic into the cargo pouch on my cammie bottoms. As I shoved the supplies into my pocket, I felt the magazine full of bullets press against my leg. I looked around the room to see if I could bring anything else. I grabbed something that looked like Neosporin and ran back to the boy.

Doc was squatting next to the boy, inspecting his foot, bending it back and forth at the ankle and pressing on the bones in his foot. The boy didn't flinch.

"I'm going to clean and bandage up his foot. Can you distract him?"

After I handed over the supplies to the doc, I ran to my backpack, grabbed something and ran back. I saw a watermelon on a bench and had an idea. I reached into my pocket and grabbed the knife I kept clipped to the edge of my pocket. The blade was only 3.7 inches long, but it would do. I stabbed the watermelon repeatedly, hacking at it roughly until I was able to pry it open.

"Hey, that's ours!" A Marine yelled at me from across the compound.

I ignored him and continued cutting off a chunk. Thinking about how dirty my hands were, I handed the piece of watermelon and the blue Gatorade to the boy. He looked down at the stuff, his face almost made of stone, eyes completely deadened. I smiled at him, took back the Gatorade and opened it, lightly replacing the twist-cap before handing the bottle back to him. I gestured for him to pour it into his mouth. He just watched me mime. Seeing that the doc was set to begin pouring the antiseptic, I tried to think of a better distraction.

I grabbed my camera from my other cargo pocket and took a picture of him, then turned the camera's screen back to the boy. He looked at the screen, looked up at me, and his eyes grew wide.

I wonder if he has ever seen his reflection. Probably in pools of water, right? Does he know this is him?

I motioned down at the picture and up at him. He shoved the watermelon into his mouth, grabbed the camera out of my hand, and gazed down at his own face. For a split second, he looked anxiously over his shoulder at the man he had entered the compound with. Seeing that the man wasn't reacting—*How could he?*—the little boy spent minutes looking at the picture. He opened the Gatorade and took a small sip. His eyes lit up when he tasted the Gatorade, and he took multiple giant swigs. I laughed at his enthusiasm, and he smiled at me, while speaking rapidly and excitedly. I scrolled through the other pictures in the camera, telling him what each one was showing. I spoke in English, and he responded in Farsi. Stone had walked off to help someone else, so the boy and I babbled back and forth nonsensically. He kept wanting to see the picture of himself.

Doc finished bundling up the boy's foot. The little boy grabbed the old man's hand, waved and smiled at me, and carried the Gatorade out of the compound, limping significantly less than before as he disappeared out of my view.

34

June 2010, AUP Station in the Town of Delaram, Afghanistan

The atmosphere of the compound relaxed once the accident victims left. The sun had started to lower, and Marines were milling about discussing dinner plans. Everyone was tired of the Meals Ready to Eat (MREs) that were stacked in a small shack at the front of the main building. Stone offered to go to town and grab us some food. The boot lieutenant peeled off a few bills from a stack that he pulled from his pocket and handed the money to the terp. The man left the Marine compound alone and walked to the marketplace.

Dumaw fired up the grill that was in the tiny courtyard. Everyone stood around talking and joking and enjoying life as young Marines do in a combat zone when there are no responsibilities or danger. Suddenly, there was a slight commotion at the entrance of the compound.

"CHESTY!"

Everyone ran up to the puppy that had wandered into the compound. I squealed and ran up to the mangy pup. Falling to my knees, I gathered the puppy into my lap and received multiple licks from her dry tongue as the men gathered around me and watched me fawn over her. "Oh my god, she's dehydrated."

"You're going to get a disease."

I ignored the men's comments and poured some water from my CamelBak pouch into my palm and let her lick my hand dry multiple times. "Chesty is a horrible name for a girl dog. Who named her?"

"One of the guys." Sergeant P watched me cuddle the mangy dog. She was my first exposure to animal life in four months. She reminded me of home and the dogs I had grown up with in Georgia.

Chesty was short for Lieutenant General Chesty Puller, a Marine Corps officer who was revered around the Corps. He had received five Navy Crosses during World War II and the Korean War and was known for being badass and not giving a fuck if Marines put their hands in their pockets, a highly debated topic among Marines. During their annual physical fitness test, Marines do an additional pull-up on top of the required 20: "AND ONE FOR CHESTY!" Calling this dog "Chesty" was a gesture of respect for a dog who always managed to pull through difficult situations.

As I rolled around on the smooth pebbles with this dog, the other Marines gave up trying to pet her. Jokingly, one of them tried to kick her and I gave him a harsh scolding. Marines have a weird relationship with dogs; the majority love the FOB dogs, but every once in a while, there is an asshole who tortures the dogs in-country. Marines were on the news in 2008 for throwing a puppy off of a cliff in Iraq. War does strange things to people, sure, but some Marines are just assholes.

Stone came back carrying meat, bread, and a bunch of grapes. Dumaw took the meat from him and threw it on the grill. Eventually, the smell of cooking meat filled the air.

I asked Stone what kind of meat it was.

"Maybe goat."

"Maybe?"

He glanced at Chesty rolling around my feet and sat down next to me. "Let's say it's goat."

I ignored the implications of his words. I looked down at his hands as he took off the cloth wrapped around one of them. The cloth unraveled and a malformed hand was exposed with missing fingers. The skin was completely healed, and it looked like the cloth was only to prevent stares.

"What happened?"

He answered that he was born this way and the hospital couldn't do anything to help it.

"What hospital? You had hospitals?"

"Of course. I went to college in Florida."

I realized how much I had profiled this man. *I am a total asshole.*

"Why did you come back to this place?"

"I wanted to help my people. Afghanistan is a beautiful place, and I want people to remember that."

I gestured around at the empty desert as he sat down and handed me a handful of warm and juicy grapes.

"This is beautiful? This is a shithole."

"Kandahar is amazing. So full of green and beauty and the history of our people."

"If you say so."

"Come and visit my family one day. You'll see. Afghans are a proud people, and we have a lot to offer."

I nodded and we continued talking about the land and the green trees of the city. He spoke of the war ruining the temples and land of his youth. I imagined the city's green.

Dumaw shouted that the food would be ready soon. Everyone shuffled up to the grill.

"I didn't realize you could grill."

Sergeant P responded to one of the other Marines' half-insult to Dumaw: "He's preparing for the Father's Day grilling he's going to have to start doing for himself."

I slapped Dumaw on the shoulder. "What? You're going to be a father? You're having a kid?"

"Yeah, the wife is due in September."

"Aw, man, that's awesome!"

"Yeah, it's a boy. I can't wait to teach him how to—"

Dumaw was cut off by a rock hitting the building next to his head. Quickly bending down, he scooped up a handful of rocks and chucked them over the compound's wall.

"KNOCK IT OFF, FUCKERS!"

Looking at me, he went back to the grill and shook his head.

"The little motherfuckering kids like to fuck with us."

"Careful, you're about to raise one of your own."

Dumaw started handing out the meat.

"Ladies first."

I looked around for a plate: "Uh … are there any plates?"

"Are you insane? We barely have food. Here." Dumaw quickly tore a flap from a box of MREs. Throwing the meat on it, he handed the "plate" to me. As I ate with my dirty hands from my makeshift cardboard plate, I kept talking to Dumaw and Sergeant P.

"I guess you could say this is Dumaw's birthday party too."

Sergeant P stood back and let his men eat first before taking his own plate. "No, shit, Dumaw? When was your birthday? How old are you?"

"I'm 23. It was last week. Best birthday ever. Remember that patrol, P?"

"Yeah, motherfucker, it was last week."

Everyone laughed as they ate. We were full, calm, and as content as possible in a combat zone.

35

June 2010, AUP Station in the Town of Delaram, Afghanistan

As people began to break off to head to their racks to sleep, I yawned and Sergeant P glanced at me.

"Ready to sleep?"

"Always. I guess I'll head to the roof."

"Nah, I got some of the guys to set up a tent for you after the GBOSS incident last time."

"Aw, really? You didn't have to do that."

"I know I didn't have to. Let the other guys sleep on the roof."

He walked me to the back of the general's building and showed me my personal tent. It was large enough for a cot or two. I placed my flak and Kevlar down on the floor. Virkler had followed me to see the sweet digs.

"Jealous?"

"Fuck no, sleeping on the roof is great."

"Thank you, Sergeant P, so much."

"Yeah, 'course."

We stood silently in the tent in the dark. Sergeant P didn't want to leave, and I didn't want him to go.

Sergeant P offered, "Want to watch a movie?"

"Sure!"

We walked over to his tent. When I entered, I saw a well lived-in area where he and the gunnery sergeant and a few others lived. The lower ranks slept in the large and smelly tents. Sergeant P got a smaller tent to share with fewer people. There was a rug on the ground, and various homey paraphernalia about the area where he slept. It felt intimate, being in his "home," where he slept and was vulnerable. Sergeant P grabbed his laptop and brought it back to my tent.

The three of us sat on the small green cot that one of the Marines had grabbed for me. I sat between Virkler and P and we began to watch a movie. In hindsight, I can't remember the name of the movie or what occurred in it. I wasn't paying attention to the movie. I was noticing how close Sergeant P was to me. Our thighs were touching as our trio gathered close enough to see the laptop's screen on my lap. His arm would occasionally brush against mine.

Virkler suddenly stood up. "I'm going to go to bed."

P and I mumbled our goodbyes and Virkler left us alone in my tent. Sergeant P and I continued watching the movie, neither of us willing to break the silence. Some of the light from outside spilled into the tent through its window above our heads. I could see his tattooed arms in the dim light, his sleeves rolled up to the elbows. I could feel the energy flowing between us, almost sparking.

I started to nod off. I was exhausted and even the spark couldn't keep me awake. Sergeant P glanced over at me and leapt up. "I'll let you get some sleep."

"No, I'm fine. Let's finish the movie."

"Well, at least lay down."

Sergeant P sat on the floor, his back leaning against the cot that I laid on. He held the laptop on his lap and I watched the movie over his shoulder. I studied his face intently—when I knew he wasn't looking at me—wondering about this man and how he was so strong and naturally authoritative, someone who would throw himself in front of a bullet to protect me. Slowly, I drifted off.

As I slept, I felt him get up, gently touch my shoulder, and say "Goodnight."

The next morning, the bright sun tore through the window in the tent and woke me harshly. The compound was beginning to stir with the sounds of people cleaning their weapons and packing things.

Once I had readied myself, which meant putting my boots back on and ensuring that my hair was still somewhat in a bun, I ventured out to the tiny courtyard.

"Good morning! Ready to go back to Delaram? We want to drop y'all on the way up the highway," Sergeant P called out to me while he was moving about, telling people to get ready for a run to Delaram. We grabbed our stuff and met the team next to the vics. I went directly to Sergeant P's lead vic with Dumaw and Owens. "What's up the highway?"

"We do patrols there occasionally."

"Let us go."

Sergeant P said no immediately.

"It's too dangerous."

"Fuck. Am I driving again?"

Owens almost paled. He was one of the good ol' boys from Tennessee who you could imagine hunting and fishing back home. His look of shock and fear was laughable.

"No! You practically murdered me up there."

Dumaw laughed and told Owens to stop being a pussy.

"Why don't you be the gunner this time?"

Everyone looked at me.

"Uh ... if you guys trust me with that."

"You know how to fire the 240, right?"

"Yeah, they taught us how to shoot that at MCT."

"Then you're good."

I climbed up into the turret. Standing between MATV's two front seats, I couldn't see out of the turret. "Uh, guys? I can't see shit."

"Then jump."

"You fuckers ...."

Dumaw grabbed a box and put it under my feet.

"Better, short stuff?"

"Yeah, thanks."

Sergeant P climbed into the vehicle. "Ah, Cannon's gunner?"

"Now that she can see with her short-ass self."

"Hey!" I aimed a kick wildly into the vehicle's cab and connected with someone's shoulder. Sergeant P laughed and grabbed my calf, squeezing gently.

"Right on. Cannon, Condition 1."

I looked down at the vaguely familiar weapon. Owens handed me the ammo up through the turret from a giant green ammo can. The rounds were 7.62 millimeters and linked together in a giant chain. Rapidly trying to remember how to load a weapon from when I did it *once* two years prior, I opened the feed tray.

"Rack it back first." Owens looked up at me from between my legs.

I reached to pull back the charging handle. I pulled.

Nothing.

I pulled harder.

Still nothing.

I pulled so hard that I was straining with both hands. I braced my back against the circular edge of the turret and drew my knees to my chest so I could place my boots on the other side of the circle and leverage my entire weight.

Nothing.

Owens looked up at me incredulously. "What's wrong? Are you too weak to pull back a lever? Get out of the way."

I dropped down the turret in embarrassment and knelt next to Sergeant P's left shoulder as Owens scrambled up and tried to rack back the charging handle. He pulled once and hesitated before pulling the second time. With a giant grinding sound, the charging handle came back slowly, crushing the sand that had built up within the weapon.

Sergeant P and I looked at each other with raised eyebrows. Owens finished loading the weapon and climbed back down.

"You point it at what you want to shoot."

"Hey, shut up. Maybe if you cleaned your weapon every once in a while …."

We left the compound and headed out to the wadis.

As we drove along, I scoured the areas ahead of me while my right finger was straight and rigid next to the trigger of the fully loaded machine gun. It was difficult to brace my legs on the box Dumaw had set up for me to stand on, so when the MATV hit a bump, my body smashed into the sides of the turret. My flak jacket protected my insides, but my shoulders were still smashed. I couldn't stumble and fall and leave the turret unoccupied and the guys unprotected, so I started to anticipate the bumps and turns. Owens had been tall enough to sit down in the sling that dangled between two sides of the turret's circle. The sling had protected him from hitting the sides, except in the harshest of driving conditions. I began to get better at avoiding the edges of the turret.

Riding in the turret made me remember the Humvee rollover training my unit had taken prior to deployment. Four of us were stuffed into a tiny Humvee simulator and rolled in every direction, quickly and slowly, back and forth, to simulate a vehicle rollover. We were randomly stopped, with the vehicle flipped in a random direction, and we had to extract ourselves quickly. With each simulation, a fellow Marine named Butler and I sang "Chitty Chitty Bang Bang" as we tumbled through the air. One roll ended up with my side on the bottom and Butler was above me. He released his seatbelt and dropped onto me, crushing me with his 240 pounds of body and gear. In the next simulation, I was on top and I had to open the Humvee door outward above me. I had released and dropped onto Butler. I couldn't reach the door through the length of the Humvee cab. Butler had to use his legs to leg press my entire body and gear high enough for me to reach the door and start pushing all 300 pounds of it upward. We strained and cursed and sweated and laughed. Rollovers are dangerous and a very real threat in Afghanistan because the

IEDs can blow up a vehicle into a wadi filled with water. In the event of a rollover, we were told to yank the machine gunner down from the turret so their head wouldn't be crushed by the rollover. During the training, Butler and I had laughed and joked while we acted like we yanked an imaginary person from the turret. Now that I was in Afghanistan, that person was no longer imaginary. It was me.

Suddenly, we hit a bump and I braced my body for the impact and dipped my head, making my body weightless so it wouldn't resist the impact. Unfortunately, another giant bump in the road was immediate and the MATV's direction changed abruptly. Not expecting the second hit, my face smashed into the buttstock of the M240G at a very high speed. Everything went black for a second, but I immediately came to, still gripping the weapon. I had evidently yelped because Sergeant P yelled at me, concerned.

"I'm good. Fucking hurt."

I ran my fingers over my face and my tongue over my teeth, making sure they were intact. When my tongue slid over my lips, I tasted copper—blood was dripping from my nose and mouth. Owens was gleeful as I hocked a giant bloody loogie into the desert.

"Payback is a bitch!"

Wincing, I wiped the blood on my cammies and hoped the sand from the wind would stem the freely flowing blood before anyone noticed.

We pulled into Delaram and I hopped down from the turret. "Fuck that shit."

Owens laughed at my face. My stomach was still churning from the impact. I grabbed my stuff from the vehicle and looked at Sergeant P. "When will I see you guys again?"

"Oh, we're always around. Where do you work?"

I motioned to the compound.

"I'll swing by when we do our trash and food runs, if I can."

"Awesome. I wish I could stay with y'all."

"Yeah, it would be great, but you have a job here and we have a job out there." He motioned to the desert.

"Alright, I'll see y'all around then. Have fun!"

Sergeant P smiled at me. "We always do."

I waved to Owens and Dumaw. Owens grunted and Dumaw waved back.

36

June 22, 2010, Camp Delaram, Afghanistan

After the men from the police mentoring team left, life went back to "normal" on Delaram. I was still bothered from being shot at and seeing the shattered bodies of the civilians from the previous mission. The only person I could have talked to about any of it was Virkler, and we were separated as soon as we checked in with Staff Sergeant Rambo. Virkler was assigned to the day shift again. I was back to being completely alone on night shift.

Twenty-four hours after Sergeant P and the boys had dropped us off in Delaram, I was working on my own, setting up a small portion of the network within the compound. I had to place the Internet protocol (IP) address on the switch to ensure it would connect properly. I navigated to the Excel document that held the IP addresses that were taken already. I chose the one that hadn't been used according to the document. I placed the IP address on the switch, verified connectivity, and casually sauntered over to COC to see if everything was okay over there.

When I walked into the building, it was clear that something was wrong. The helpdesk that was attached to the COC was bustling with activity. Everyone was yelling at each other in panic. Through the window to the COC, I saw lieutenants and captains yelling and ordering people to "find out what the fuck happened."

I asked one of the Marines at the help desk what was going on.

"The grunts were on a foot patrol and there was an explosion."

The blood drained from my face.

"Hey, uh, I lost connection."

Someone manning the COC was looking down at their computer in confusion, as other people in the COC began to realize they were dead in the water too. Everyone in the help desk scrambled to find out what had happened to the communications between the COC and the other units. There was still radio communication to the patrol, but all connections from the COC to anywhere else were gone.

I went completely numb as I realized that there was probably a connection between me adding the switch earlier and the entire COC going down. I sprinted back to the other building and quickly attached my laptop to the console port on the back of the switch. I logged in. Every cell in my body was screaming, and I was sure I wasn't breathing. I yanked all of the cables out of the switch. As the green lights shut off, my trembling hands placed the laptop back onto the table and I raced back to the COC.

Communication was back up. I stood in the center of the help desk, which was now calm as we watched the COC try to find out what had happened as the nine line came in.

I ran back to my desk.

It has to be a different patrol. It can't be them. It can't be them. Please, God, don't let it be them.

I searched the table of the wire guys to see if I could find the phone number of the AUP station. When I found it, I dialed the number.

Please pick up, anyone, pick up.

The line went dead. No one answered.

I dialed again. Someone picked up.

"What the fuck do you want?"

The voice was sharp.

"It's Cannon, wh—"

"Hang up the fucking phone, Cannon."

The voice sounded weary now.

"Who w—"

"Get off the fucking phone."

The line disconnected.

I stood there as the realization flooded my body and my brain started to process what was possible.

When I reached the COC, I sat down on a bucket and placed myself where I could hear what was happening. The grunts were using call signs that I didn't know. I couldn't understand much, and no one could identify the injured.

"They won't say his name over the nets."

Fifteen minutes, 30 minutes ... some amount of time passed before I heard it.

"We lost him."

The COC seemed to collapse with frustration and sadness in one collective breath.

"Warhawk heading back to base."

Everything moved in slow motion after that. I walked outside of the compound and stood waiting for the grunts to pull up next to the cans at the bottom of the hill, as they had multiple times before. While I waited, my mind went over what I had done. I had probably connected the switch five minutes after the explosion. I took down communications when they were trying to call in medical help. Communication was down for maybe seven minutes. I tied up the phone line for another four minutes. That's 11 minutes … 11 minutes that he was struggling to live. I cost him 11 minutes.

The vehicles pulled up and I sprinted down to them. Coming to a sudden halt, I watched the men climb out, looking for Sergeant P's face in everyone. Red, Dumaw's best friend, fell out of the vehicle, white-faced and sobbing openly. Blood covered his shirt and pants. He looked me in the eye and I knew he wasn't seeing me as his face twisted. Following him, holding Red up, was Sergeant P. Relief flooded my body when I saw that he was okay. I started to run toward him when he saw me, but he shook his head for me to stay back.

"Get everyone to the chaplain."

One of the guys spoke, "Someone has to watch the vehicles."

His voice was shaky.

"I got it."

Everyone glanced at me when I spoke.

Sergeant P and Owens carried Red between them, his feet dragging on the ground. He was in such shock, he couldn't stand.

Sergeant P, Owens, Red, Martin, Salgado…. Where is Dumaw? Oh fuck, no, not Dumaw.

The tall Black gunnery sergeant stayed too.

"Go, Gunny, I got this. Go to the chaplain."

"No. No. No."

He didn't look at me; he was looking at the lead vehicle.

"They can't come back to this."

I walked over to where he stood and looked at what he was looking at.

Blood covered the outside of the vehicle. My stomach lurched. There was so much blood, streaks of it, a spray pattern of an explosion.

Without saying a word, I ran back up to the compound, burst into the help desk, and looked around at what I could find. I stuffed a trash bag into my cargo pocket, grabbed a container of bottled water, and a broom. Everyone asked me what I was doing and I ignored them. I sprinted back to the vehicle.

The gunny was still standing where I had left him. "Go away. You shouldn't be here."

He still didn't look at me. I ignored him and I started pouring water on the blood. The water collected dust and blood as it fell into the sand below the vehicle. Gunny grabbed a bottle of water and we cleaned together in silence. I used the broom to scrub the outside of the vehicle where I could reach. I climbed into the front seats and collected the bottles of dip spit and empty cans of energy drinks and filled the trash bag I had brought.

The gunny climbed up to the top of the vehicle and I followed. "Go away."

I stayed silent, in shock.

"You shouldn't be seeing this. I couldn't protect him, but I can protect you from—"

He was kneeling on the cammie cargo net that draped over the top of the vehicle. One knee touched the cargo net and he put his head in his hands and sobbed.

"It's my fault. I shouldn't have let them keep walking. We had already found one IED. I shouldn't have let them keep going. He kept walking. I failed him. I failed him. I failed …."

He sobbed openly. I watched the broken leader silently and he finally looked me in the eye. "Cannon, I failed. He's dead because of me."

I reached out and touched his knee.

"No, he's not. You didn't fail him."

I did.

The gunny collected himself after a few moments.

We started to clean the cammie netting.

Something hung in the cammie netting. I reached down to pick it out. When I looked closely at it, my stomach heaved. It was a shard of stark white bone with part of the Marine Corps digital cammie pattern stuck on it. I looked at the cammie netting more closely. Bone was everywhere, caught between bits of Dumaw's cammies and covered in blood. I looked up at the gunny. We had noticed at the same time. Without a word between us, we gathered bits of Dumaw's body. My tears mixed with his blood as I quietly cried and cleaned. I started a pile of the pieces big enough to grab and held them in my hand, and I poured water over the bits that were too small. I went over every inch of the cammie netting meticulously, to make sure none of the grunts would have to see their friend's body on their vehicle for the rest of their deployment. When we were done, I held Dumaw's bones and blood and cammie bits tightly. I gripped them so hard that one shard of bone made a crease in my palm that remained for hours.

When I climbed down from the vehicle, I looked at what I held in my hand. *What do I do with … him?*

I didn't want to bother the gunny with that question. I unceremoniously placed what remained of the lower half of Dumaw's body into the trash bag. I didn't go back to work.

37

2017, California, U.S.A.

When I write, I try to place myself back in the moment to truly capture it. While trying to write about Dumaw, I felt detached and panicky at the same time. I tried to get inside the memory of that day, but it was like my mind was revolting, throwing up mental blocks and not allowing me to relive the experience. I suppose that is for a good reason.

But at night, the blocks fall away. For some reason, falling into a deep sleep can cause your mental protection to drop away and contorts your brain in ways that make you doubt your sanity.

I have had a few nightmares about Dumaw that repeat themselves. One starts with Sergeant P and I wandering through a sandstorm. We get shot at, but we don't care. We are trying to find Dumaw in the sandstorm because we can hear him screaming. We are rushing to find him, dodging bullets and explosions, and he is screaming. We can't find him for what seems like hours. When we finally come across his mangled body, the dream turns to slow motion and I can't call for help because my radio isn't working. I wake up screaming.

The second one might be based in reality. I'm not sure. When I was cleaning out the vehicles, I went to the back of the fourth vehicle to clean out the large area that can hold a few troops. I think I started to open it and got a glance inside before the gunny slammed the door in my face.

"That's where—"

When I think back on that time, it's hard for me to remember what actually happened. Did he slam the door before I saw anything? Or are my dreams real? Something happened with that fourth vehicle that my mind has twisted and warped into nightmares.

In the second dream, I open the back of the vehicle where Dumaw's body was held as he died. In the second dream, sometimes I open the door and blood drips down slowly from the floor onto the sand. Sometimes I see his body.

I don't think I actually saw his body. No one has told me or verified any of it, but would they have gone to the chaplain with his body still in the back of the vehicle? Or did they drop it off at some morgue facility prior? I didn't even think Delaram had a morgue area, but that doesn't make sense because other people died, too. Where did they process the dead bodies? Either way, my brain fills in the blanks. Sometimes I see him, sometimes it's just pools of blood at the bottom of the vehicle, and sometimes the gunny reaches me in time to stop me from seeing it. I wake up screaming in the dreams where I see his body.

The third nightmare is just Red's face looking at me as he gets out of the vehicle. No actor from any movie can capture the look of shock and disbelief and horror I saw in him. He looks at me with dead eyes that turn accusatory, until I wake up crying.

I don't feel justified in having these nightmares. I wasn't there. I didn't hold Dumaw while he died. I only heard what came through the radios, relayed from a person at the AUP station. Perhaps that is why I didn't tell anyone how affected I was for so long. Leaders can tell their Marines to "go talk to the chaplain" all day, but if someone feels like they don't have the right to ask for help, what good will telling them to go to a chaplain do? The only people who could help me—the men of PMT—were busy holding themselves together. I told no one, because how on earth could I have the right to need help when I wasn't there? How could I even tell them I might have cost them the time that might have saved him? They probably would've hated me. So, I turned the loathing in on myself.

I'd like to say to the members of Dumaw's platoon, who saw and experienced so much more than I did, that I know you have nightmares and regrets like I do, but you … you were there. I'm sorry if I've brought up things you don't want to think about or talk about. But I know you think about them, either consciously blocking them out with alcohol or drugs, or dangerous acts, or subconsciously dreaming about them. I hope you are getting help. It's time to deal with the memories. I carry the pain of Dumaw's death, and your pain, as we still experience it. I'm sorry that our friend and brother died.

Semper Fidelis, Marines.

38

June 23, 2010, Camp Delaram, Afghanistan

Staff Sergeant Rambo asked if I had finished installing the switch.

"No, Staff Sergeant."

"Why?"

Silence.

"Well?"

"I dunno, Staff Sergeant, I think something was wrong with the IP I gave it."

"What do you mean?"

He pulled up the Excel document.

"The next IP to use is right here. It didn't work?"

I looked at the spreadsheet.

"Where did you get this spreadsheet?"

"On the sharedrive. Come on, Cannon, you know this."

"I ... I guess I had a different one."

"Well, use this one. Get it done."

"Yes, Staff Sergeant."

I avoided that switch all day. I went into the tent where it lay to look at it. My laptop was still connected and lying open on the table I had thrown it on. I stood in the doorway of the tent and just looked at the switch.

I also avoided Staff Sergeant Rambo all day. I didn't want to be asked about the switch. Instead, I scoured the sharedrive to find our IP address scheme documentation. I found five copies of the spreadsheet, similarly named, and opened the first one on the list. Sure enough, the address I had used was taken by a device in the COC. I had used a duplicate address. The lack of communication at the most important time of military operations was my fault. Shaking my head at the stupidity and horror, I deleted the extra—and very wrong—copies of the spreadsheet.

When Virkler came for his shift, he looked at me with concern. Ever since I had told him Dumaw had died, he treated me like I was going to break in two. I didn't tell him any details, but he could tell I was extremely bothered.

"You okay?"

"I'm fine. Look, Staff Sergeant Rambo needs this switch installed next door. I didn't get to it today. Just use .72 for the IP address and it should work."

"Alright. Want to grab some food?"

"I'm not really hungry."

"You need to eat."

"I'll come sit with you."

"And eat."

I rolled my eyes and walked to the chow hall tent with him. As I rounded the corner of the HESCO barriers that formed the line outside of the tent, I stopped so abruptly that Virkler walked into me.

"What the heck, Cannon?" His eyes followed my gaze.

The grunts were immediately ahead of me in line. I saw the backs of Sergeant P and Owens. Red was standing in front of them, facing me, and he looked directly at me. His eyes were still deadened, and his gaze made me look down immediately. Red wasn't wearing bloody cammies anymore, but he looked like death.

I turned back to Virkler. "I'm really not hungry. I'm going to go to sleep."

"Uh, okay? You really need to eat."

"I'll see you later."

I slunk off to my can in shame. My feet crunched the rocks with every step and the noise grated in my ears, boring into my brain.

Fucking noisy, fucking feet. Why the fuck are you so loud? Why the fuck are you so fucked up? Why did you fuck up? What the fuck is wrong with you? If you had just opened the other document, Dumaw might be alive. You dumb fucking fuck. Fuck.

Later on, I came across a gathering of Marines by accident. I walked up to Dumaw's memorial service and stood far away from everyone. No one noticed me. Everyone was gathered around the boots and rifle display. Their body language showed defeat. I stayed for less than a minute before walking away. I was an imposter in that heartbreaking moment.

I shouldn't be here.

The Warhawk's Prayer

Blessed Saint Michael, Archangel of Battle,
We pray you watch over our souls.
And should we walk into combat this day,
We pray you be our shining armor and protection
Against the snares and fires of these wretched demons we face,
Who believe themselves our equals,
Guide our rounds to pierce their flesh and into the empty blackness
these wicked men call hearts.
We shall take violent vengeance against those who have trespassed
against us,
And stolen our Brother out of cowardice and fear.
We shall rain down upon them the Raging Fires Destruction brought
forth from the depths of Hell itself,
Born of our anger, our agony and our pain.
The full weight of our violent rage shall come down upon them and crush
their blackened hearts,
And we shall repay these wicked men with death.
Each and every corrupt and twisted soul to cross our path shall be slain,
That we may send them to the Gates of Judgement.
And if, in your wisdom, we should fall in Righteous Battle,
We pray you take us gently and with compassion.
Guide our fallen through the Holy Gates unto the Almighty's domain,
That we may stand among the Just and Saintly.
Oh Saint Michael, Prince of the Heavenly Host,
We beg of you, sharpen your sword, ready your shield, and fly with us
into Battle.

Written by Lance Corporal Alex Aron Daniel Salgado
Police Mentor Team RCT-2
in the days and weeks following the loss of Corporal Joshua Dumaw, who was KIA
on the evening of June 22, 2010, in Nimruz Province, Afghanistan.

39

June 2010, Camp Delaram, Afghanistan

I sat in the technical control facility (TCF) alone. At some point during the time I was with the grunts, the communications equipment for RCT-2 had been moved out of the tents and into a plywood building erected by the Navy Seabees. The building was spotless and kept out sand and dust extremely well, considering it was in the desert. It was well-lit, unlike the old networking tent, and the tan plywood was splintery and new.

It was 0200 and everything was quiet. I was simultaneously doing Marine Corps Institute classes and watching *Weeds*. The drama in *Weeds* made me feel better about my own life drama. We were still in River City from Dumaw's death, which meant that all outside communication was cut off until his family was contacted. When I received the email, I knew it came from within Afghanistan.

Come here.

I read the email, got to my feet, and walked to the help desk next to the COC where William worked. I stayed on the porch and waited for him to come out to meet me. I didn't like being summoned, but I knew he would come find me anyway, and I hadn't had a conversation with another person in days. My vocal cords needed some exercise and I needed to talk to someone.

He came outside and smiled at me. I looked at him and didn't smile back.

"What's wrong with you?"

"Dumaw died."

"Who?"

"One of the guys from the missions I've been going on."

"Well, that's what happens to people outside the wire. It's a risk they take."

"I could have been on that patrol. I almost was."

"Well, you weren't."

"K."

"Why are you so bothered? Were you more than friends with him?"

"What? No!"

"Good."

I was simultaneously sickened and angry at his accusations.

"I took down comm when they were trying to call in a medevac. I don't think they could get help."

He sat and watched me as tears filled my eyes. Survivor's guilt is a weird thing.

"Look, William, I've been thinking. I don't think I can do this."

"Do what?"

"Have this baby."

"Well, you are having it, so—"

"I can't. If anyone finds out, I'll be arrested. Everything I've worked for will be gone."

"So, what are you saying?"

"I dunno. I would have to—"

I stopped talking and dropped my eyes to the ground. My throat swelled up and I swallowed hard.

"You'd be that selfish? To murder a child?"

"Not selfish, William. I had sex in a combat zone. I went against orders. I could be court martialed and placed in the brig if someone finds out."

"Exactly. If you try to get an abortion, I'll turn you in. They'll arrest you and you'll be placed in the brig and you won't be able to get an abortion. Then I'll have the child taken from you because clearly you are an unfit mother."

"William, no, everyone will know when I have this kid that I broke the law. I'll be arrested anyway."

"At least my child will be alive. I'll raise her and you'll finish your time and get out of the military."

"I'll be kicked out. Dishonorable discharge. I'll lose my benefits, everything."

"So? You don't need a job. You'll be a mother."

"All of my benefits … my school … if I'm dishonorably discharged, I lose the GI Bill."

"You don't need school. Raise your children."

"But—"

"Dammit, if you do this I'll turn you in, I swear."

I started crying.

"Look, I'll order more prenatal vitamins. Everything will be fine."

40

July 4, 2010, Camp Delaram, Afghanistan

The chow hall air was damp with sweat. The third country nationals (TCNs) loaded my plate with steak and lobster and green beans. The plate steamed from the heat of the food. It was a feast that I hadn't seen before in Afghanistan.

I guess they made a special delivery for the Fourth of July. Where the fuck did this lobster come from? Isn't Afghanistan landlocked? And ice would melt in a second out here.

As I exited the chow hall, my eyes adjusted to the blinding sun and a large gust of oven-hot wind engulfed me and my food. The wind elegantly deposited the usual amount of sand on both.

Of course.

I crunched my way over to the large tent that served as a dining hall. I swung open the door and entered darkness. As I stood and waited for my eyes to adjust to the lack of blinding sun, I tried to focus on the faces before me in the tent.

All Georgians.

They stared at me as I passed and sat down alone. I was used to the stares at this point, so I avoided all of their eyes and focused my attention on the tiny little American flag on the center of the table. It looked flimsy compared to the giant flag that hung at the top of the tent.

I was so nauseated.

Swallowing the bile that had crept into my throat from the small walk from the chow hall, I looked down at my plate. I poked the rubbery lobster.

I fucking hate lobster.

I picked up my fork and knife and tried to cut into the steak. After I sawed at the tough steak for what seemed like an hour, I managed to cut off a small piece. Taking a small bite, I chewed the tasteless and leather-like meat. Stopping mid-chew, I opened the napkin that lay next to my plate and vomited into it. Wiping the bile from my mouth, I sat and looked at my plate, shuffling the green beans from side to side.

I need to eat something. This baby needs something.

I looked at the meat again and heaved.

And if you feel like the whole wide world is raining down on youuuu ....

I lamented the song lyrics in my head.

Everything is so fucking hot. It's so hot here. I don't want hot lobster and steak. I want ice. I want ice cold watermelon. I want ....

My mouth began to water at the thought of a juicy slice of cold watermelon. I imagined an ice cube on my tongue, slowly melting. I'd let the cool, melted water slide down my hot throat and I'd feel it enter my belly and gently slosh around. Even the watermelon the grunts had was hot and sticky. I wanted cold.

I'm not even hungry. I want to be cold. I'm salivating at the thought of being cold.

Even our water was unbearably warm. Pallets of bottled water had been air dropped on base, exploding open and scattering bottles of water several feet in every direction. Water disappeared quickly, and we had to dig with our hands into the sand to find stray water bottles in order to drink. If we were lucky enough to find one bottle of water in the dusty sand, we would crack it open to pour water that was over 100 degrees and tasted like carrots into our mouth. Harot water. 0/10 recommend.

I glanced around at the Georgians in the chow hall. None of them were paying attention to me anymore as I reached over and plucked the small American flag from the center of my table.

I threw my plate into the trash and pocketed the American flag.

Happy Birthday, America.

41

July 2010, Camp Delaram, Afghanistan

River City was lifted, and I immediately called my husband, Adam, in America. It took three days for him to answer a phone call.

"Hey."

"Hey."

The time delay between responses made communication difficult.

"Look, are you somewhere alone where I can talk to you?"

"No. Let me go outside." I heard sounds of him opening a sliding door. "Okay, what's up?"

I didn't want to tell him about Dumaw. I couldn't.

"Remember last year when we discussed swinging and the possibilities of me getting pregnant?"

"Yeah …. Why?"

I took a deep breath. "I'm pregnant."

His laughter resonated through the earpiece.

"Oh yeah? By who?"

"Just a guy. But hey, are you okay? Are we okay?"

"I'm good. You're the one pregnant in Afghanistan."

"Yeah. But how are we?"

"I said it then and I'll say it again, it's okay."

"Are you sure?"

"Yeah, look, I gotta go. Love ya, bye."

The phone disconnected before I could respond. I hung up the phone, both relieved and a little disconcerted.

He was too cavalier. And he didn't ask me how I was. And he hasn't heard from me in a month. What the hell?

I called back. There was no answer.

I tried calling back every day, multiple times a day, for three weeks.

42

July 2010, Camp Delaram, Afghanistan

I was on the phone with a contractor from Leatherneck who was telling me what to do.

"Go change the MTU on the TACLANE to 1423."

"Are you sure?"

"We have a maintenance window of four hours to do this. They expect your communication to go down."

"If you say so."

It was 0200 and I was the only person in the newly built Technical Control Facility. I walked over to the room across the hall and changed the Maximum Transmission Unit on our encryptor. I walked back to my desk and picked up the phone.

"Done."

"Okay, hold on."

I poked around my computer while I waited for Simon to check my connection from Camp Leatherneck. He was one of the main engineers in our Area of Responsibility (AOR). I had never met him, but we had cultivated somewhat of a friendship over the months of these middle-of-the-night maintenance windows.

As I tried navigating to Facebook, I saw another email come in.

Come here.

I ignored it but felt a sense of dread settle in the bottom of my stomach. Simon came back on the phone.

"Hey, it worked. You're back up."

"Cool."

"Hey, are you okay? You've sounded different."

I sat in silence, shocked that someone who was miles and miles away could sense that something was wrong.

"Uh, I'm fine."

"Are you sure? Your voice sounds … different."

I sighed. "There's just a lot going on out here."

"Hey, look, just let me know if you need to talk ever. I've been around the block a few times and I never sleep."

"Thank you. But I'm fine. I'll be fine."

"Alright. Enjoy the rest of your shift."

"Always." I responded sarcastically.

We disconnected and I sank back into my hard metal folding chair.

Bing.

Where are you?

I sat upright with a jolt. Almost robotically, I walked outside and into the compound where William sat on the front porch of the COC.

"Why didn't you answer?"

"I was working."

He looked at me suspiciously as he lit his cigarette. He took a long drag and sat down on the wall with his feet on the bench seat. "You've been emailing your husband."

"What? How did you know th—"

"Why are you emailing him?"

"I …. Wait, how did you know?"

"You don't think I know what happens on your computer?"

"You're reading my emails?!"

"Don't contact him again. He isn't your family anymore. You're carrying my child. You will go back to America and get a divorce before she is born. You will not talk to him again. You will marry me, so she won't be born out of wedlock."

My mouth dropped open and my stomach turned cold. Somewhere in the back of my brain I laughed that this wasn't the kind of "cold" I was daydreaming about.

"I can't just stop talking to him."

William ignored me. "And while we are on it, I know you have access to Facebook. Don't think you can try contacting him through that either. I'll know."

My brain was screaming with questions and fear. *This is the man I'm going to raise a child with? He expects me to marry him. I can't marry this! He tracks me wherever I go; he wants me to rely totally on him, barefoot in the kitchen, popping out babies ....*

I finally realized why I was so terrified of the situation. I saw my mom stay with someone who hit her, hit me and my sister, who shot a television .... She stayed because she couldn't afford not to stay. She didn't have an education or a career, so she was tied to someone who treated her and her children like refuse. I was watching history repeat itself, from my mother, through to me. I would be forever tied to someone, incapable of breaking away from a situation that would cause my independent soul to decay, my fiery love of life to wilt .... I would slowly become a shell of the wonderful woman I was supposed to be.

How will I support myself? If he reports me for being pregnant, I'll lose my career; I'll go to jail. He will take my baby from me. I won't be able to finish my degree.

My thoughts flashed to the Marine Corps Captain chevrons I kept tucked in the little folds on the inside of my cover, just behind the eagle, globe, and anchor insignia; chevrons of motivation, of what I knew I was capable of. My dream of finishing my degree and commissioning as an officer, Captain Cannon, wavered in front of my mind's eye.

So, either I go along with this, doing as he says until I get out of this country, or I lose everything. I can figure this out.

William continued talking. I was shifting through possible solutions to this impossible situation, full of terror like a panicked rabbit cornered by a self-assured fox. I wasn't capable of listening until a word jarred my distracted thoughts and brought me smashing right back to earth. "Wait, what?"

"She'll be raised Catholic."

"But I'm not Catholic."

"Neither am I, really. I don't agree with how they interpret certain parts of the Bible."

"I'm not even sure I believe in God anymore, William."

"Why not?"

"Dumaw? War in general? I don't want to raise my child to believe in some guy in the sky who doesn't see the swallow fall."

"Dumaw wasn't a swallow. He made a choice to be in the military."

"It doesn't matter; I don't want to raise her Catholic."

"We will raise her in the church."

"I'm not okay with this."

"I'm not okay with having a child with someone who doesn't fully believe. You said you did."

"Things changed."

"So, change them back."

At this point, the sky was beginning to turn light blues and pinks. William finished his cigarette and tossed the butt into the sand. "Let's get breakfast."

"I'm not hungry."

"Your daughter is. Eat something."

We walked to the chow hall. I was sick to my stomach as I saw the alternate paths of my life ahead of me. One path, married to William, forced to do as he pleases because I have no career, no education, and no other choice. Another path, in jail because I didn't acquiesce, with my daughter taken from me, deemed an unfit mother, with a dishonorable discharge, no career, and no education. Another path?

The sun broke as we descended the hill, and I felt my back grow hot as the rays struck it. After ten hours of darkness, my eyes strained at the bright and relentless morning sun.

William and I went to sit in the extended tent. I walked to the side of the back-most table that faced the only entrance to the tent. William put his hand on my shoulder, "No, sit on the other side."

"I can't sit with my back to the door. We can both sit on this side."

"Sit on the other side. I want to see your face while I eat. We need to discuss some stuff about our child."

I slowly slid my tray to the other side and sat down with my back facing the door. Having my back to the door made me anxious. Someone could come up behind me without me knowing. I heard the door open and turned around to see who it was.

"Why are you looking at the door? Are you expecting someone?"

"No, I just can't not look."

"Stop."

We sat in silence. The door opened again. William watched my face to see if I would look again. My eyes flickered over as someone came into my peripheral vision.

"Stop looking at other people."

"Why does it matter if I look?"

"Why does it matter if you don't?"

I didn't respond. My throat began to close up and I couldn't breathe. I was in a combat zone, and I was being forced to not be aware of my surroundings. Every nerve in my body screamed to look as the door opened again. I felt helpless, completely at this man's mercy, the man who dangled everything I loved over a precipice every day. I didn't look, and William smiled. "Good. See? You only need to look at me."

I pushed the canned peaches around my plate and sank further into myself.

43

July 2010, Camp Delaram, Afghanistan

"We can go to Harry Potter land."

As William waited for me to speak, I shook my head, jolted back into reality—I was actually living this life. It felt like everything had closed in on me and I couldn't escape. I was determined to make this work for my baby. William wasn't a bad person, right? He had a daughter already and had sacrificed a year of his life to come to a combat zone to get enough money to give her a good life.

He's just concerned because there are a bunch of men out here and I'm vulnerable. It's understandable. I can make this work. He makes good money and I'll need someone to support me if I'm dishonorably discharged from the Marine Corps at 20 years old for being a whore.

I smiled at him. "Yeah? I love Harry Potter."

"Me too. We can take the girls and explore."

"That would be nice."

Images of the four of us walking through the live experience of my favorite book series floated through my head.

We could get wands and drink Butterbeer. Yeah, this can work.

William smiled at me and relaxed into his seat. "You'll be a good mother." Then he walked me back to work for shift changeover.

All the Marines gathered around in a group, bullshitting and talking shit to each other. Everyone avoided me completely until Staff Sergeant Rambo came in and sat down at his desk and looked at me. "How was last night?"

"It went well."

"Good. Leatherneck was happy?"

"Yeah."

I had completely dropped all formal phrasing from my vocabulary as I spoke to the SNCO who was two ranks higher than me. I didn't mean to be disrespectful, but I was having a hard time catching my breath from the walk back from the chow hall. Staff Sergeant Rambo began telling the guys what they needed to do for the day, and I stepped back.

Suddenly, I started to feel faint. My knees weren't locked, which notoriously causes fainting in the military, and I hadn't been standing for that long. I stepped back again, stumbling, as my vision began to turn white. I focused on Staff Sergeant Rambo's desk through the white.

Don't pass out. Don't pass out.

I fell against the wall and slowly slid down with my hands on my knees. I got really hot and suddenly very cold, then went back to hot.

"Cannon." Staff Sergeant Rambo's voice was sharp. "Someone get her a chair!"

"I'm fine!" My voice snapped. "I just need to—"

I slid farther down the wall until I was sitting. I put my head in my hands and tried to stop the world from spinning, between flashes of hot and cold.

Everyone stared at me.

I can't be weak. I can't show that something is wrong. I'm fine. You're fine. Get up.

I struggled to get to my feet and leaned against the wall. "I'm fine."

Fine. You're fine.

Once the shift changeover was done, I walked out of the TCF alone.

"Cannon, wait!"

I turned around to see Staff Sergeant Rambo running after me. I stopped and waited for him to reach me.

"Yes, Staff Sergeant? I'm sorry about what happened in there. I don't think I've been drinking enough water."

"Then drink more." His voice wasn't mean, it was factual.

We stood in silence.

"Cannon, hey look, I understand that deployments can be tough. This is your first one, right?"

"Yes, Staff Sergeant."

"Is your family okay?"

Without warning, tears flooded my eyes. "I don't know. My husband won't answer the phone or any of my emails."

Staff Sergeant Rambo studied my face as I looked at the ground. He took a deep breath and sighed. "I don't know if you've noticed, but I'm not wearing my wedding ring."

I looked at his hands. They were white and soft, and the ring finger on his left hand was empty. I looked back into his eyes questioningly.

He continued. "When I went home on R&R, my wife threw her wedding ring at me and said she never wanted to see me again. 'We are getting a divorce.'"

He was no longer the SNCO who I took orders from; he was a man forced to be thousands of miles away from the woman he loved, who probably wouldn't have stopped loving him if he had stayed in America.

"I'm so sorry."

"All I'm saying is, we are all going through some personal stuff. You just have to buckle down and keep going, because what is happening here, your job, is what matters now. You can't force someone to be there for you. America doesn't understand what goes on here and you can't spend your time and energy on someone on the other side of the world."

I fought back the tears as I thought about how much I appreciated his words, but he didn't understand. He couldn't.

"You can talk to me, you know."

I paused for a very long time.

I can't tell him what's happening. I'll be court martialed. I'll be sent to the brig. Should I tell him? Can he help? No. He is bound to his duties by the Uniformed Code of Military Justice. I can't tell him anything.

"I'm fine, Staff Sergeant. Thank you."

He studied me for a minute longer. "Okay. Don't be stubborn, Cannon."

I laughed bitterly, turned, and walked away.

44

July 2010, Camp Delaram, Afghanistan

I lay on my bed in my silkie bottoms and shirt. I was freshly showered, with the usual layer of dust gathered on my dampened skin during the walk back.

William had said he would come by my can after he got off work. I had told him it wasn't a good idea because two new girls had moved into the tent I was sharing with the lance corporal. I didn't know their sleep schedules, in fact I knew nothing about them, and it was possible they would be around when he stopped by. I also didn't want him around.

"I'll come in the back."

"I dunno. I don't want to get caught."

Getting in trouble for a man in my can would just be the icing on this shitcake.

"Just leave the back of the tent open."

"William, I don't want to do anything to get into trouble."

"I'll be there around nine."

I looked at my watch. 0855. He'd be by any second. I rolled onto my left side and faced the back of the can. There was a giant zippered square door on the back of the tent. Because the bathrooms were so far away and my bladder seemed to have shrunk exponentially, I had begun stepping out of the back of the tent to relieve myself, between the air-conditioning units, whenever I woke up. No one was ever behind my can, but if someone had walked back there around 1300, they would see a groggy and grumpy female trying ridiculously hard not to pee on her feet and sometimes failing.

My ears strained to hear if the new girls had fallen asleep yet. One chuckled. *She must be watching something on her laptop. Fuck. I hope it's distracting.*

Three sides of my bottom bunk were blocked from view. The only opening was the left side, the one facing the rear of the can.

I heard the zipper start to come up from the bottom of the tent. It slid up slowly but deliberately. I bolted upright and gazed around the sheets that blocked my bunk to make sure no one was looking out from their bunks.

When William stepped in, I gestured to him to hurry over before someone saw him. He was so tall that I was sure his shadow had cast over another bunk when the sun came in through the open tent flap. I zipped it shut and sat down on my bed next to my pillow. I closed my legs and brought my knees up, hugging them to my chest. "William, why are you here?"

"To make love to the mother of my child."

We were both whispering.

"No, I don't want to. People are in here."

"Do you not feel well?"

His voice was suddenly concerned.

"No, I don't."

"Are you eating?"

"They keep running out of food during midrats."

Midrats were the "middle of the night" rations for people on night shift. I was lying to him. They didn't run out of food. But I couldn't eat chicken cordon bleu for the fifth day in a row.

"I'll find you some food. You'll feel better."

He leaned over to kiss me. I reluctantly kissed him back. He put his hands on my shoulders and squeezed.

"Lay back."

"William, I don't want to do—"

He shoved me backward. I lay down in silence. I couldn't let the other girls hear.

William pulled down my silkie shorts. I lay in silence. When he unbuckled his pants, I started to shake my head and opened my mouth. He placed his hand over it.

"They will hear you."

His hand remained over my mouth as he proceeded to shove inside of me. I'm five years old again.

At one point, I looked over to my weapon that rested against the flight bag. The magazine of bullets was next to it. My knife was in my cammie bottom pocket, less than three feet from me.

I didn't fight back. If I yelled, I would be found out and arrested.

You're fine. You're fine.

By the time he was done, I had journeyed around the world and back. I had gone to the days of playing "the floor is lava" with my best friend on the bus in elementary school. I had played songs on my flute in my head, purposefully imagining every placement of my finger to form the notes, to keep myself from making a sound. "Whisper to their Souls" was drifting through my head. I was riding down the streets of my hometown on my bicycle with my sister. I was anywhere but in Afghanistan.

I didn't remember him leaving. I remember noticing my pillow was wet from tears, but I did not remember when I started crying. I remember pulling the knife from my pants pocket and laying back down on the bed.

I pulled up my shirt and pulled down the top of my shorts. I opened the knife and traced my stomach, right where my baby was.

I could just stab myself now. If I did it quickly, I could probably slice myself open enough to kill her and myself before I went into shock. If they found me in time, they would be so worried about me that they might not notice her. The doctors would. But I would be protected, right?

I pressed deeper into the skin above my uterus with the blade.

I could do it.

Just do it.

Do it.

I burst into tears and flung myself onto my left side. I could see the now-zipped doorway and the air-conditioning tube that ran along the side of the wall to the ceiling and deposited six feet above my head.

It's so fucking hot.

I took my knife and, through the blubbery tears, sliced the AC tube multiple times. Cold air poured out onto me directly.

Why the fuck didn't I do that months ago? Fuck. I'm fucked.

I started to cry again, not holding back for fear of being found out. I cried loudly, sobbing into Pongo, the stuffed Dalmation dog I had slept with as a child and had brought to Afghanistan, and no one heard.

45

July 2010, Camp Delaram, Afghanistan

The Internet was slow. I tapped my foot impatiently as I waited for the web page to load. When it finally did, I read the information and wrote down a phone number on a piece of paper. I walked into the server room of the TCF and sat cross-legged on the floor next to the green tactical box that held unused equipment.

"Hello, you have reached Planned Parenthood of San Diego. Please listen to the following options before choos—"

I pressed 0.

I don't have time to listen to menus. Get me a person.

"Hello, this is Nurse Trisha, how may I help you?"

"Hi. I have a few questions."

"I'm sorry, there seems to be a delay."

"There will be. I have some questions?"

"Okay, what are they?"

"What's the latest someone can get an abortion?"

"We don't perform abortions after the first trimester."

"So, 12 weeks?"

"Twelve weeks."

"How much do they cost?"

"It depends on how far along you are. Do you have insurance?"

"Yes, Tricare."

"Oh, well, Tricare doesn't cover anything regarding an abortion unless the baby is the result of a rape or in cases of incest. Is this true for you?"

"No, not the result."

"Then you'll need to use Planned Parenthood. We have options for people who can't pay the full amount through outside donors. How far along are you?"

"Six weeks."

"Well, that is approximately four—"

I was rapidly doing calculations in my head, and I cut her off.

"How much is a 12-week abortion?"

"Um, approximately 900 dollars. The cost of medicine varies. But may I ask why you would wait? The further along an abortion is, the more invasive and dangerous the procedure."

"I, uh, I kinda can't get to a center right now."

"Ma'am, I'm sure your life is busy, but your health matters in this situation."

"Am I able to just walk in?"

"You'll need an appointment. If you decide to walk in, we might be able to see you, but we can't promise anything."

"Okay, thanks for the help."

"Have a good day!"

I hung up the phone and sat with my head in my hands, continuously doing the math.

I got to Afghanistan in March. Deployments are typically 6–7 months long. It's the end of July. August makes six months. September makes seven. I'll be 12 weeks along September 17th. Is this possible? Can I do this?

I blocked out the thought that this was my child I was so excited about. I blocked out the thought this was the child I had wanted so desperately. I pushed those thoughts out of my head and started building a wall around the part of my heart that had jumped for joy when I saw the plus sign. Brick by brick, I built the wall and dehumanized the child I was carrying. And I placed a few more bricks around the memory of William coming into my tent.

46

July 2010, Camp Delaram, Afghanistan

I Googled my parent unit that was stationed in California. Once the Internet let me slowly navigate to the webpage, I wrote down the number for the Officer of the Day's desk. The Officer of the Day is a randomly assigned junior officer or a staff non-commissioned officer who stands a 24-hour duty at the regiment. The OOD is in charge of all people and property within the command during their 24-hour shift. All domestic abuse incidents, drinking and driving arrests, and Marines jumping from the third deck balcony with ponchos as parachutes were the bane of the OOD's existence.

I walked over to the phone and dialed the number.

"Good morning, sir or ma'am, this is Combat Logistics Regiment 17, Captain Sullivan speaking. How may I help you?"

"Good evening, sir, this is Corporal Cannon. I am looking for my husband who works in Communications Company."

"Umm, who is your husband?"

I told him my husband's name and rank.

"Have you tried his cell phone?"

"Yes, sir, he isn't answering."

"Well, try back later."

"Sir, I'm in Afghanistan and he isn't picking up the phone."

"Maybe he's busy."

The captain was nonchalant. I wasn't getting anywhere with him.

"Sir, he hasn't answered in three weeks. Or my emails."

There was silence on the other side of the line.

"Corporal?"

His voice was suddenly business-like.

"Yes, sir."

"What did you say his name was?"

He gathered my husband's name and the platoon he was supposedly in.

"Please hold on."

The phone was set down. I heard the captain relay the story to his assistant duty, a gunnery sergeant, who said, "Oh no."

Five minutes passed before the captain picked up the phone again. "What's your email?"

"savannah.cannon@afg.mil, sir."

"Alright. I talked to his commanding officer. They are getting in touch with him now. You should receive an email from me when it's okay for you to call back."

"Yes, sir, thank you."

"Sure thing. Stay safe, Marine."

I hung up the phone.

Fuck. I guess I didn't think the CO would get involved. He's going to be in so much trouble. Well, hell, good. That will teach him not to ignore his wife who is in a combat zone. Fucker.

I received an email about ten minutes later.

Call the duty phone.

I rang the OOD number again.

"Good morning, sir or ma'am, this is Combat Logistics Regiment 17, Captain Sullivan speaking. How may I help you?"

"Sir, it's Corporal Cannon."

"Yes, here he is."

The phone was handed to my husband, who said hello in a cheery voice.

"Hey, what's up?"

I heard him laugh to the OOD.

"Yes, sir, I've got it. Thank you."

"I'll leave you two alone."

"Thank you, sir."

The officer walked away from my husband and left him on the duty phone. Once the officer was out of earshot, my husband hissed at me.

"What the FUCK do you think you're doing? Are you fucking crazy? I got dragged into the CO's office!"

"You were ignoring my emails and my calls! What was I supposed to do? I emailed your dad and your brother. Neither of them is responding to me either."

"Yeah, I told them what you did. I don't want anything to do with you."

"What? Why?"

I knew why.

"You're fucking pregnant from someone else in Afghanistan!"

"There's a lot going on out here, I need to talk to you."

"Since the CO is making sure I talk to you, go ahead, what do you have to say?"

His voice was so sharp that my mind went blank. How could I explain everything that had gone on in the last few months?

"I need a friend. *Please*. You said you would always be my friend. We haven't seriously spent time around each other in almost a year and a half. Between your deployment and mine—"

He cut me off. "I. Don't. Want. To. Be. With. You."

"Please!" I was crying at this point. "Please, please! You said you would stay with me, even if I got pregnant. Remember? It was a risk. Remember what you said to me when we got married?"

The line was silent.

"I love you, please don't do this."

"Do not tell the command that I am not answering your phone calls. I don't need this shit."

"No, I won't. I won't say anything to them again. I promise. I just needed to know why you weren't answering. Just please answer my emails, or something."

"Yeah, sure."

"I love you."

"Bye."

I hung up the phone and wiped away my tears before walking back to my computer. I put on *Weeds* again and judged Nancy's life choices.

47

July 2010, Camp Delaram, Afghanistan

During the morning changeover, I overheard the other Comm guys talking: "Did you go see him yet?"

"Nah, and what the fuck is he going to do for me? I'm not re-enlisting and they won't move me to another station with only two years left."

"He could move you to another unit within the station."

"And miss out on HQ's fantastic treatment of us? No, thanks. I'll just stick with the evil I know."

"It's your life, bro."

"Yup. What about you? Asked him to move you to Pendleton yet?"

"Yeah, he said he would work something out. He said I would have orders in the system within a few weeks."

"Dude, that's awesome. I mean, you're an idiot for re-enlisting, but you'll get to see your girlfriend in California."

"Yeah, I'm pretty happy about it. But I'm not telling her until I have orders in-hand. You know the Marine Corps."

"Yeah ...."

Another Marine walked up and joined the conversation. "Are you guys talking about the monitor?"

"Yeah, they are all here for a few days. Go talk to him."

"Why? He can't do anything for me."

"Always go talk to your monitor when they do these roadshows. If you plan on staying in the Marine Corps, this man dictates every aspect of your life: When you get orders, where you get orders to, how long you get orders for .... They are the gods of the Marine Corps."

"I bet they have people offering to suck them off daily to get away from Headquarters and Service Company."

"Fuuuuck, I know, right?"

Staff Sergeant Rambo came in and changeover commenced. Upon its conclusion, I quickly walked out of the compound and down the hill in search of the monitor. Luckily, the base was small, and I noticed a congregation of Marines near a can that I knew wasn't occupied on a normal day. As I walked up, everyone stopped to stare at me.

"Is this where the monitors are?"

One of the men gruffly replied in the affirmative with disdain. Trying not to show my eyes rolling at his manner, I swung open the door of the can. My eyes tried adjusting to the interior that was much darker than the blinding sun of the desert. Blinking rapidly, knowing that people on the inside would be watching me as I tried to see again, I strained my eyes to make sense of the blobs in front of me. Slowly, I could make out multiple desks facing the door, with single chairs next to them that were turned toward the desk in a consulting manner. There were pieces of paper taped to the front of the desks with what I determined were Military Occupational Specialty numbers.

Each MOS has a monitor that determines the career of the people within its field. The monitor can see what the Marine Corps needs at each station and in each unit and can adjust Marines' orders to benefit the Marine Corps. No matter what, the monitor puts the Marine Corps first. Family doesn't matter, sometimes rotation time (time between overseas assignments) is upheld, but in a time of two wars it was often ignored, and certainly the Marine's desires were ignored. Needs of the Marine Corps went first.

I saw a desk with 06XX on its piece of paper and made my way to it. The master sergeant was fiddling on his computer with no one around him, unlike every other desk in the can.

"Good morning, Master Sergeant."

"Marine! Good morning!"

He was all smiles. It was so weird to see such happiness in the desert.

"Are you the Data monitor?"

"Sure am, what can I do ya for?"

"I would like to know my options. I'm Data."

"Out here? What on earth are you doing at a combat unit?"

"They needed technical people, Master Sergeant. And they thought I was a man when they sent the roster out."

He looked me up and down, "Marines are idiots."

"Yes, Master Sergeant."

"Well, sit down! Let's see what we've got."

I sat down in the folding chair to his right and relayed my name and social security number to him. He typed away, pulling up my information, and I glanced around the room at the other monitors at work. Everyone looked so plump and refreshed.

"How long are y'all here?"

"We bounce around the bases every few days. Only in Afghanistan for two weeks."

"That's why y'all are so happy."

"Indeed. Okay, now this is what we have. You can go to Japan for two years unaccompanied."

"Well, I am married to another 0656 actually."

"Oh, what's his name? Cannon?"

"No, that's my maiden name. Didn't change it. His name is Rollio."

"Yeah, I wouldn't have changed my name either."

He looked up my husband in his system and told me there were no plans for orders yet, but he was up for them soon.

"Can we get orders somewhere else together?"

New place, new start?

"I can only change your orders. I can't change his."

"Okay. What about Base?"

"Oh, you want Base Tel? There is a spot open."

"Really?"

"Yeah, but a warning, everyone hates it. The op tempo is slow, you don't deploy, and the work is monotonous. I can keep you in a deploying unit, easy."

I remembered the last two years of constant field operations, no weekends, 18-hour workdays. If I wasn't in the field, I was in a class trying to learn stuff to use in the field. My leave had been denied a few times because the op tempo was so high and the Marine Corps came first. Deploying units in a two-war world was horribly tough. We were great at what we did, fighting wars, but our mental and physical health suffered the consequences.

A slow op tempo? Sign me up!

"Sorry, Master Sergeant, but I need to focus on my family right now. We've had two back-to-back deployments. It isn't exactly the best environment for a marriage."

"Oh yeah, the Marine Corps in general isn't exactly the best environment for a marriage."

"So, I can really get moved to Base?"

"Yeah, Marine, you're in the middle of a combat zone. You can ask for whatever the fuck you want. There are motherfuckers who haven't ever deployed, who are sitting on their asses in garrison. Take a look at this."

He swiveled the computer screen around to face me. There was an Excel spreadsheet with names and dates in different colors.

"Green means never deployed. Same rank as you."

There was a decent amount of green.

"Oh."

"Yeah, watch this."

He selected a name in green and copied it over to a different area. I wondered whose life I had just impacted with my desire for an easier ride.

"There, now he will be taking your place at CLR-17. He will be deployed within six months."

"Whoa."

"That's the Marine Corps. But hey, you're set. Enjoy Base. Your orders will be for October."

October! I'll be about six months pregnant. I wonder if I'll be showing by then, checking into my new unit. Great, I'll be THAT female Marine.

"Thank you, Master Sergeant!"

"Enjoy the States."

"Oh, trust me, I will."

48

Five months earlier: February 2010, San Diego, California, U.S.A.

We strolled off to the Home Depot paint department to find a good color to repaint Jim's bedroom. We were dating, which is difficult to explain since I was married to someone else. I had met Jim through work, about nine months previous. He was a contractor in cyber security, and we had worked together to re-image the laptops my unit needed for our upcoming deployment. We hit it off through our mutual love of smart-ass remarks.

I was head over heels for this guy. There were a few times that my marriage came up, but I swore to him that it was okay, because it was. My husband was in a relationship with someone in the Navy while he was on his deployment, and he and I had been discussing a divorce anyway. Jim and I'd had a few rough patches since we'd started seeing each other in July. For a while, he wouldn't answer text messages, but sometime around New Year's, things changed. We had spent the majority of the past two months together in some capacity.

"Okay, so what color are you looking for?"

"I don't know. Just something that's better than the boring white that it is now."

I picked up a swatch of colors and showed him a baby blue. "It matches the color of my room back home in Georgia. It's very peaceful and I love this color. Get this one."

He studied it.

"I promise, it doesn't overwhelm the room."

"Alright."

He put in the color at the paint desk, and we stood waiting for the mixture to be done.

"My husband is coming home from his deployment in two weeks."

"Yeah? Isn't that when you leave?"

"Yeah, it's looking like we might see each other for like two days before I leave for my deployment."

"Are y'all still getting a divorce?"

"I don't know. I honestly don't. I want to say yes because we won't have seen each other in over 14 months by the time I get back. And they are talking about extending my deployment to 14 months, so it would be roughly two years without seeing him. We stopped really communicating while he's been gone. I've been busy with field ops, college, regular work, and his ship's communications seem bad. The last I heard; he really likes the Navy chick he is seeing."

Jim didn't say anything, so I continued.

"Plus, I really like you. Like, enough to pick out paint with you."

Jim laughed and we put the paint in the cart to take it to checkout.

"So, if we have a giant 'Welcome Back' and 'Have a Good Deployment' party, would you want to come?"

"With your husband there? Uh, no thanks."

"It's not like that. He wouldn't care."

"Yeah, no, I'm not a fan of going to parties where the husband of the girl I've been having sex with is going to be there, regardless of your 'swinging' arrangements."

"Uh, he told me he didn't care. I'm leaving anyway."

"I guess we will see. I'm not comfortable with that."

"Okay."

Two weeks later, Jim and I were laying in his bed at one in the morning. I was supposed to be on base in an hour to leave for Afghanistan. "So, do you want to keep … doing this … while I'm gone?"

"Seven months is a long time. Let's just see what happens when you get back."

"Of course, yeah."

We lay in silence for a little bit.

"So, your husband was okay with me dropping you off for your deployment?"

"I wouldn't say okay. No, he wasn't, but we've argued for the past few days when he's been home. You can't fix a marriage in 36 hours when one of the parties is leaving for seven or 14 months. And I'm not sure I want to fix it."

"Yeah, because you like me or something." He was teasing me.

"Yeah, or something. And thank you for letting me borrow your sleeping bag from when you were in the Marine Corps. I guess my husband lost mine while he was on his deployment."

"Yeah, of course. Just bring it back. It's great for camping."

"Yeah."

We lay in silence in each other's arms. I was anxious to get going but wanted to savor every moment while I could.

"We better get going unless you want to be late for your first deployment."

We got into his car and Jim drove me to base. It was dark in Oceanside and hardly any cars were out on the roads. We pulled into the staging area. Everyone else was stacking their bags in various piles and hugging their sleepy families. Everyone looked tense in the harsh floodlights that barely cut through the darkness.

Jim got out my bags and threw them on the correct piles for me. Suddenly, it was time for me to go.

"I got you a present." He reached into his car and pulled out a tin of chocolates. "Try not to eat them all on the bus in one sitting."

"You know me too well. Thank you, Jim. That was sweet of you."

"It's not every day that you deploy to a war zone."

"Will you email me?"

"Yes, Savannah."

He rolled his eyes. We hugged and gave each other a quick kiss before he got back into his car and drove away. I placed the tin of chocolates in my cargo pocket and boarded the bus.

49

July 2010, Camp Delaram, Afghanistan

I leaned back in the roll-y chair and put my boots up on the table, shifting back and forth to try and find a good position to bring some feeling back into my ass. I pressed my computer's space bar, which un-paused VLC Player, and began watching the next episode of *Weeds*. The two wiremen on night watch were huddled together in the corner behind me, ignoring me. One of the men was a sergeant, the Marine Corps Martial Arts instructor I had bitten in the first few weeks on Delaram. Ever since I had bitten him, he had been avoiding me, even when we worked directly together on a project.

He is sitting awfully close to his lance corporal for such a large room. I wonder….

My mind dismissed the next thought in my head, and I focused on ignoring my own deteriorating life instead. *Weeds* was good for focusing on other people's bad decisions. If I thought too much about how my decisions were unfolding, I would have had a panic attack.

Bing.

My browser window flashed. My heart rate spiked, and I looked at the computer's clock.

It's 2200. It can't be William. He should be asleep. But he's the only one who messages me.

Confused, I braced myself, swallowed hard, and opened up the browser tab.

HEY! HOW HAVE YOU BEEN?!

Relieved by the cheery tone, I saw the message was from one of my lance corporals, who had deployed with me from America and had also been placed on the Georgian Liaison Team. However, Norred, as a male, had been sent out to another Forward Operating Base with the Georgians, while I remained on Delaram. I hadn't heard from him in months.

I'm alive, Norred. How are you?
I'm good. It's crazy out here. Half the time we walk around in silkies. No one gives a fuck.
Is it safe?
We have some mortar fire occasionally. There was an incident a few weeks ago but it's fine. What about you?
Same.

He was replying too quickly. He was excited to have access to the Internet and to talk to a friend who spoke English. But his replies were too cheerful and happy, and I wanted to reach through the computer and choke him.

NO, NORRED, MY LIFE IS SHIT AND I HAVE NO IDEA WHAT I AM DOING AND I FUCKED UP AND I COULD GO TO JAIL AND I HAVE TO ACT LIKE I'M FINE 24/7 EVEN THOUGH I WANT TO PUKE AND SLEEP AND CRY AND ….

My fingers were posed over the keyboard ….

Do I tell him?

As more responses came flooding in, I shook my head and placed my hands in my lap to wait for the barrage to end.

Did you hear about Cash?
No?
She was pregnant. They medevaced her.

HOLY. SHIT. She was pregnant? I'm not the only one? I need more details without giving myself away.

She was pregnant?
Yeah, man, they medevaced her in May.
Did she get into trouble?
Nah, dude, she was seven months pregnant. She got pregnant in America. WTF?!

Seven months pregnant? How the fuck didn't she know?

All of the girls were lined up before deployment and tested for pregnancy. I remembered holding my cup of pee in my hands in front of all of the men and walking up to the Navy corpsman, in a giant warehouse, to see him openly test my pee. I had tried to hide everyone's view of the doc as he dipped the pregnancy test into my still-warm cup of pee. It horrified me. What if I had been pregnant then? I would have been told by a doc in front of 100 crass and rude men, and it would have perpetuated the idea that female Marines get pregnant to get out of deployment. Fuck. That. No wonder she didn't go through the pee gauntlet. I still had no idea how she had gotten out of it.

Yeah, remember that asshole from the G-6? Jim? He's the father.

My heart went cold.

Jim. My Jim?

Are you sure?

I did the math rapidly in my head.

Seven months … that means she got pregnant in … October? November? When he and I were starting to date. So, Cash got pregnant outside of a combat zone. And she isn't married so she doesn't have to worry about getting slapped with an adultery charge.

Things had been weird with Jim then. He went back and forth with me, yanking me around, being sweet and then ignoring me for a few days. He had always said Sam Cash was just a girl who was obsessed with him and wouldn't leave him alone. It made me hate her for bugging him. In fact, I had been so fed up with the awkwardness that when I saw her, I approached her outside of the Internet café on Camp Leatherneck and yelled, "Hey, Cash!"

She terrified me. She was tall and thin with dark hair and a gaze that clearly told me to go fuck myself. She stood with two other female Marines I didn't know.

"What?"

"Do you mind if I talk to you?"

The other girls took the hint and walked away.

"What?"

"So, we've never met, or talked, really, and I just wanted to … you know … meet you. Because things feel weird, and I know you're friends with Jim and …" I trailed off, hoping that she would help me along with my grand attempt at being the "bigger" person.

She stared at me like I was a disgusting piece of trash. "Yes, we are friends. And you are married."

"Ah … yes … kinda."

"I want nothing to do with you." She practically spat at me.

"Oh … ah … okay."

She turned and left me standing by myself outside the Internet café.

Thinking back now on how my face had burned with embarrassment when she walked away, I wondered if she had known that she was pregnant then. Based on her reaction, I guessed so. Her hatred of me was palpable.

Yeah, I'm sure.

Hey, Norred, I have to go. Something went down across base. TTYL.

I quickly closed the tab before he could respond.

As I bolted to my feet, my roll-y chair shot across the room and banged into the wall behind me. The wiremen looked up in shock as I dashed out of the room. I went into the server farm and pulled the phone onto my lap. I pulled my notebook out of my cargo pocket and rapidly dialed the call center's phone number and another phone number I had written in the notebook's margins.

"Hello?"

"Hey, Jim, it's Savannah."

"I figured by the fact I don't know anyone in Indiana."

Gah, he is always such a smartass!

"How have you been?"

I was bursting to know if it was true, if he had lied to me about Cash, for months, pitting me against another woman so he could play us both. I wondered if I was the fool.

"Great. You?"

"Things are shitty."

"Yeah?"

"You stopped emailing."

"So did you."

"You know how it is out here."

There was an awkward silence. He and I had exchanged a few emails while I was on Camp Leatherneck, but the distance proved to be too much. I still had the sexy pictures he had emailed me printed out and stuffed into my bag. He had posed shirtless in front of the newly painted baby blue walls we had picked out together.

"I heard about Cash."

"Oh …"

"Is it yours?"

"She says so."

"Did you not get a paternity test?"

"Not yet."

"Jim, she got pregnant when you and I were—"

"She's lying." He was so quick to say that.

"Well, did you fuck her?"

He was silent. I tried to play it cool, like my heart wasn't breaking at getting lied to.

"When was it born?"

"July 8th. It's a girl."

"Congratulations." I said it bitterly and fell silent. He said nothing.

"What's her name?"

"Guilliana."

"What?"

"RIGHT! How weird is that? I call her Ghouls. Sam hates it."

I laughed bitterly again, imagining Cash's death glare as Jim mocked the name she had chosen.

"Well …" I got the information I needed. Her behavior towards me made so much more sense. I knew that when I hung up the phone, that would be it between us. We wouldn't even remain friends.

"Goodbye, Savannah."

I set the phone down and cried bitterly into my hands.

50

It is common knowledge that human brains aren't fully developed until well into adulthood, the late twenties or early thirties. The science behind how younger brains are lacking developmentally is pretty straightforward: myelin is a substance that covers the nerves that transmit information between brain cells. As a child, a teenager, and a young adult, this substance is thin and causes the transmissions between brain cells to be weak and inefficient. This is especially important in the function of the prefrontal cortex, where we make our decisions and solve our problems. When a young adult makes a decision that is less than optimal, it might simply be because their brains aren't capable of transmitting the signals between their brain cells.

So, for sure, the best thing to do is to take a shitload of underdeveloped brains and place them in a war zone to deal with isolation, death, and the dregs of the world.

July 2010, Camp Delaram, Afghanistan

My pregnancy began to overtake my brain. All of my other problems slid to the back burner as I struggled to survive in 120-degree heat at almost two months pregnant. Isolation, unanswered emails from my husband and his family, Jim getting someone else pregnant while we were dating, Dumaw's death, William's actions ... all of it faded to the background as I scrambled to decide what to do.

Facing the music, for my bad decision at 20, was something I couldn't accept. I began to sink into myself further and further. Every second my brain was whirling, trying to figure out what to do to avoid jail and a dishonorable discharge. I stopped eating, although not by choice. I was filled with such constant panic and fear that I couldn't eat. I spent hours researching prior court martial cases, the laws that people were prosecuted under, and ways I could get help. I researched how many ways I would be screwed if I was dishonorably discharged, including losing my GI Bill. In the past, women who became pregnant while in the Marine Corps had the option to leave the service; however, that was before the two wars affected force readiness necessities. I had never heard of it happening.

I sat on night watch, alone in the TCF building. The wiremen had disappeared.

If I manage to convince the Marine Corps to let me leave active duty because of my pregnancy, I will be in the clear. If I can hit my three-year mark in the military in December, then I will be able to retain my GI Bill benefits. If I manage to hide how far along I actually am until December, I will be able to leave the service, have my baby, and retain my education benefits.

If I lose my education benefits, everything will be ruined. That's the only decent reason I joined the Marine Corps.

If … if … if …. My underdeveloped brain swirled.

I will be forced to leave behind everything and everyone I know in order to not be prosecuted under the Uniformed Code of Military Justice (UCMJ). The UCMJ's statute of limitations is five years. I will cut everyone off for five years. I can do that, right?

How will I live? How will I pay for anything? How will I pay for the birth? Diapers? Getting out after three years in the military as a pregnant 20-year-old with no education won't offer me many options, regardless of how useful my job had been while in the service.

I looked for jobs. I wasn't qualified for any of them.

William …

My mind replayed our interactions.

This IS his child. He has a house already. His first daughter needs a mother, and I am already in love with her sweet little fat rolls. He seems like an amazing father. He will marry me; he said so already. He will treat me well. We can be happy.

I ignored the tug in the back of my brain telling me what a marriage born of necessity looks like.

You can't doubt this decision. How else will you be able to have this baby?

I gently laid my hand over the bottom of my stomach while I pondered other possibilities of my future with William.

But … what if I had a miscarriage? That would solve everything. That would solve ….

I yearned to be without this noose around my neck, to have a normal deployment with just the expected fear and death. I walked outside.

The night sky glittered like diamonds being rolled around a darkened blanket. Silence permeated the base, and I felt like the only person in the world.

I wonder if there's another world out there, with another me standing outside and looking at the night sky, who isn't pregnant, who didn't join the Marine Corps, who stayed on Camp Leatherneck, who believes in God ....

I thought about the various ways I had read about miscarriages occurring throughout the years. Scarlett O'Hara had been shoved down a stairwell. Another woman drank herbal tea that caused contractions. Blunt force trauma seemed to be the cause of a few miscarriages.

There aren't many stairs around here ....

My mind was at war. Two very different parts of me fought back and forth between an intense desire to have and love this baby and an intense fear of punishment and abuse. My mind volleyed thoughts like a tennis match with 80 different tennis balls. Back to this side, back to that side, back, back, back. Each voice began to get louder in order to be heard over the others.

LISTEN TO ME!

My mind screamed. I placed my hands on either side of my head and squeezed hard until I saw stars.

JUST FUCKING SHUT UP!

My mind went numb as the voices silenced, although they were still there ... silent, but there. I walked to the concrete bunker that had protected me from mortars for the past few months. My eyes stared straight ahead, without seeing, as I balled up my right fist. I pulled my hand up over my head and, with voices beginning to scream again, rapidly slammed my fist into my lower abdomen. My abdomen clenched tightly around my child, my body automatically protecting the thing I loved.

No, fuck, stop protecting her. I can't do this. I can't get into trouble. I can't do this, I can't, *I can't, I can't!*

Bursting into tears, I pulled my fist up and brought it down again. Again and again, I tried so hard to hit myself with full force, but my body doubled over and my fist slowed before making contact.

Doubling over in pain, I sobbed openly and laughed insanely at what I must look like, like my arm was possessed, trying to hit its wielder.

Stop hitting yourself, stop hitting yourself.

Images of my sister forcing me to punch myself in the face, when I was younger, flashed through my mind.

Stop hitting yourself.

Mocking ….
I laughed at the utter insane nonsense that I was doing. I laughed and then sobbed in a wild, animal-like tone of despair. Snot ran from my nose, and I wiped it on my sleeve as I slid into the sand in the bunker.

I'm sorry, I'm sorry, I'm so sorry, I love you, I'm sorry. I'm sorry.

I held my lower abdomen, full of sharp pains, and cradled the baby inside of me.

I'm sorry ….

Suddenly, the martial arts instructor wireman, the one I had bitten on the thigh a few months ago, stepped into the bunker. He looked down in disgust at me, sobbing, holding my stomach, alone in the dark. He was silent for a few seconds before he spoke.

"You need to get help."

He walked out of the bunker, leaving me alone in the sand.

51

July 2010, Camp Delaram, Afghanistan

I am on patrol, carrying multiple weapons and two backpacks. Sergeant P and I come to a corner and stack against each other on the edge to provide cover before proceeding around it with purpose and intent to kill. There's a crowd of civilians in the street and they turn to us as we round the corner. Their faces are filled with hatred and they swarm us with malice in their eyes. I raise my weapon and point it at a man who morphs into a small child and starts to run at me. Horrified, I continue to aim at the child. "We can't shoot!" Is the voice Sergeant P? I look around. I don't see him anymore. I am alone but surrounded by an angry crowd of dirty and laughing children and spitting men and women in brightly colored robes, all massed around me, pressing in on me, pushing me down. I can't raise my weapon anymore. I waited too long to act. They crowd above me. Angry and laughing at my pain, they press down onto me. There's a Marine taking pictures of my terror. "This is so cool!" I feel like they are sitting on my chest, restricting my breathing, and I struggle to inhale. I feel my chest try to rise, but the weight is too much. I try to breathe. I try. With the strangled breath that I can muster, I start to scream ....

I bolted upright in my bed, the nightmare reverberating in my mind, and I realized instantly that something was seriously wrong. I couldn't breathe. I was drenched in sweat and the air around me was thick and so hot that my vision seemed wavy. I struggled to sit up and found my bed wet with sweat. I swung my feet to the edge of the bed and tried to stand. When my feet hit the floor, I yanked them back with a yelp of pain.

The floor must be 110 degrees!

The AC tube dangled loosely from where it ran down the corner of the can. I had been without air conditioning for God knows how long and left to bake in the Afghanistan desert heat with my can as an oven.

How long was I asleep?

I swallowed hard and realized my throat was cracked.

I must have actually screamed to wake up.

I tried to breathe and still couldn't. Almost passing out, I put on my flip-flops, grabbed my rifle, and limped to the tent flap two feet from my bed. I struggled to lift the zipper and fell out of the can into the blazing sun.

The 120-degree air felt like cool water pouring down my throat, filling my lungs. I realized the camp was silent when I couldn't hear the usual drone of the generators. I looked around and no one was in sight.

They must all be working. Only night shift would be in the tents right now. What the fuck happened? Why aren't the generators running?

I walked to a bunker and collapsed in the shade. I felt drained of everything. Looking at my watch, I realized it was 1400 and I had five more hours until my shift started.

Shit. I can't go back to that oven.

I laid down in the sand and closed my eyes. The nightmare came flooding back to me and I bolted upright again.

Nah. I'm good. I don't need sleep.

I entered the can and dressed quickly before heading to work five hours early.

As I walked to the compound, I passed a giant group of Communications Marines, including Virkler, Ski, and Rambo, standing next to the large unit sign for RCT-2.

"Hey, what's going on?"

"We are taking unit pictures."

"Oh, what about me?"

"Are you part of our unit? Get out of here, you dirty PTADer."

Someone yelled from the crowd, pointing out my temporary assigned duty status away from my parent unit to RCT-2 for six months in a combat zone. Tears stung my eyes and I blurrily watched them huddle together for their unit picture before I trudged into work.

52

August 2010, Camp Delaram, Afghanistan

William met me on the porch, and we walked down the hill to the chow hall. It was 0500 and the sun was breaking harshly over the horizon as we made our way down the sandy slope.

"The Wizarding World of Harry Potter just opened in Florida."

He waited for me to respond. "Oh, that's cool."

"Yeah, looks like they have everything. Butterbeer, wands, you name it."

"Mmmm, Butterbeer. I wonder what that tastes like. The books make it seem so amazing."

William watched me as I practically salivated in the sand, and he smiled.

"Let's go. Like I said before. Let's take our children when we leave Afghanistan."

"Amy too?"

"Haha, yeah, of course. You'll be her mother."

"I'd like that."

We smiled at each other.

See? This is good. He really is good. He cares about his children having a good mother, he wants them to be raised with Christian values, he can provide for us …. It is a little presumptuous that I'll be Amy's mother though. What about her real mother?

"Did you get any more pictures of her from your family?"

"Yeah, do you want to see them?"

"Of course, I want to see more of my daughter."

So, I'm going to raise two babies. I'm 20. I guess I'll be just like everyone else from my hometown.

We were approaching his can where he lived with about ten other contrac-tors. He told me to stand outside while he opened the door and went inside. I wasn't supposed to be in his sleeping area, but I had broken that rule almost two months ago, so I was able to picture him rummaging through his things. His bed was fourth from the left, bottom bunk. I shuffled back and forth on my feet as the sun began roasting my back. When William walked out of the can, he was holding a few pictures of Amy. Her face was so cute and chubby, and my heart ached to think of holding her.

"I can't wait."

"Me either. You'll be a good mom."

"I hope so."

We made our way down to the chow hall. I grabbed the food that looked appetizing, Special K cereal and Silk soy milk. Silk didn't have to be refrigerated, so it was perfect for transport through the desert. William encouraged me to put more food on my plate.

"You need to eat more."

"I'm trying. Nothing seems appealing, and I really just want an orange or some fresh fruit."

"You're having cravings?"

"Just fruit."

"Are you taking your vitamins?"

"Yeah, of course. And I stopped taking those ridiculous malaria pills. They gave me technicolor nightmares. I just can't get the idea of fruit out of my head."

I hadn't seen fruit since the grunts had that watermelon. Fruit was scarce so, of course, that's what I obsessed over.

"Good. I'll see if I can find some fruit for you in the next few weeks."

"Thank you."

"Anything for you and my baby."

See? He'll take care of me.

We walked into the dining tent, and he held the door for me to proceed ahead of him. The dining tent was occupied with Georgians who were intensely watching the television that was newly installed on the far wall. The Armed Forces Network (AFN) was showing a news segment about Russia's wildfires. Scenes of flames and destruction were filling the television. When an image of fleeing families overtook the screen, the Georgians erupted into a din of cheering and celebration. They were hugging each other and jumping up and down in ecstatic glee at Russia's suffering.

"Why are they so happy to see Russia burn?"

William watched the Georgians celebrate and said nothing.

"Hey!" I caught the attention of another American in the tent. "What's going on?"

The American shrugged and went back to his breakfast. William chided me for speaking to another man and so I continued to watch the celebration in silence, admonished. A Georgian saw I was watching them closely and spoke to me in broken English:

"Rossiya [Russia] burn! Rossiya deserve dead. Rossiya bad. Bad, bad. Sakartvelo [Georgia] hurt. Rossiya hurt Sakartvelo. Fire good. Teach Rossiya."

He went back to cheering and clasping his arms around his comrades. I turned back to William. "Stop worrying about it," he said.

"But William, I was sent to help the Georgians originally."

"Well, you're not now. Focus on the thing you should care about the most—our child."

We went back to eating. I shifted the contents of my bowl around and acted like I ate occasionally. I was torn between what he wanted me to do and what I wanted to do.

I feel so stuck, like I can't turn in any direction without causing irrevocable damage. Every move I make is scrutinized. I feel like I can't breathe.

My throat started to close up, aching with the prickling urge to cry.

"Finish your food."

"I'm not hungry."

"She's starving. Eat."

Amid the shouts of the Georgians and the scenes of the fleeing Russians, I swallowed the rest of my cereal with a tight throat.

53

August 2010, Camp Delaram, Afghanistan

Day after day, hour after hour trudged on, repeating like an alternative version of a Bill Murray movie with not so many fun antics and more heat and misery. Hell's Groundhog Day. I stopped eating completely. Sleep was non-existent from the operations or my nightmares. I didn't even flinch or run for cover when mortars exploded near me. I'd sunken into despair. Virkler tried desperately to drag me out of it. He knew I wasn't okay.

Against orders, he woke me up every day and walked me to the chow hall to try and encourage me to eat breakfast (which was technically dinner, as he would wake me in the afternoon at 1700), then he walked me to our changeover and passed off his duties to me with all of the other Data Marines. Then Virkler left with his laughing friends. I started taking night classes when I hit the fleet in 2008. I was determined to get the degree I thought would save me from the life my childhood had set me up to live. Classes as an active duty Marine meant giving up my six hours of sleep time during field ops to take finals. My degree was worth staying up for days.

Virkler would run up to meet me hours later, after goofing off with the guys in their can. He wore sweats, his rifle slung across his shoulders, and we talked for hours. We talked about our childhoods, our relationships and how they were broken and shattered; we spoke of our hopes and dreams and our desires to be writers. He emailed me rough drafts of his work and I edited them and sent them back. He was always quite terrible with the editing process, but I suppose most creative people are.

We spent hours discussing all sorts of atrocities, but we didn't speak about Dumaw and I didn't speak about William. Some things were just too raw to talk about.

Virkler and I would talk until midnight or sometimes later. I always made sure he left before 0200, though, so I wouldn't have to answer William's accusations about speaking to another man. I didn't like how guilty he made me feel for interacting with anyone but him.

One night I couldn't handle the turmoil in my head anymore, so I told Virkler. Sobbing on the top of the bunker we had climbed onto, looking at the stars, I confessed I was pregnant. In a spill of words that spewed from my mouth like a busted fire hydrant, I told him everything ... almost. I cried about my concerns about my husband. I cried about my fears of jail and of my future with no career and no degree and no money and no support, all while being a scorned member of my conservative Southern community. I cried until my lips were swollen and snot covered my sleeves, only to be dusted with sand.

And he listened.

By the time I was done and silent, he was holding me. I clasped my hands, wringing them, visibly shaken. He held onto me tightly, as though trying to keep me from breaking apart. He was silent while my body shook, and I tried to regain my composure. "I'm sorry. I'm sorry."

"For what?"

"For crying. For being so unstable. For telling you this and burdening you. For getting you in trouble with the guys for being my friend."

"Fuck them. And don't say you're sorry for having feelings. Don't ever apologize for that."

I choked a sob of laughter and clung to him. Virkler knew he was out of his depth.

"Look, I want you to talk to my brother."

"Huh? Why?"

"He's older; he knows more about the world and its shitty experiences than me. Trust me, he can help."

"How?"

"I don't know ... be another person to talk to outside of this shithole? Someone who can support you when I'm not around? Someone you can bounce ideas off of?"

Someone outside of this sand-filled fishbowl who can't turn on me? I wonder how I can talk to him without William finding out. What if William is watching the call logs? What if he sees I called Planned Parenthood? Fuck.

"Okay. Yeah."

"Talk to him. I'm serious. This is a lot to handle by yourself."

Virkler gave me his brother's phone number and I wrote it down in my notebook. He proceeded to hold me for the next hour while I calmed down. Every second he was there, I knew he was sacrificing his sleep. Every single second he was there, I knew he was an unparalleled source of comfort and an anchor in that sea of sand.

The next day, Virkler didn't wake me for breakfast. When I got to changeover, I was told he had been sent out to work with another unit while I had slept.

"When will he be back?"

"A month? Maybe two."

I didn't see Virkler again. My one friend was gone. I hadn't even gotten to say goodbye.

54

August 2010, Camp Delaram, Afghanistan

William and I were inside of a bunker. I stood with my back against an inside wall. It was dark in the bunker, and no one could see us. He stood in front of me. We were arguing. "I can't do this, William."

"Stop saying that. You can. You'll be a great mother."

"No, I can't do this. I'll be punished. I can't. I can't."

He grabbed me by the shoulders and shook me. I began to cry and continued to blubber, dissolving into a bout of uncontrollable insanity. "I can't. I ... I have to get an abortion."

William was filled with rage. His fingers dug into my shoulders, and he shoved me hard into the side of the bunker. My back slapped against the concrete and my hair, which was in a tight bun, protected my head from the impact. Shocked, I looked at him and continued to cry. He shook me again and then abruptly let me go. Still filled with rage, he wheeled back his right hand and hit the bunker with his open palm, full force, right next to my head.

"You CANNOT be that selfish. You will NOT get an abortion. You will have our child and raise it and we will be happy! Do you understand me?"

Still crying, I nodded my head, snot running from my nose as the tears silently fell. I quickly wiped my nose with the sleeve of my cammies; moon dust began to coat my wet arm. With my agreement, he relaxed. His right hand was still next to my head. He reached up with his left hand and tilted my chin up to him. And then he kissed me.

Everything began to scare me. From Americans getting murdered on our own bases by the Afghans, to the threat of jail, to mortars and gunfire, to bases catching on fire while Marines slept, to my nightmares, to my fear of

William turning me in if I didn't do as he wished. I wasn't safe anywhere. I stopped sleeping completely, and my mental stability disintegrated rapidly. Like a cornered and injured rabbit, I was wide-eyed and panicked, jumping at every movement and sound.

There comes a time when a person becomes so fearful, for so long, they begin to slide into paranoia. My descent into the depths of that darkness came soon after I lost my one touch with reality—Virkler. There was no longer someone I could trust to keep me grounded.

As a Communications Marine, I knew exactly how much information could be intercepted by the people who built and maintained the network because I had taken classes about communications security, and I had seen firsthand the access we had. The worst enemy to have is a systems or network engineer. They have the ability to control and see everything you do. There is a type of moral and ethical responsibility for engineers when they design and maintain systems of communication. But not everyone is ethical.

There were no cell phones using an outside cellular network for me to use. There was a white line that was installed on Delaram around the end of July for an Internet café, but we were constantly in River City from people dying and the café was closed. There was only the Marine Corps network, run by Marines and contractors—the same Marines and contractors who were bored, petty, vindictive, and particularly interested in the only female Marine around. I began to believe my every move was being watched, and after William told me to stop emailing my husband without telling him about it, I had every right to think that was true.

Voice over IP calls can be monitored by call managers; Exchange servers retain copies of all emails, and keyloggers can be installed on computers to send every keystroke you make to another person's computer without your knowledge. Everything can be monitored. I became paranoid, and I knew enough about the Internet to know that my paranoia wasn't unfounded.

I became sneaky. I sent emails to my husband and immediately accessed my repository within the Microsoft Exchange server and erased every copy of my emails. Microsoft Outlook 2007 allowed people to do this to their own accounts without requiring administrative access, which was good because I wasn't an administrator of the Exchange server. I don't remember how I figured this out, but I know that the best way to learn something is when your life or livelihood is at stake. I began to learn other covert ways of communicating. I accessed the wireless Internet white line once and scrubbed my presence from the Internet. Xanga, Myspace, all records of my awards and recognitions from high school and college: everything. I ensured it was erased. I contacted website administrators and told them to take down information about me. The only thing I kept open was my Facebook. The only things about me on the Internet were things I wanted out there.

Some might ask how I prevented my incoming emails from being read, it was easy—everyone had stopped responding to me. I hadn't received mail since March.

As for verbal communication, I didn't speak to anyone in person but William and only when it was absolutely necessary. Everyone else seemed fine with that. The conditioning started by the commanding officer, that all Marines should avoid me, was fully in place. They ignored me when I entered rooms. Everyone's eyes slid over me and they talked around me. During changeovers, orders were spoken in my general direction and then everyone left me to sit alone for 12 hours. I forgot how to use my voice. It was strange to feel reverberating vocal cords when I had to respond to William. I was able to call Virkler's brother a few times when I knew William was asleep. Alex tried to support me, a complete stranger, as much as he could from America. But I felt like my calling him was a burden that he didn't need, and I eventually stopped calling.

Twelve hours a day of no communication with anyone for a month leaves a lot of time to think. Coupled with vast isolation and paranoia, I began to daydream about multiple different universes: one where I wasn't pregnant, one where I was pregnant and not in the Marine Corps, and one where I was dead. Some of the daydreams would morph into nightmares. I began to consider my life in every scenario.

Not pregnant:
Travel the world
Join a community band
Finish my degree
Pregnant and not in the Marine Corps:
William's wife
Mother of Amy
Living in Arizona
Dead:
… I made a list of what songs I wanted played at my funeral.

The most comforting scenario—being dead. I could die, and all of the pain and discomfort and fear would be gone. If I died by an IED or a mortar, I wouldn't even have to do it myself. No one would think I was a coward; I would die an American hero. I fixated on this and hoped that the Afghans would suddenly become target experts and end my self-inflicted misery. Any explosion could be the one. I began to welcome them.

With these thoughts came the guilt.

Dumaw actually died a hero. It should have been me. I almost went with them on that patrol. I should've .... He would've been safe. I would have died. I should have. He had a pregnant wife. He was so mangled from the blast .... He was so tall. If it had been me, I would've been disintegrated from the stomach down. No one would know I had ever been pregnant. Everything would be better. His family would have him alive and in their arms. They miss him, I'm sure. I can't even get an email response.

Thinking about death made everything calmer for me. I was no longer panicky. I had a solution. I had a way out. I was back in control.

55

August 2010, Camp Delaram/D1, Afghanistan

So, there I was, kneeling on the dusty, sand-covered floor of my can. My loaded rifle was tossed on my bed, and I held the pregnancy test in my shaking hand. I had so desperately wanted to pull the trigger, to end all of the pain and confusion, but I held my lower stomach and looked at the test.

This is my reason to live. This child, my baby.

I didn't sleep that night. I cried bitterly into my pillow.

My mind still flirted with the idea of death. It seemed to ebb and flow with my ridiculously raging hormones. I was too much of a coward to do it myself. My mind imagined the bullet traveling down the barrel of the rifle and connecting with my throat. And then I remembered the man from my unit in the U.S., who had been in Iraq when he put his rifle to his throat. I had met him after he had fully recovered; his face was severely disfigured. It takes a steady hand to take your own life with a gun. One slight hesitation at the last moment and your finger can pull the weapon slightly to one side, putting the bullet off its deadly path and down a painful and embarrassing trajectory instead.

****

During the next changeover, Staff Sergeant Rambo informed me that I would be traveling outside the wire again. I immediately perked up. "When will the grunts be here?"

The thought of seeing a friendly face suddenly filled me with hope.

"It's not the grunts coming. The Georgians will be coming to pick you up and take you to Delaram 1."

My heart and hope were immediately crushed. I wouldn't know anyone. Delaram I (D1) was located close to Delaram II (D2), the main camp where I had spent the last five months. We didn't call Delaram II "D2." It was simply Delaram. The D1 camp had been given to the Georgians and promptly forgotten by most Americans. NATO forces gathered there, but no one paid it any mind. I was getting sent to D1 to grab a decommissioned switch.

"That's it, Staff Sergeant?"

"That's it."

A different hope filled me.

What a glamorous mission. Maybe I'll hit an IED.

I went to my can and grabbed my stuff for the mission. The Georgians' convoy was waiting for me. When I walked up, an uglier version of Victor Krum greeted me in Georgian and silently ushered me into the back of an MRAP (mine resistant/ambush protected) vehicle.

The same vehicle Dumaw bled out in the back of ....

I sat in the back of the vehicle by myself, while the non-English speaking Georgians drove to D1. I replayed Dumaw's death in my head over and over, hearing the screams over the radio and imagining the floor of the vehicle covered in his blood, while the grunts tried to save his life and stop his lower body from bleeding out. I saw the vehicle door open and saw his blood dripping from the back. My brain wouldn't stop playing it over and over.

By the end of the relatively short trip to D1, I was sick to my stomach and on the verge of fainting. When the vehicle stopped, a Georgian walked over to the back of the MRAP and opened the door for me. I stood up and instantly began to sway back and forth. A Georgian saw me and sprinted over. He knelt on one knee and held out his hand to take mine. I shook my head at him and he stubbornly refused to let me try to get out of the vehicle. Tacitly, he made it known that I was to use his knee as a step down from the relatively high cab. Suspiciously, I allowed him to take my hand and guide me down, gingerly stepping on his knee as I went.

I weigh 200 pounds right now!

The Georgian didn't even flinch. When I was standing safely on the ground, he smiled at me and took both of my hands into his, and then he bowed. The gesture of kindness caught me off guard, and I was too shocked to say anything before someone else guided me away from him and into the area of the base where I was to grab the switch.

The buildings of D1 were half pressed wood built by Seabees and half bombed stone buildings. As I approached the half-stone/half-sandbagged building, I saw a tall tower made of stone standing alone.

"Russiya."

The Georgian pointed at the tower when he saw my gaze.

Russia? Are Russians here? Shiiiit.

Immediately on guard for the Georgians and the Russians to be at close quarters near me, I pulled my weapon up to the ready position with my finger straight and slightly off the trigger. After seeing the reaction of the Georgians as Russia burned, I wasn't willing to be engaged in further cultural disagreements. The Georgian led me into his Command Operations Center.

"SHIIIIT. CANNON?!"

Adjusting my eyes to the darkness, I wheeled around to see a Marine I had originally deployed with waving at me from the other side of the room.

Of course, he was one of the Georgian liaisons sent here with me. Of course, he's here … with his Georgians.

Franklin wasn't wearing cammies. He was sitting on a cot at the edge of the COC in green-on-green shirt and skivvies. It was surreal to see him, a tangible element of my life before everything had gone so terribly wrong.

"You aren't wearing cammies."

"Yeah, man, the Georgians don't give a shit."

"Where are the Russians?"

"Huh?"

"I don't know, one of the guys waved at the tower and said Russia or some shit."

"Oh, I guess the Russians built it when they were here in the '80s."

"Oh."

"Yeah, so how have you been? You look like shit."

I let out the breath I had been holding with an audible *whoosh* and let my rifle fall, dangling from my body.

"Things fucking suck."

"Yeah, man, this place blows. Georgians smell like shit."

I quickly looked back and forth at the multiple Georgians standing around us. "Hey!"

"Man, they don't know a lick of English. They are the dumbest, smelliest people I've ever met. Isn't that right, bedro?"

He stood up and clasped hands with the nearest Georgian, who grinned and nodded at him. "Bedro?"

"Georgian for 'brother.'"

My mind flashed to the image of the Georgian helping me from the vehicle and my loyalty landed with the Georgians. "It's still rude."

A Georgian walked up to us and gestured for me to come with him.

"What does he want?"

"Fuck if I know."

I followed the Georgian over to a computer. He began talking to me in Georgian, gesturing at the computer.

"Uh, hey Franklin, aren't you supposed to be their IT support?"

"Yeah, why?"

"I think he's asking me to fix his computer."

"Man, fuck that. I can't figure out what they want."

I sighed and looked back at the gesturing Georgian. He was miming with his hands, covering his ears. I, like an idiot, kept trying to ask him questions. He kept miming the same thing over and over.

"This is frustrating. Okay, let me sit down and figure it out."

Did the computer work? Did it connect to the network? Did it ... have sound?

I worked with the computer briefly. The computer was in a language that I couldn't read. I navigated to the control panel by memory and changed the language to English, before running it through its paces. When I saw that it was muted, I unmuted it and played sound.

The Georgian jumped up and down like a teenage girl and clasped me by the shoulders, cheering.

"Jesus, Franklin, they just wanted sound."

"Cool."

"You seriously couldn't just try? What do you even do all day?" I was irritated and on edge. Franklin ignored me. I put the computer back into the language the Georgians wanted and stomped out of the COC, grabbing the switch I was to decommission.

I ate alone, surrounded by Georgians, in a brightly lit chow hall. I hadn't eaten or slept in over 48 hours, and was stumbling with sleep deprivation as I tried to make it back to the vehicle I had arrived in. I planned on curling up under the vehicle to sleep. No one seemed to care where I was or what I was doing. I had become invisible again, which is what I wanted. However, I was intercepted on my trek by a Georgian. He motioned for me to follow him.

Sure, just follow strangers, Savannah, that's smart. What's the worst that could happen?

I laughed bitterly to myself. I was too tired to argue with someone who didn't speak my language, so I walked behind him. He brought me to a can and motioned for me to go in. I heard female voices ... American female voices. Shocked, I opened the door to the can. The FET.

The Female Engagement Team was a group of female Marines specifically trained to be the Marine Corps liaisons with the local women and children of

Afghanistan. I had volunteered to be one when I was on Camp Leatherneck because the FET was supposedly the only way a female Marine could see any action or go on any patrols. I had been told that my job was too important to be FET, so I watched other women from supply and admin positions "train" and conduct "tryouts," while I inventoried equipment in the hot sun.

But Congress had stopped the FET from engaging in any missions for over five months, starting at the beginning of 2010. I remembered Sergeant P mentioning they came out briefly, but they were told to stay on base.

So, this is where they ended up.

I walked into the can and headed directly toward the only empty cot I saw. I started to set down my 90 pounds of equipment and the switch when a particularly bitchy-faced sergeant called out to me. "And who the fuck are you?"

"Cannon." I offered no other information.

"You can't be in here."

"Oh yeah?"

Fucking fight me.

"We are full."

"This cot looks awfully empty."

The girls looked at each other, shocked into silence. I flopped onto the completely empty cot and closed my eyes at last, immediately falling asleep.

Within what must have been seconds, I was jolted awake to the cot being kicked. "Move. This is our staff sergeant's cot."

I was fed up. "There is literally no equipment or anything anywhere near this cot."

"Well, she's coming back tonight. She's been out for a few weeks."

"Well, then she can wake me up when she comes in. I'm not going to sleep on the floor when there is a perfectly empty cot right here."

"Cunt." The Marine didn't even try to be quiet with her insult as she and the others walked outside the can.

"Fucking cock-sucking bitches." I spoke aloud to the empty can. I could hear the females outside the can, insulting me. I put my head back down onto my arms and drifted off again.

Clank. Clank. Clank.

I was jolted awake again.

ARE THEY FUCKING THROWING ROCKS AT THE CAN?! ARE YOU FUCKING SERIOUS?!

Seeing red, I walked outside holding my rifle like I was going to butt stroke someone across the face.

"HEY, FUCKFACES! KNOCK IT THE FUCK OFF BEFORE I FUCKING PUNCH YOU IN THE FUCKING FACE. SOME OF US ACTUALLY FUCKING WORK AND DON'T GET TO SIT AROUND AND SHOOT THE SHIT FOR MONTHS BECAUSE WE'RE THE GOD DAMN SPECIAL TEAM THAT CONGRESS TOLD TO SIT DOWN."

Again, shocked silence.

"FUCK." I screamed into the air.

I slammed the door and threw myself down again to sleep.

Throughout the night, they stayed up and laughed and talked loudly, smoking and shooting the shit like a bunch of people who had no worries in the world. My anger at them was amplified when I awoke, once again, to them sticking their burning cigarettes into the can's ventilation system. As cigarette smoke filled the can, I struggled not to cough and give them the satisfaction of knowing I was affected. I breathed through my cammies to smell sweat instead of disgusting cigarette smoke. I knew if I walked outside again, I would murder one of them. When I looked at my watch, it was 0300. They were still awake.

When I awoke at 0500, I slammed the door loudly on the way out while they slept.

Fucking disgusting cunts.

56

August 2010, Camp Delaram, Afghanistan

Simon cleared his throat and told me to fix one more thing on the encryption device.

I walked out of the room and into the main server farm across the hallway of the TCF. After fiddling with the encryption settings, I re-entered my area and picked up the phone again. "Done."

As Simon checked that the network traffic was routing from Camp Leatherneck to my location on Camp Delaram, I trailed my fingers over the top of the plywood desk, brushing the sand into a pile and then squeezing the mound between my fingers. I sat down on the table and let one leg dangle, barely touching the floor.

"We're good. You're up."

"Alright." The lack of usual excitement was noticeable in my voice. A network coming back up is a source of excitement and relief. We both fell silent—our work completed and only the night lying ahead. He sat in his TCF hundreds of miles from me. We had never met, and neither of us knew what the other looked like.

"You okay?"

"Simon, I mean ... I—"

He stayed silent and waited for me to continue.

"No. No, you know what? I'm not okay. I'm so fucking tired of being miserable. How do people live like this? In such constant misery?"

"What do you mean?"

"This country, this world ... everything is falling apart, people are dying and being tortured, and families are ripped apart because of selfishness and war and greed and stupidity ...."

As I trailed off, my mind started to wonder if I was even speaking about the war anymore.

"Cannon, look, that's just life, right? People get knocked down, but they get back up."

"Do they?" My scornful tone practically torched the phone handset.

"Yes, they do. In fact, my wife is leaving me. We are getting a divorce and I—"

I rudely cut him off. "See? Even you're getting a divorce!"

"Well, I chose to remain out here for two more years. She fell in love with someone else. And I'm getting over it. Work helps."

"This is fucking bullshit."

"What?"

"Love. Marriage. All of it. Everyone always leaves. Always. I can't fucking stand it anymore. I just want to … give up."

Once I had verbalized it, I felt better, like a weight had been taken from my heart and placed onto his. Simon's tone changed and became wary. "What do you mean, 'give up'?"

"I just … I want to … I just don't want to be here anymore."

"You mean Afghanistan?"

He was hoping for a reassurance that I couldn't give him.

"No … this world. There is no good in it. I don't want to live in a world with no good or love. Give me one good act you've seen this week."

Simon was silent.

"See? Even among fellow Americans, we are so shitty to each other. I'm tired of being so alone and so … I'm so fucking tired." I cried silently. Tears streamed down my face.

"Hey, look, you're going to be fine, right? You have, what, a month left before you go home?"

"Supposedly three weeks."

"See? And you can go home and enjoy everything America has to offer."

I barked a cruel laugh.

"Everything America has to offer? Like what? I have no friends. I have no family there. My husband won't speak to me and my entire unit in America hates me because of what he's telling people. I'm leaving Afghanistan to go back to an even worse place. At least here, I'm in an environmental stalemate where I could die a martyr."

"You have to stop talking like that."

"Do you know how easy it would be?"

"Stop. You'll be fine. Go back to America and get some In-N-Out. You'll be fine, and all of your problems will buff out. They always do."

I stayed silent for a minute or two and listened to his breathing. I'm sure he was scrolling through work on his computer while we were on the phone. I couldn't hear him typing, though, which would have immediately triggered a hurt disconnect from me. He finally spoke again.

"Promise me you'll be okay."

"I'm not going to make any more promises that I might break."

"Promise."

"Goodbye, Simon." I hung up the phone and disconnected it from the wall so he couldn't call me back. I shut my laptop and stared at the small and now crumpled mound of sand and moon dust on the table.

"Hey!"

My head snapped up to see a wireman standing in the doorway.

"Shit, you scared me."

"There's someone outside asking for you."

My heart shuttered to a stop.

"A contractor?"

"Nah, some Marine."

A Marine? Who couldn't come into the TCF? Who the fuck could it be?

"Who?"

"Do I look like your fucking secretary? Get your ass up and go look."

Bewildered and wary, I grabbed my rifle and slung it over my shoulder as I walked into the hallway. The buildings erected by the Seabees were all the same: one main hallway down the center with doors on each end that led to steps to the sand and various rooms on each side of the hallway. The TCF was special because it had a fake floor that allowed us to run cables between the tall server racks that held our equipment. But if you've walked through one of these buildings, you've walked through them all.

The hallway stretched out ahead of me like some cartoonish display. I had one small hope of who could be on the other side of the door, but—

Could it be …?

I pulled the door open to the night.

And there stood Sergeant P.

57

August 2010, Camp Delaram, Afghanistan

Sergeant P's presence came as a welcome shock. He stood at the bottom of the three stairs leading to the TCF, looking at me with the self-assured calm that always emitted from the man who feared almost nothing.

He had just showered. His face was uncharacteristically clean, with small drops of water quickly evaporating and dangling from the lobes of his ears. It was strange to see him so clean. His cammies were even clean—no streaks of sweat, dust, or blood anywhere.

"Hey! Wow, you came!"

"Of course I came. I told you I'd come by to see you if I could, didn't I?"

I was breathless with the surprise that someone wanted to see me, and that this someone was him. His sleeves were rolled up slightly, exposing his tattooed arms to the elbows.

"Yeah, but it's been so long I thought that you'd forgotten me."

It had been over a month since I had seen Sergeant P. It was from afar at Dumaw's memorial service as I'd stood very detached in the background, before leaving in disgrace. Sergeant P was focused on his men and hadn't seen me. Before then, it was when he was carrying Red from the bloody vehicle. A lifetime had been lived and lost since he had made his promise to see me again.

"We've been pretty busy out at the station."

"Yeah?"

"Fuck yeah, I'll tell you all about it."

I glanced over my shoulder at the now closed doorway to the TCF. I was extremely anxious that a wireman might come out and start rumors about me talking to a strange man. The last thing I needed was for William to hear more rumors. Luckily, Sergeant P was astute and sensed that I was uncomfortable.

"Want to go eat? I'm starving."

I looked at my watch. I was never hungry, but it was 2330 and I guessed as good a time as any to practice the charade of eating. We headed off to midrats.

We entered the chow hall tent, which was dimly lit and empty.

"Oh yay, chicken cordon bleu ..." I said sarcastically, while smiling at the TCN (third country national), who scurried out to scoop the cheesy blob of fried chicken and ham onto my plate, for the fourth time that week. "Why the fuck can't there be any other kind of food? I'm tired of the same thing over and over."

"Hey, you could be eating MREs."

Sergeant P's remark reminded me I had access to hot food, even if it was the same food and even if it was all that was left for midrats. The TCN spooned canned peaches onto my plate next. They slid from the spoon like slimy pale orange slugs. I suppressed the urge to dry heave; my face contorted into a grimace. Sergeant P noticed my every move. "What's wrong?"

We had left the chow hall and were carrying our trays into the separate eating tent.

"I miss fresh fruit so much. Crisp, fresh, clean ... I think about how spoiled I was in America. If I wanted fruit, I could go get it at any time. Shoot, I didn't even like fruit that much. Now I have to force slimy fruit into my mouth, and I would kill for a piece of fresh fruit."

"You guys don't get fresh fruit?"

"I haven't seen anything fresh since y'all had those local grapes at the BBQ, fruit or otherwise. They run out of soy milk and veggies within 12 hours after getting a convoy in, which also rarely happens."

"You'd think you'd get more fruit. I know convoys haven't been getting through, but damn."

We sat down and ate. Sergeant P ate like he hadn't seen food in weeks, and I pushed the peaches around my plate.

"You really need to eat."

I ignored him.

"So where are the other guys?"

"Around. Showering, shitting, the usual. We needed to do a trash run and I managed to get them a night here to try and grab a real shower and a night without watch."

"Awesome. Y'all need it."

He had finished and we stood up to leave. Upon reaching the TCF, Sergeant P turned abruptly to me. "Hey, I forgot, I need to do something. I'll come back up to you in a bit."

Panic quickly overcame me. The likelihood he would leave and not come back again was high, simply based on the importance of his position and how often the grunts came and went with the dangers of combat. "Please don't go."

"I have to. I'll be back, really quick. I promise."

He strode off with a purpose and left me standing and watching his back fade into the darkness.

I sat in my rolling chair with my feet up, cradling my stomach underneath my cammie blouse. I had started watching *Big Love* after finally finishing *Weeds*. As I sat there, I felt it—something slid out of me. As the substance soaked my panties, a sudden cold overcame me. It felt like my period.

Am I miscarrying? Will my hedonistic prayers be answered? Fuck, what if I'm miscarrying?

I walked outside the TCF and sprinted to the nearest porta-john. The tan porta-shitter, as it was so lovingly called by the Marines, was silhouetted against the backdrop of the never-ending desert. The moon shone directly from behind, so when I opened the door, I could see nothing, but I could smell it. Attempting to adjust my eyes to the darkness, I realized it was an Afghan porta-shitter. There was no place to stand on the inside—you had to climb atop the plastic cover that occupied the space generally used for standing. Once you had climbed inside, I realized you had to drop trow and squat over the giant hole in the center of the cover.

Mouth agape, I decided against climbing atop the plastic cover in the darkness and tried looking for some toilet paper to wipe myself to see if I was bleeding.

There was no toilet paper.

Don't Afghans use their hands? Oooooof course.

I sighed and gave up, unbuckling my pants. I stuck my right hand down my pants and slid my fingers inside of myself. Pulling them out, gingerly avoiding all articles of clothing, I lifted my fingers up and tried to see what color the substance was. The moon's light was bright enough to show ....
Clear. A giant glop of clear .... Fuck.

I pulled my fingers apart and watched the sticky liquid pull and expand between my fingers. It was so sticky that it didn't break apart. I could see the moon between the clear glop.

Look, the moon is shiny.

Half laughing, I wiped my fingers on my cammies, buckled my pants back up with a few loud clinks of the belt buckle, and headed back inside.

58

August 2010, Camp Delaram, Afghanistan

Less than ten minutes after wiping my sticky hand on my cammies and returning to my area in the TCF, I heard a distant *thud, thud, thud*. Springing to my feet, I left the room empty and practically skipped to the door. I grasped the shiny silver doorknob and pulled the door open to see the side of Sergeant P's body. He scanned the area with his entire body, and only turned back to me once he was done. This gave me ample time to study his body as he turned. He was solid, with broad and muscled shoulders that stretched his FROG top taut. His light brown hair was cut short, so short for a grunt, and he didn't have a cover on. The lack of a cover was something I was unaccustomed to. Even during a time of war, POG ranks were fixated on following the useless Marine uniform regulations, like covers at all times outdoors. Grunts clearly didn't give a fuck.

He wasn't carrying a rifle. He had an M9 pistol strapped tightly to his right leg. The holster had two straps fastened around his right thigh, allowing me to see how thick his leg was. It was extremely ... solid.

I glanced up from admiring his body to see him watching me take in every detail. He was on the same step as me and he stood tall and close, self-assured. A cocky look came into his eye, as he drew up with a large breath that expanded his chest.

Catching my breath, I moved to pass him and he followed me down the stairs. "I'm glad you came back."

"Why are you so worried?" He laughed in a manner that suggested he was a god.

"Gee, I have no idea, Mike." It was the first time I had said his first name, and the sarcasm helped mask my attempt to tiptoe into an area of insubordination to see how he responded. We were both enlisted NCOs, but he was a sergeant and I was a corporal. Fraternization rules were laid out between officers and enlisted, but people had been charged under the UCMJ for inappropriate behavior within enlisted ranks before. Marines don't call each other by our first names; we aren't the Air Force.

"Nothing is going to happen to me, Savannah."

"You're not invincible, no one is."

"I am. Too much has happened to me for it to be otherwise."

We both fell silent. All Marines are cocky; we are trained to be the best, to be fearless in the face of death, to kill with our bare hands within seconds. We are built up to be invincible, because that is what we must be in combat. Tripoli, Iwo Jima, the Frozen Chosin, Fallujah ... those historic battles were fought with invincible men, who stared death in the face with a resounding sense of superiority. If Mike felt invincible, it was because he was. He was a healthy young man primed to look death in the face every day. *Fuck death, I am death.*

"How are you doing?" I didn't know how to come out and speak about Dumaw.

"The guys are ... they are pretty fucked up."

"You. How are YOU?"

"I'm good, man. You know, of course it was bad. Fuck. It was fucking bad. But—" He trailed off.

We had walked around the TCF to the other side, the side whose door no one ever used. The entire desert lay before us and we both stared hard into the darkness, intentionally not looking at each other. We stayed silent as we both replayed our versions of Dumaw's death. He eventually spoke again.

"This isn't my first deployment."

Of course it wasn't. A grunt sergeant in the Marine Corps during a time of two wars?

"I mean, I've seen people die before. Marines, ragheads, both. Fuck, during Fallujah there was a Marine whose head was blown off a few feet from me."

My breath caught, and I jerked my head around to look at his face. "You were in Fallujah?" Fallujah was the battle of the decade. My combat instructors, my drill instructors, and my old master gunnery sergeant spoke of Fallujah with such reverence and awe that I had begun to think of the Marines of Fallujah as mythical creatures who I could only hope to meet one day. *And it's him.*

"Of course, I was fucking in Fallujah. Went to Iraq twice. We fucking invaded the city and shot shit up. The one patrol I was in, when the guy died next to me, we were rounding this corner ... city invasions are tough, you know. There are high buildings and all sorts of fucking hideout spots for people to pick you off."

He glanced at me quickly. "I mean, you know."

Remembering my brush with the rooftop shooter, I nodded. He continued.

"So, we were going along, and we were keeping our eyes out for fuckers and we rounded this corner and started taking fire. We were shooting back, but we were completely exposed out there, you know. Our vics weren't like how they are now. They were metal cans with canvas doorways. So, we hit this ambush and we can't tell which way is up. We try to take cover and ... KERPLERT!"

He motioned to his own head exploding. "Dude's brains were all over me."

My jaw might have dropped open at this point. He looked at my expression. "He was dead instantly."

"Fuck."

"But Dumaw—"

My heart began to break. I knew what was coming next.

"Dumaw was different. He... Fuck... He was such a good man, you know? Goofy as fuck, but good. I knew him. He was my fucking Marine. In Iraq, I was just a fucking dumbass PFC who didn't know his ass from a hole in the ground. That guy died in Fallujah and he wasn't my Marine. Sure, he was A Marine, but he wasn't MY Marine. You know? Everyone else who died? I didn't know them well at all. But Dumaw—"

No .... No. Fuck. Here it comes. You need to hear this, to know what happened while you were listening.

"Savannah, I fucking put him as point-man. We were going to check out an IED, so we could call it into EOD. We had already gotten one and marked it for them. And we kept going. He kept walking and he stepped on that pressure plate—"

He cut off abruptly and looked at me hard.

"You know those fucking cowards use pressure plates to detonate the explosives while they hide in the fucking hills and watch? Did you know that? Those fucking cowards."

His voice had turned from pained to furious. His entire body tensed; his fists were clenched. I reached out and placed my hand on his arm. He shook his head and seemed to shake himself back to the present.

"When he stepped on it, the explosion knocked me down hard. I couldn't hear anything ... until I could hear him screaming."

The back of my throat got tight and burned as I remembered.

"Red got there first. He was holding Dumaw and ... Dumaw was missing from the waist down. His legs were completely gone, and his body was pouring blood. We got him into the back of the MRAP—"

Sergeant P's voice caught. I slid my hands down to his and gripped tightly. He looked into my eyes, but he wasn't seeing me. "We tried so hard."

"I know."

"So hard."

Tears were falling from his eyes. I looked as hard as I could and tried to absorb some of the pain spilling from this invincible god.

Stop hurting, please stop hurting.

"He kept asking us if he was going to be okay. We kept telling him he would be. But he knew. He knew. He told us to tell his wife and son that he loved them and that we better take care of them. We kept trying to call in the nine-line, but they wouldn't come. The risk of attack was too much, and no one was close. So, we held him and, you know, Doc gave him some morphine to ease the pain, but he was missing half of his fucking body, so we watched him die fucking slowly, with his screams eventually stopping.

"Do you know the fucking worst part? The fucking WORST FUCKING PART?!" He yanked his hand from mine and wiped his nose angrily with his sleeve.

"What?"

"EOD couldn't even come to us to detonate the first IED that we had found because there were so many others around the region that they had to take care of first. So, we were forced to stay there for fucking hours, the whole goddamn night with Dumaw's blood covering us, holding his fucking mangled body. We had to sit next to him for hours. Fucking hours."

"Fuck."

"The guys had to see that. Red had to see that; he had to hold his best friend and watch him die a long and painful death while sitting in a pool of his blood."

The words fit what I had heard happened. They explained Red's face as he was carried from the vehicle. They explained the trauma-stricken faces that blamed themselves ... everyone blamed themselves.

Still gripping each other's hands, we stared back out at the desert where the sand had soaked up the blood of our brother.

59

August 2010, Camp Delaram, Afghanistan

Sergeant P and I looked off into the desert for a long time in silence. After a while, he turned to face me. "So, what's going on with you? You look like hell. And you keep flinching."

I looked at him and ached to tell him what was going on. I felt as though he could help, somehow. The desire to tell him everything churned in my stomach and rose to my throat, only to pour out of my mouth.

"I ... I'm pregnant."

"What?"

"He ff-f-force—" I stuttered and broke down into tears as Mike looked at me, not in shock, but in a calculating way that made his eyes grow extremely hard with sudden understanding.

"Who."

It wasn't a question; it was a demand. I wrung my hands together and began backpedaling once I saw the look of angry determination on his face.

"No, no, it's fine, he ... It's fine."

"Who the FUCK touched you?"

Relief flooded over me and then a sudden panic as Mike stood up and grabbed his pistol, unholstering it. "I'll fucking kill him. Tell me who fucking touched you."

Sobbing, I reached out to him and grabbed his arm and tried pulling him back down beside me.

"No, please, no, you can't kill him, you can't. He's the only way I can even have the baby. Please, fuck, no, it's fine."

"No, it's not fucking fine. What goddamn Marine raped you?"

I was in full panic mode.

Would he kill him? He couldn't kill him. He could totally kill him.

"He isn't a Marine. Look, I'll be fine. I'll figure it out. Just please, please promise me you won't do anything stupid. Don't do anything stupid for me. I'm not worth it."

"No one would know. There are ways, and the guys and I would make sure no one would fucking find that fucker. Ever."

The thought of a dozen men coming to my rescue both humbled and terrified me. I longed to have William hidden in some wadi with a bullet in his brain.

How would they account for the missing bullet? He can't commit a crime for me. I would forever owe a blood debt, as stupid as that sounds. And the rest of the guys wouldn't do that for me.

"Please, Mike. I appreciate it, but please, calm down."

Mike looked furious. I was seeing the wrath of someone who knows how to kill and doesn't shy away from the act. I suddenly felt so cared for … that I had to talk someone down from murdering someone who hurt me. The relief that flooded over me was intense.

It could be over.

No. No. William has a daughter and I need him.

"Look, you're one of us, okay? No one fucks with us, with me, with the people I care about. No one. I don't give a shit. You're like a sister to me … I mean … a hot sister I would totally—"

He broke off as I laughed. The laugh was cleansing, and I felt like everything was suddenly going to be fine.

"I'm serious, Savannah. You say the word. He's gone."

I still gripped his arm, and I wasn't sure if I was holding him down or if I was clinging to him to hold me down.

With his other hand, he returned his pistol to his holster and reached into his cargo pocket. When he held out his hand to me, I gasped.

"A tangerine!"

I was in disbelief.

"Here, it's yours."

"You went to go find me some fruit. That's why you left."

"We get fruit occasionally. I was saving this one for a patrol. Go ahead, eat it."

"No, I can't. You need it more than me."

"Just eat it."

"Thank you."

My voice grew soft with the 'thank you.' I began to peel the fruit and the fresh citrus smell filled the air. With every peel, the citrus juice sprayed its sticky wetness all over my fingers and hands. Breaking apart the tangerine, I handed him half.

"Hey, let's take a walk."

We came back satiated and relaxed. The sun was beginning to rise and I could see his face more clearly.

"I have to get back to the boys."

"Thank you. For everything."

"I'll see you again, next time I'm around."

"I can't wait."

We smiled at each other and he turned to walk down the hill, away from me. The desert sky was turning shades of pink and red as the sun rose.

Red sky at night, sailors' delight.

Red sky at morning, sailors take warning.

The old rhyme ran through my head as I watched my skin turn pink with the sky. Finally feeling at ease for the first time in months, I walked back into the TCF.

60

August 2010, Camp Delaram, Afghanistan

I walked down the hill after changeover. This time it didn't bother me to see the men laughing and joking together while avoiding me. I had the memory of last night to replay; the tangerine had stained my fingers a bright sticky orange. I was able to look at the laughing men as I stood completely apart, separated by more than just gender. As I leaned against the wall in the back of the room, I noticed how different they were from me. They were still children. Without saying anything, I walked out without being noticed and practically glided down the hill. Their exclusion was fine with me. I could stand being alone again.

I needed to pick up my laundry before going to sleep. Staff Sergeant Rambo said I would be leaving Delaram soon. Soon meant today? Tomorrow? Two weeks? No one knew. I didn't have a replacement and the regiment was loath to let a body go so easily. But still, I needed to start packing and shipping my things back to America. I had dropped off all of my sandy, sweaty clothes to the laundromat the day before to be washed by the TCNs. It was time to pick them up.

Before I passed the tents that contained the throned toilets, I turned left toward the laundry tent. Between the laundry tent and the bathrooms, there stood a large tan bladder of water. It spanned more than the length of a tent, approximately 25 feet long by 15 feet wide. As I walked up to it, I noticed streaks of dust and sand covering the tan plastic. I touched the thick, hot material that bulged from the strain of holding water. The bladder was higher than my waist. My fingers left tracks as I drug my hand back and forth. The dust came away easily and caked on my fingers. As I brushed my fingers together, I watched the dust fall onto the sand on the ground. I started poking the plastic with my fingers, testing the strain of the fabric. I could see the fabric strands as I looked closer. Plastic-covered fabric.

I wonder what would happen if I sliced a hole in the bladder with my knife. Would it explode outwards, sweeping me off of my feet? Or would the water sink too quickly into the sand?

I looked around for the hole used to fill the water bladder. It was bigger than the palm of my hand and had a handle that needed to be turned. It was locked.

Lame.

I flicked the water bladder once more and walked into the laundromat.

Delaram was infinitely smaller than Camp Leatherneck, but its amenities were better. Leatherneck had food, yes, but the rest of their amenities were horrible. The mattress I slept on at Delaram was like a cloud of heaven, while Leatherneck had thin, hard mats. Another amenity that Leatherneck failed on was their laundry services. Once a week, we were expected to walk a mile to the mat on Leatherneck and turn in our laundry in our white mesh laundry bags. The contractors on Leatherneck were so inundated with dirty laundry that they would toss the whole bag into an industrial washer with about six other mesh bags at the same time. The clothes were "washed" and "dried" all while staying in the mesh bag. When you picked up your laundry, the bag was tossed to you, shades grayer than before. Balled-up socks were crusted shut with sand and chunks of clothes that hadn't separated in the wash were crusted together and wrinkly. The clothes never smelled clean and were never folded. I wrinkled my nose at the chunky bundle of sandy, still sweaty gray clothes, but accepted that was just how laundry was done in-country.

Delaram, though, oh Delaram. You got the laundry situation down right.

I walked into the tent and leaned against the pressed wood counter that had been built just inside the doorway. A fresh smell filled the room. Individual sized washers and dryers lined the right side of the tent, and on the left side there were wooden cubbies labeled A through Z. The very tan gentleman saw me come in and bustled up to me. He took the piece of paper I had in my hand and immediately set off to the cubby labeled CA–DE. When he set down my mesh bag onto the wooden counter, he motioned for me to open the bag. Loosening the strings, I gazed in at the laundry that had been neatly and perfectly folded into color-coordinated piles. Light green, dark green, tan, and all of my thongs individually folded into colorful squares.

I was no longer embarrassed that a strange man was touching my underwear and folding it. Anything was better than a gray bag of dust rudely tossed to me by an angry man on Leatherneck. Somehow, the men on Delaram managed to keep my brights brighter, and they smelled amazing. Laundry day on Delaram was a bright spot for me in the land of death and unhappiness.

I nodded and thanked the man, as I tied up my bag and put it under my arm for the journey to my tent. He waved at me while sticking my paper through the center of a giant receipt spike. I walked toward my tent and noticed a Marine standing outside of my door.

"What's up?"

"The CO wants you."

"What? Why?"

Getting summoned by the commanding officer was always a toss-up. Either you were being praised or you were in deep shit. It was never the former.

"Dunno."

"K, hold on."

"You're telling the CO to hold on, not me."

"Well, if the CO wants me to walk in holding a bag full of my underwear then yeah, I'll come right up. Jesus fuck, just hold on."

I walked into my tent and quickly tossed my bag onto my bunk in the back of the tent. My eyes still hadn't adjusted to the tent's darkness before I was back outside and sprint-walking to the commanding officer's office. Heart pounding, I knocked on the doorway. All of the things I had done wrong swirled through my head.

What does he know? Fuck. What does he know?

The CO called out for me to come in. Shaking, I opened the door and stepped in, snapping to attention front and center of his desk. My eyes were fixed over his head.

"Good morning, sir. Corporal Cannon reporting as ordered."

I stood swaying in silence. My knees were locked, and I was rapidly approaching unconsciousness, between the nerves and the heat and the fear. I felt his eyes studying my face as I stood stiffly. What seemed like an eternity passed before ….

"At ease."

I snapped to the "at ease" position, with my legs apart and my hands behind me in the small of my back. My rifle had smacked my leg multiple times during this process, and my right arm was wrapped awkwardly around the buttstock as I clasped my left hand behind my back. My eyes met the CO's eyes.

Here was the man who told people to avoid me, who told everyone they would be punished if seen with me. This was the first time I had seen him since the day he yelled at Ski for throwing me over his shoulder and making me laugh … four months ago.

"Cannon."

"Sir."

"Hand over your rifle."

61

August 2010, Camp Delaram, Afghanistan

My mouth dropped open. "What?"

There was no "sir" added to my response. All the blood rushed from my head to collect in a pool at my feet and I felt my stomach drop deeper than I had ever felt it before. And I was suddenly cold, as if I were in the Arctic instead of in the middle of a 120-degree desert.

A Marine's rifle is their life. During deployment, it becomes an appendage to our bodies. We train with it, we sleep with it, we lean it against the wall or across our laps as we use the restroom. The resounding smack of a rifle against our body is the comforting reminder that our safety is at our fingertips. The seven-pound, eight-ounce rifle is always present, always comforting, always painfully there.

"Hand over your weapon, Marine." The CO's face was firm as he stood warily behind his desk.

"But sir—"

My hand went instinctively to the barrel of my rifle, around my right side, and I grasped it tightly.

"Now, Marine."

Shaking, I unslung the rifle, swinging the black three-point swing around and over my head. Holding the barrel in my left hand and the buttstock in my right, I pulled the rifle close to my body and looked at the CO's face to make sure he wasn't joking.

He wasn't.

Incredulously, I pulled the bolt to the rear and locked it. Fastened to the rear, the contents of the rifle's chamber could be seen. Inspecting it officially, my voice shook. "All clear."

He reached out his hands and grasped my rifle, pulling it from me. I let go reluctantly. He inspected the chamber for rounds, then slammed the bolt to the front and closed the flap to hide the bolt. Then he placed my rifle on his desk and sat back down.

"Corporal Cannon."

"Yes, sir?"

"Do you want to tell me why I got a call from RC-Southwest's general this morning saying we had a Marine who wanted to kill themselves?"

WHAT? "What ... do you mean?"

"Exactly."

A Marine Corps general? What the actual heck?

RC-Southwest, or Regimental Command Southwest, was the international military command in the southwestern portion of Afghanistan.

"I don't know, sir." Never a truer statement had been said.

"So, you can't explain why, during the regimental general's brief, a contractor from Leatherneck stood up and told a bunch of Marine officers there was a Marine who wanted to kill themselves out on Delaram?"

Simon. Oh. Fuck.

My shoulders sagged as I realized this was actually happening. "Oh."

"Oh." He was mocking me. "Do you realize what that looks like? That a contractor has to tell A GENERAL THAT WE AREN'T TAKING CARE OF OUR MARINES?"

"Yes, sir."

"So, is it true?"

"No, sir. I didn't say I wanted to kill myself."

"What did you say?"

"That it would be so much better if I wasn't alive."

The CO studied me firmly. Decades of leading troops into battle, and he was watching the weakest link begin to fall apart in front of him.

"Why? Why on earth didn't you come to me?"

I almost snorted with laughter, choking. I immediately turned it into a cough to cover it up.

You made it very clear that I wasn't wanted here.

"I don't know, sir."

"What on earth could be so bad that you would think that?"

I said nothing. We stared at each other in silence for a few moments. It seemed like he hoped the silence would convince me to speak. He lowered his gaze first and sighed, shuffling the papers on his desk.

"You're going back to Leatherneck today. Your command already knows about the situation."

Shame filled me further, if that was possible. "Yes, sir."

"Be on the flight line at 1500."

"Yes, sir."

"You're dismissed."

"Aye, sir."

I turned and walked to the door of his office, leaving my rifle on his desk.

God dammit, Simon.

My mind swirled in panic and confusion.

What the fuck is going to happen to me now?

I needed to tell William what was happening; maybe he could help. What if I was found out? He needed to know.

One of the helpdesk Marines asked where my rifle was.

"Fuck off. Where is he?" I motioned to the desk where William usually sat. The Marine, abashed by my bitchy response, shrugged and turned away from me. I wasn't going to find William, or any help, here.

I walked out of the compound and didn't look back.

I started packing my stuff furiously into my black gorilla box—a toughened footlocker sold to the military to hold extra gear. I had bought the gorilla box from Delaram's tiny postal exchange in anticipation of heading back to the United States a few weeks previous. I rearranged item after item in the box, trying to make more stuff fit, so I would have to hand-carry less of it out of country. Everyone loves to have their stuff handy, but 200 pounds is 200 pounds to lug from country to country, on flights back to the U.S.

Once I was fully packed, I stacked the stuff I would hand carry next to my can's doorway. Flight bag, military backpack, seabag. They probably weighed 250 pounds together. I gave my footlocker a lift and guessed that it weighed about 150 pounds.

How did I get so much crap?

Leaving my stuff by the door, I began dragging my gorilla box down the small steps and past the rows of cans to the post office.

With each step, my breathing became more and more labored. The sun scorched my hands and the back of my neck. I could feel my skin burning.

Drag, step. Step, drag.

I repeated the motion again and again, over and over, and my heart began to physically hurt. I looked down the row to see how much farther I had until I'd reach the post office. I couldn't even see it yet.

Drag, step. Step.

I stumbled, my legs gave way under me, and I fell to my knees, cracking both against the sharp rocks. I gasped in instant pain and tears filled my eyes. I placed my hands on my knees and sobbed, rocking back and forth; I cried from shock and pain and shame. Then I sank back onto my ass and looked up again to find the post office, willing it to appear closer.

You have to get up. Literally no one can help you right now. Look around. There is no one. This is all you, all you, so get up. Get up, Savannah.

I can't.

Yes, you can. You have to. You have to. Get. The. Fuck. Up.

I stumbled to my feet, placing my hands on my knees, remaining bent over. Whether it was the heat, or the situation, or the weight of the gorilla box, my vision began to go black, and I fell backward.

Get. Up.

Stifling my tears, I stood up again, and felt more of that stupid sticky liquid fall out of me and onto my underwear.

Blegh. Let's go. You need to go wipe now. Get this to the post office and find a bathroom. Stop whining and go.

I shuffled the rest of the way, what seemed like a mile, and tried to focus on not passing out again. Swaying, my vision blurry, I tried to fill out the import forms for my box to make it back to America. My brain faltered and the exasperated postal assistant corrected my form multiple times.

"I'm sorry."

My speech was slurred.

That's weird. Fuck, I need water.

The assistant dismissively waved at me and put my box behind the counter with ease.

Stumbling to the bathroom, I pulled down my cammie pants and flopped onto the toilet. I tried to pee, but I had nothing in the tank. Giving up, I wiped, just to see how much clear liquid had fallen from my body. I looked down at the toilet paper. It was everywhere. It covered my underwear, it covered my thighs, and it had leaked through my cammies.

Blood.

62

September 2010, Camp Delaram, Afghanistan

My hands shook as I tried to clean myself up. I kept wiping, over and over, and blood kept coming. I spat on the toilet paper and wiped my thighs down; bits of white toilet paper stuck to my leg as I scrubbed, and the toilet paper disintegrated. I knew that my time to get to the flight line was coming, so I quickly bundled up a huge wad of toilet paper and thrust it between my legs to stem the flow. Girls are used to this when we run out of tampons or pads.

Just treat it like a period …. Except it is your baby dying.

Quickly, I stood and pulled up my shorts and then cammie bottoms. I wrenched my body around to see if the blood had soaked through my cammie bottoms and was visible. It was. There were two bright red spots showing directly in the lower center of my ass.

Fuck. And everyone stares at my ass.

I walked outside and grabbed a handful of sand and threw it against my ass, rubbing some of the sand into the blood. The sand clung to the clots and dulled the brightness of the blood. I did this a few times, until it looked like I had sat in oil and had the cammies washed a few times.

Fuck.

I looked at my watch.

One hour to get my shit to the flight line. I can't miss this flight.

With stellar compartmentalization skills, I walked back to my can and did one last sweep of the area to make sure I wasn't missing anything. My corner of the tent was empty, except for the memories of everything that had happened there over the past five months. That slit in the air conditioning tube would no longer blow slightly less hot air directly onto my face while I tossed and turned. I would no longer have to listen for the sound of the zipper sliding up in the back of the tent. I would no longer have to lay in bed and wait ... wait for whatever was going to happen next. It was happening.

I didn't think I'd leave here alive. I'm ... I'm finally leaving.

Picking up my flak jacket with the Kevlar hanging from the front, I put it on. Then I picked up my bright green sea bag and placed it onto my shoulders. I put my backpack in the front of my body to free my hands and braced myself against the can's wall to pick up my flight bag. I stepped out of the can, letting the door swing shut behind me, before starting the arduous trek to the flight line.

I remember nothing from that walk but pain and the attempt to stay conscious.

When I got to the tarmac, I was surprised at how different it looked compared to the two times I had previously been there. Once was five months ago, when I was dropped off by the Osprey in the middle of the night on the large rock. The second time was during that awful sandstorm with Virkler and the WPPL. Now, four months later and in the light of day, the area was transformed. The flight line was no longer sand and rock; it had been blasted flat by tons of dynamite that had been detonated and had dulled our senses to the mortars. It had been paved in gray concrete that was almost blindingly white when the Afghan sun struck it.

There was a small crowd of people standing around in the open sun. There was no cover or protection. I walked up and asked the nearest Marine if this was the crowd for the 1500 flight. He nodded curtly, before turning his back to me and returning to his conversation with his buddies.

Does everyone know? No, they can't. They seriously can't. Stop being paranoid. These fuckers just suck.

I plopped my stuff down and made a small cover from the sun with my flak jacket before I fell asleep. I knew I would wake up at the slightest increase in motion or noise, so I wasn't afraid of missing the flight.

1500 came and went. I woke in a panic less than 15 minutes later, thinking I had made a mistake and the plane had left without me. Jolted to my feet, wide-eyed and crazy looking, I ran to the nearest group of men. "You're 1500, right?"

"Yeah, dude, calm down. It's late."

"Fuck."

Everyone started talking about the "hurry up and wait" expectation of the military. "You need to hurry, hurry, hurry, just so you can sit and wait, wait, wait ... and wait a little more." (Usually because Motor Transportation—the MOS responsible for driving and maintaining vehicles—was always fucking late).

I crawled under my flak tent and fell back asleep.

Around 1730, a loud roar filled the air. A large, gray CH-53 Sea Stallion helicopter started on the other side of the flight line. Everyone gathered their shit and headed in that direction.

Is that my flight? WHY THE FUCK IS NO ONE TELLING ME ANYTHING? No one was really in charge. No one knew me and no one seemed to know each other, except for groups of four or five Marines. It was with complete faith and lack of knowledge that I put on my stuff and joined the line of Marines heading to the helo.

****

During the second to final week of boot camp, Marines undergo what is called the Crucible. This 54-hour event began in 1996 as a culminating event to prove the transformation from civilian to United States Marine. It is hell for almost all Marines.

According to Oxford Languages, a crucible is "a situation of severe trial, or in which different elements interact, leading to the creation of something new." In metallurgy, a ceramic or metal container in which metals or other substances may be melted or subjected to very high temperatures is considered a crucible.

Personally, I completed the Marine Corps Crucible with a broken ankle that I continued to hike on for 15 miles, with no sleep and very little food. When the Eagle, Globe, and Anchor was placed into my hand by Staff Sergeant Barto, during that cold March morning in 2008, I certainly felt transformed into a Marine, but I had no idea what a true crucible was and what it meant to be completely transformed until I was standing on the tarmac at 1730 in the blazing hot Afghanistan sun.

It was hot. It was hot and sandy. It was hot and sandy, and I was bleeding profusely while carrying a shitload of stuff across that flight line. My throat got tight, and my eyes started welling up from the load. It wasn't just the physical load that I was lugging; it was the mental load of everything that had happened and everything I had done and seen. It was the emotional load of knowing that my baby was dying, and I was ignoring it. It was thinking about how I hadn't gotten to say goodbye to Virkler or Sergeant P. It was thinking about how none of the people I had served with out here, except for those two, would give a shit that I left without a word. It was the fact that every step closer I got to the helo was a step farther away from the place that had ruined me—or, rather, where I had made the decisions that had ruined me. Every step toward that helo made me realize that I was breaking away from who I had become ... and from William. Such a transformation felt as though I was burying the girl I used to be in that Afghanistan sand and stomping on her viciously with my combat boots. I hated her ... me ... more, with every step I took.

The line of Marines was slowly leading into the back of the helicopter. With slow shuffles and steps, I moved my stuff bit by bit closer and closer to the bird, and the scorching sun hurt my eyes. I could see the shade of the back of the bird expanding ... almost there.

Just hold on a little bit more. You can do this, you can.

The heat grew, with the wavering heat lines shining over the concrete, proving hydration did exist in the desert in the form of a watery horizon. The line crept forward slowly, and I was close to the entrance of the bird when it suddenly stopped. Everyone was pushing equipment into the center of the bird to make more room for the last of us. As I stood in the increasing heat, I wondered how it was possible for the sun to get any hotter.

God. Dammit.

The weight crushed me, and I felt my world closing in. I was breaking and I felt tears leak out of my eyes.

The fucking exhaust!

We were standing directly in the line of the helicopter's exhaust. It was pouring boiling hot air onto our faces and bodies. Once I realized this, I laugh-choked a sob.

The only way out is to keep standing here and subjecting yourself to this heat. The only way out is forward .... You have to stand here, in line .... You can't leave. Do you feel that? It feels like my face is melting. I can't turn away. What the fuck am I doing here? Turn and run! FUCK.

My face was burning; it felt like a million needles. The two tears that had leaked from my eyes evaporated into nothing before they got to the middle of my cheeks.

HURRY ... THE FUCK ... UP ... JESUS CHRIST

Finally, I made it into the bird. I sat on the right side of the bulkhead and sat down with all of my stuff piled between my legs. I placed my head on all of my shit and drifted in and out of consciousness.

63

September 2010, somewhere in the Afghan sky

The helicopter whirred into the air. The smell of JP-8 surrounded the cabin and seeped into my nostrils as I lay my head down. The noise was overwhelmingly loud, and the helo seemed to creak and rattle as if all of the bolts were purposely loosened to allow parts to easily shift. As we reached altitude, we began to bob up and down in the air like a ship riding tumultuous waves. Up, up, up, I was pressed down into my seat until we reached the apex of the lift, and then we dropped rapidly back down. My body lifted slightly out of the seat with each drop. Press down, lift, press down, lift ....

Bobbing like a fucking bottle in the ocean. I'm going to hurl.

My stomach clenched and tossed from the bobbing and exhaust smell. One particular drop of the helo lifted my head from my pack, and I looked around to cover the fact that I was being tossed up and down. The Marine next to me looked at my face warily.

"If you are going to toss your cookies, don't get it on my shit."

He shouted, trying to be heard over the props. I arranged my Kevlar helmet face-up on top of my pack and placed my face into it. If I threw up, the splash-back would, hopefully, be contained. It was uncomfortable to press my face into my helmet, but the smell of my own stale sweat embedded in the Kevlar's gray interior pads was better than the smell of gas. Your own stench is bearable, sometimes a little enjoyable.

Another sudden drop brought my head up again. Looking around, I attempted to pass the time by gazing at the helo's interior. There was a pipe running vertically up the bulkhead ... and it was leaking black stuff.

Starting to panic, I tried to catch the eye of the Marine who told me not to vomit on him. He was dead asleep with his head back and mouth wide open.

Turning to my other side, I poked the shoulder of the Marine to my left to grab his attention. I motioned to the wall, where the questionable black stuff was pouring down. The Marine leaned over and stuck his mouth directly over my ear, screaming into it: "OIL."

I looked at him with an *And that's okay?* expression. He leaned back over, exasperated.

"IF IT ISN'T LEAKING, THAT'S WHEN WE DIE."

I gave him a sarcastic thumbs up and went back to suppressing my vomit.

September 2010, Camp Leatherneck, Afghanistan

When the helo landed, it was completely dark. Huge floodlights cut the darkness and blotted out the stars I would've been able to see on Delaram. Instead of a quiet base, Camp Leatherneck was a clusterfuck of noise and light.

One of the floodlights was directly next to a fence that seemed to lead inside Camp Leatherneck's flight terminal hangar.

So, what now? Where do I go? I have no fucking idea where my unit physically is. Maybe if I start walking left I'll end up walking in an area I recognize.

I started to lug my stuff in the direction the crowd was moving when my arm was gently tugged. "Corporal Cannon?"

I whirled around, but the weight of my equipment swung me farther than I had expected to go and I stumbled. Regaining my balance, I tried to adjust my eyes to the brightness directly behind the individual who was speaking to me. His face was darkened by the shadows and my eyes took a few seconds to recognize my old unit's commanding officer standing in front of me. "Sir. What are you doing here?"

"Picking you up, Marine."

This commanding officer was the nicest officer I had ever met. He was a major, well-educated and soft-spoken, and he treated everyone like a person, which is rare in the Marine Corps. One time, while I was setting up his Afghanistan computer for the first time in March, I had seen something gold and shiny on his desk. He saw me studying it and picked it up, handing it to me to study. "It's a sextant."

"Whoa, cool, like the ones in the books?"

He had laughed good-naturedly. "Yes, like the ones in the books."

"That's so cool! I've never seen one before. I only know how they are described in books. Does it work?"

"Come here."

He had led me outside into the night and we stood on the back steps of the command building, for an hour or so, while he showed me how to use the sextant to focus on the stars. I was clumsy and discovered I had the nautical navigational skills of a rock.

He gave up eventually and held the sextant in his hands, while we discussed astronomy and the impact of light pollution and GPS on the deteriorating ability of humans to navigate the earth. We had parted ways after that, and I hadn't seen him since.

He was short in stature; his shoulders bent forward. He had the leathery look of all Marines over the age of 30, and he looked … sad.

I knew he had come to retrieve me because he had been dragged into the general's office and had heard the story. My face turned red with embarrassment.

"Corporal, this is Chaplain Reed, and this is Lieutenant Smith."

He gestured to the two individuals hanging behind him. There was a tall Naval chaplain and a short female Marine looking at me anxiously.

"Good evening, sir, ma'am."

The two creeped me out. People would always joke that Naval chaplains are known in the Marine Corps for being creepy and a little too friendly with the male Marines. That female was looking entirely too eager to be there and practically leapt forward when she was introduced. I stepped back in distrust. The major leaned forward to take my flight bag.

"No, sir, I've got it."

"Don't be ridiculous, we have a vehicle right here."

They loaded my bags into a white SUV, while I stood awkwardly next to it. When we climbed in, the chaplain sat next to me in the back, while the LT drove and the major rode shotgun. We rode in silence for a while, until the chaplain spoke.

"So, how are you?"

"Fine, sir."

He looked like he wanted to keep talking, but I looked out the window and ignored him.

This fucking stranger better not act like I'm his fucking friend. Clearly, he's only here because I'm "suicidal."

I even made the quotation marks in my head when I thought that.

I'm not suicidal, I guess … I mean, I wouldn't mind dying; in fact, I would welcome it. But is that being suicidal? Nah. It's morbid opportunism.

I almost laughed at my reflection in the SUV's back window.

The major tried next: "So how was it out there?"

"Oh, you know, sir … it was war."

I laughed loudly for a few seconds before I realized I was laughing alone. I quickly trailed off while the LT shifted uncomfortably in her seat. Silence permeated the white SUV for another five minutes or so.

I have fucking lost my marbles. Or maybe their sense of humor just sucks.

"We are going to take you to get medically cleared."

"Right now?"

All I wanted was a shower and sleep. I hadn't taken a shower in over 48 hours or slept in just as long. I could feel the blood soaking my thighs.

"Yes."

Suddenly, I was scared. I was a terrible liar, and I had no idea what to tell the Navy doc. Would he be able to diagnose my physical, *fuck, or mental,* state?

The SUV pulled up to some large tan tents. Everyone exited the vehicle and walked toward the tent flaps. The major opened them and motioned for me to enter first. I ducked my head and walked in.

64

Sexual assault in the military is an epidemic and has been for decades. Sexual Assault Prevention and Response (SAPR, pronounced "saper") was originally implemented in 2006 by a Department of Defense (DoD) directive that gave guidelines to the different branches of the military to help military members, government workers, and federal contractors who were sexually assaulted while serving overseas. Prior to my deployment in 2010, we were given a quick brief on SAPR training that was implemented by the Marine Corps Order 1752.5A, written in February 2008. It was summarized as the following:

"If you are sexually assaulted, you can report it in two ways. 1.) Restricted reporting means that your identity will not be given to anyone. You will get medical care. You will be protected, but the person will not be investigated. 2.) Unrestricted reporting means that your identity will be given to the command. An investigation will occur. You will get medical care. You will not be able to maintain privacy.

"You are able to report to three types of people: a chaplain, a military medical facility, or a Uniformed Victims Advocate (UVA). **Each of those are to maintain your privacy, while you get medical attention and you are given an option to have a restricted or unrestricted reporting.** If you tell anyone but those three, you will automatically have an unrestricted reporting."

****

September 2010, Camp Leatherneck, Afghanistan

There was a Navy chief standing just inside the tent, waiting for our group of misfits. "Is this her?"

Huh? "Is this her?" Who the fuck is this guy?

202 • SAVANNAH CANNON

"Yes, this is Corporal Cannon."

"Okay, come this way."

I was led behind the desk that the Navy docs used to check various ailments of Marines and into a very small room made from curtains. A blue medical table was set up within the tent. There was nothing else within the room. The LT, my old CO, and the chaplain were all within earshot of the curtained "room." There was no auditory privacy, but the medical tent was completely empty at this time of night, except for the five of us.

"Take off your blouse and I'll get some vitals."

The chief didn't tell me his name, but he exited the room briefly while I peeled off my blouse; my green skivvy shirt was clinging to me with sweat, or was it chills?

When he returned, he wheeled in the usual blood pressure, heartbeat, and temperature apparatus with one hand while holding a sheaf of paper in the other. He placed the papers on the table on which I was now sitting to hide the blood stains that were reappearing on the back of my cammies.

"So, are you feeling well today?"

"If I felt well, would I be here?"

Stupid motherfucker.

He sighed and wrapped the blood pressure cuff around my arm. He placed a stethoscope on the inside of my elbow while he pumped the air into the cuff. He listened intently, tapping his foot while the pressure deflated. He shook his head. "That can't be right. Your blood pressure is extremely low. Have you been drinking water?"

"What water? This is a desert. I've been traveling all day."

"You need to drink water."

"Mmk ...."

We were irritated with each other. He had to stay late at work for a mental case and I was irritated with his lack of a decent bedside manner. He picked up his papers and started asking questions without any emotion. "How do you feel?"

"Fine."

Do I tell him?

"Do you have any feelings of hurting yourself or others?"

Only a list.

"No."

"On a scale of one to 10, with one being little to no interest and ten being lots of interest, answer the following questions: What is your interest in usual activities?"

"What the heck is a usual activity out here?"

"Look, just answer the questions."

I was shaking at this point. I felt another chunk of blood fall from me as he picked up his pen again.

I have to fucking tell someone.

"I … I think I'm miscarrying …."

I burst into tears after I whispered this to the medical professional so the crowd outside the curtains couldn't hear.

"What?"

"I'm pregnant and I'm bleeding a lot."

"How are you pregnant?"

"I was … f—"

"You were what?"

I was openly sobbing at this point. My stomach was heaving, and I started blacking out again.

"… forced?" He finished the word for me.

I nodded.

The Navy chief walked out of the room. I laid on the table, curled into a ball, holding my stomach, bawling.

"She said she was raped and now she's miscarrying," the medical professional announced loudly to the room.

65

September 2010, Camp Leatherneck, Afghanistan

So, the shit hit the metaphorical fan. The 24 hours that followed were a blur. Everyone in my command was notified of my assault, and my privacy was non-existent. I gasped when I heard the Naval doctor breach protocol. All of the things I had tried to do in the past three months to protect myself and to protect my baby were for naught.

The commanding officer, above my commanding officer, was told. NCIS was notified. My name was plastered across documents and all of my privacy was gone.

It was no surprise that I was assigned a suicide watch—someone to follow my every footstep to ensure I didn't off myself. Even though I had no weapon, everyone else had a weapon. I guess it would have been easy for me to grab someone else's gun and shoot myself. The Marine Corps likes to pride itself on its efficiency and thoroughness. In the whirlwind of those days, no one thought to take away my Gerber knife, with 3.7 inches of sharpened metal, neatly clipped to my pocket.

After the Navy corpsman's bout of unprofessionalism, I was released, still bleeding and without having received any medical care, into the hands of my suicide watch. She was a short Marine, who I knew in passing. Coincidentally, she was also the Marine rumored to have gotten pregnant in Iraq. She was too cheerful, and I hated everything that came out of her mouth. She brought me back to the crowded room of no airflow, where I had originally slept when I had arrived in Afghanistan. When the door opened, the stench of smelly women swept out of the door and into my face and I gagged. My bunk was still empty, and the thin and hard mattress looked miserable compared to my bed on Delaram.

I desperately needed a shower. I hadn't had a shower in almost two days and sweat and sand and blood caked my body. I started to open my pack and search for my hygiene bag full of soap and shampoo. "I'm going to grab a shower."

My suicide watch seemed surprised and stumbled over her next words.

"Uh, I, uh, I don't think you can leave."

"Says who? I need a shower."

"Well, it's late and I'm tired. And you can't leave without me."

"It's—" I glanced at my watch. "It is 2000!"

"Yeah, well, I don't want to go. I have to be up at 0600."

Dear lord, yeah, don't want to cut those ten hours of sleep short.

"Well, I'm going to take a shower. You can come with, or you can stay."

"Do not leave."

"This is ridiculous. I'm going to take a shower."

I grabbed my thin towel, some fresh skivvies, and my hygiene bag and sprinted out the door. She attempted to follow me, but I remembered the layout of that area of Camp Leatherneck from my night runs there months ago, so I was able to lose her quickly. The absence of a rifle was suddenly a real bonus.

Panting, I rounded a corner into a living area I did not recognize. Unfamiliar Marines were milling about, smoking and insulting each other. I caught the attention of the closest one, a scrawny and sunburned male without a blouse on.

"Where are the showers?"

He motioned in the general direction and I immediately set off that way. I felt his eyes and the eyes of his buddies follow me as I left. I wondered if they could see the blood dripping down to my knees.

I came to an area that looked like it could possibly hold showers. There were two identical tan tents, with men going in and out of one. Taking a shot in the dark, I entered the other one. Black rubber mesh covered the ground, and a line of benches ran along the inside of the tent to the right. About six showers lined the left-hand side of the tent. I set my stuff down on a bench and stripped down. I peeled my skivvy shorts from my blood-encrusted thighs and tried to see if the bleeding had continued.

Why the actual fuck is it so dark in here? I can't see anything.

My eyes strained in the dimly lit tent. A string of lightbulbs hung from the ceiling, and only two worked to light the 20-foot-long tent.

I stuck my fingers between my legs. They came away dark and wet. Sighing, I walked to the nearest shower and went to turn it on.

No water came out.

I tried the second one. There was a slight leak.

Buck-naked, I walked back and forth between the stalls, trying each one in turn. Thankfully, the last stall sprang forth water with a vengeance and I stepped in ....

... into a pool of slime and gunk.

WHAT THE FUCK?

I tried to see what was at the bottom of the shower, to cause disgusting water to reach the middle of my right calf. The tent was so dark that I could see nothing but dark water.

Screw it. I want a shower.

I stepped in with my other foot. Something wrapped around my leg. I attempted, and failed, not to gag. I began to heave, fighting a mental battle of wills to hold in my disgust and horror at what could possibly be at my feet.

Just don't think about it, it's probably nothing but soap and water and maybe some hair .... Oh my god someone else's disgusting hair.

I threw up on my feet.

Scrambling to wash the blood, sweat, sand, and now vomit from my body, I took the world's fastest shower, dressed rapidly in clean skivvies, and hightailed it back to the area of base that I knew.

66

September 2010, Camp Leatherneck, Afghanistan

When I reached the dark and smelly area where all the other women were sleeping, I placed my hygiene bag full of shampoo and soap on my bunk quietly. The sergeant who was supposed to be watching me snored loudly as she slept. I reached into the pocket of my cammies that were hanging on the bunk and pulled out my knife. I flicked it open a few times to work out the sand before I left the tent.

They take my rifle to prevent me from killing myself but neglect to make sure I don't have any other weapons. What idiots.

I walked out of the can and drifted aimlessly toward an area I hadn't been before. When I reached the area surrounded by guards, I asked them for Simon.

"He is a contractor, works for MEF. Tell him Corporal Cannon is here."

Unwillingly, one of the guards used a phone to relay my message. I waited patiently outside of the ECP of the compound for a few moments, when a man walked out and stared at me.

"Cannon?"

"Hey, Simon."

"Let's take a walk."

It was strange to finally see this man in person after months of only hearing his voice. We left MEF's ECP and walked a few blocks until we saw a cot that had been set up next to a concrete bunker. We sat down, both of us with a huge sigh.

"Why did you go to the general, Simon?"

"How do you not understand why? You've been getting … different over the last few months, and your last comments were pretty serious. You hung up on me. How was I supposed to know what was happening over there?"

"But the fucking GENERAL?! Do you know what they did?"

"They took your rifle; I can see that."

"And put me on suicide watch and yanked me from Delaram. I'm a fucking tourist attraction now."

"Where is your suicide watch?"

"Asleep."

Simon sighed and put his head in his hands.

"I'm sorry, Cannon, but I don't regret it. I probably could've gone another way—"

"Like telling, oh I dunno, anyone else lower in rank?!"

"Like telling someone else in rank, yes. But you needed help."

Simon was probably late thirties, with brown hair that was starting to gray. He looked stressed around the eyes, probably from engineering the entire region of Afghanistan for thousands of troops at war.

I slumped against the side of the bunker, dejectedly. "I don't know what I'm supposed to do."

"Go back to America. I don't think you understand how detached you are, we all are, from society. We live where every day is Groundhog Day. There is nothing fun to do besides hope it is Mongolian BBQ day at the chow hall."

"We didn't even have that on Delaram."

"America will be so much better. If you want ice cream, you can get ice cream. If you want to call up a friend, you'll have a cell phone to do it. There won't be only sand and heat and war to depress you. You can leave an area without getting stared at, you can sleep for days if you want. Just go back to America and remember what is going on here isn't forever."

"It's forever for the people who live here, though."

"You can't take in everyone else's pain like that. This region has been at war for hundreds of years. This is their lot in life and they accept it."

"Because they have to."

"Cannon …."

Simon sighed again. He was starting to realize I would argue with anything he said. I didn't understand how Americans could compartmentalize the experiences they had in a war-torn country.

Just go back to America and act like everything is okay when people are living like this every day, not knowing that life isn't full of disease and death and terror, just a little ways around the globe? No wonder people think Americans are so selfish.

"So, is that what you do? Leave Afghanistan and just act like bad shit doesn't happen here?"

"It is a job. That's all I can see it as. If I see it as anything more …" He trailed off and looked at his hands.

"How's the wife?"

"She actually filed for divorce."

"Oh, Simon, I'm sorry."

"Nah, don't be. We've both made choices that brought us here."

We sat in silence for a few minutes before Simon stood up from the cot.

"I need to get back to work. There's a maintenance window tonight to fix some stuff."

"Okay, enjoy."

"And you enjoy America. Keep your head up, Cannon."

67

September 2010, Camp Leatherneck, Afghanistan

I woke up as my suicide watch came back from the head, slamming the door shut behind her.

"Let's go. We have to be at work by seven."

I threw on my cammies and made sure my hair was still secure in its bun. I was completely dressed and ready to go before she had gotten halfway through her routine. I sat on my bed in silence as I waited for her to finish.

When she was done, we left for the compound where I had worked for almost two months before leaving for Delaram. The walk to work was about a mile through sleeping areas and other compounds full of working Marines. We passed one empty block where people were playing volleyball in the dirt and rocks. They were laughing and joking as they bounced the ball back and forth over the net. I stared at their blatant happiness, weirded out by their loudness and their delight. The sergeant didn't even glance at them.

When we entered the compound, flashing our IDs at the guards, we headed to the long building in the back. There was a wave of disruption as people recognized me. Everyone was welcoming at first, until they noticed I didn't have a weapon. Then the wave of whispers began, and people avoided eye contact with me.

I walked into the data area to rejoin my old coworkers when the sergeant called out.

"Where do you think you're going? You're going to hang out with Radio and Wire."

Radio and Wire Marines were located in a room down the hallway from Data. They were known for not doing much of anything but laying out gear and inventorying it, only to pack it up and do it again the next day. There was an unspoken feud of sorts between the Communications Marines. Data Marines were the smart ones, and we looked down on the "lowly" Radio and Wire Marines. This relationship stemmed from as far back as communications school. When we enlisted in the Marines, the Data Marines were selected based on our capabilities and scores on the ASVAB (Armed Services Vocational Aptitude Battery Exam) and the needs of the Marine Corps. Radio and Wire Marines didn't have to score as high on their tests to be placed in their schools, and if a Marine attending the data course failed out of the course, they were re-tread, or dropped, to a radio or wire course. This isn't to say that all Radio and Wire Marines were dumb, but there was a certain level of elitism that Data Marines had developed over the years.

I didn't want to hang out with the Radio and Wire Marines. I knew I could do their jobs, based upon old exercises when the Marine Corps wanted all Communications Marines to be able to do all communication jobs. But we had less than three weeks left before we would start rotating back to America, the turnover for me to start working with them would take longer than it was worth, and I was miscarrying.

Irritated, I followed her into the Radio and Wire room. Everyone was sitting around, shooting the shit, and hanging out. The whispers almost immediately started up.

"Cannon, you'll be running lines in new buildings with Roberts and Sabim" some Radio sergeant barked at me.

"Uh, Sergeant …?

"What?" His voice was annoyed and harsh.

"Uh, I'm not sure I should be doing that."

"And why is that?"

"Just, medical reasons."

Someone whispered into the sergeant's ear.

"I don't give a shit if she's pregnant. She's not getting out of work."

"Yes, Sergeant."

Face flaming in embarrassment, I walked out to the smoke pit where everyone was sitting around discussing the green belt training they had gotten to participate in while I was on Delaram. Marines were wrestling everywhere, men and women, and everyone was laughing and joking together. Their comradery only made my ostracization more apparent.

"What about you, Cannon? Why don't you at least have your gray belt?"

"I worked. Not really time for much else."

"Yeah, you look like shit."

"Thanks."

"I mean, really, you completely lost your ass. What happened?"

I replied harshly as everyone's laughs filled the air. "We didn't have four chow halls to choose from so we could stuff our fat faces. Y'all must've gained ten pounds each. Maybe I didn't lose as much weight as you've gained it."

I stalked off in anger. No one followed me.

When the truck came, I went with Roberts and Sabim to start running cables. When we pulled up to the developing part of the base, I went inside the empty building, which smelled of new plywood and construction. The two male Marines started unloading cable from the truck, placing it on the stairs for me to carry into the building. After a few trips, I started to feel lightheaded. I slid down the wall of an empty room and curled into a ball as sharp pains began to fill my abdomen.

Roberts and Sabim entered the room. Roberts took one look at me and forced Sabim out of the room, with Sabim complaining the whole time.

"Come on, man, just leave her alone."

I laid there, moving in and out of consciousness, and could vaguely hear the Eminem song the men had put on while they worked.

"Don't know what I'm going through, but I just keep going through changes ...."

Weird, I don't know that song ....

68

September 2010, Camp Leatherneck, Afghanistan

When we returned to the compound, a lieutenant was waiting for us. She was bright-eyed and nervous, like all young officers who have no idea what is going on and can't relate to their troops. She told me to follow her, explaining excitedly who she was, while we walked through the bright plywood halls of the building. "I'm your UVA."

"What?"

"I'm your uniformed victims' advocate."

"I don't know what that is."

"I facilitate all interactions with you and the command to ensure you are properly taken care of during this time. I can accompany you to medical appointments and be your voice. I'll make sure no one treats you poorly during this time."

"Oh." *Sure you will. And I am sure you can stop the whispers and the gossiping and the lack of privacy.*

We were still walking past open doors with Marines coming in and out constantly. The LT was walking ahead of me, guiding me toward a conference room.

"Where are we going, ma'am?"

"I just want to ask you a few questions."

"But I don't want to talk about it."

She stopped and looked concerned that I wouldn't bend to her immediate command. "Just come in here."

Not willing to completely disobey an officer, I walked into the conference room and walked around the table to sit facing the only door. The LT sat down across from me. "I can't help you if you don't let me."

"Well, with all due respect, ma'am, I didn't ask for your help. I have no idea who you are."

"I told you, I'm the UVA."

"I went to the corpsman for medical help and told him something he was legally required to keep quiet about, and now you're here, and everyone out there knows something happened to me. I didn't want or ask for this."

The LT shifted uncomfortably in her seat before she spoke again.

"There are some investigators from NCIS who are coming to speak with you."

I paled at the mention of the Naval Criminal Investigative Service.

"I'll be right back."

"Ma'am, I just wanted to get medical attention. I didn't want this. I don't want an investigation."

If they investigate and find out it was William, he'll be arrested and he will tell them I did it willingly, which, yeah, I did at first, so I was in the wrong, and then I'll be arrested and sent to the brig for adultery and having sex in a combat zone and ....

My voice started to get panicky. "I don't want this. I don't want this."

She looked at me with pity. "I'll go get them."

She stood up and walked out of the room. Two civilians in khakis and dark blue shirts entered the room almost immediately. The LT stood in the corner as the investigators began.

"Good evening, Corporal Cannon. We are here because an unrestricted report was filed concerning a sexual assault case you were a victim of."

"I didn't file a report."

"One was filed for you by the commanding officer."

"Don't unrestricted reports have to be requested by the victim?"

The investigator patiently responded. "Unless other parties have been informed of the assault, then they are mandated to report it and it becomes unrestricted."

"Aren't medical people outside of the mandated reporting? I told a Navy doc. He wasn't supposed to tell anyone. So, you're telling me that because he opened his mouth and told my commanding officer, I have to endure an unrestricted report? Where my name and the details of the assault are released to the command? And there is an investigation?"

The investigators looked back at the LT and exchanged looks. The discomfort level in the room had risen to peak capacity.

"Yes, I'm afraid so."

My mouth dropped open. "And that's it. I get no say."

"You don't have to participate in the investigation."

"Yeah, I won't … since I didn't ask for it."

The second investigator began to shuffle papers around while the first investigator continued.

"Corporal Cannon, I have to say that if you don't assist NCIS with this investigation, the perpetrator will probably not be caught."

Good.

"And the likelihood he will do it to someone else is high."

"I didn't want this investigation. I wanted medical help."

Which I didn't even fucking get.

"Okay, then please sign here."

The second investigator shoved a piece of paper across the table to me. I read the legal jargon that included stuff like: "The undersigned did not consent to discussing the events and willingly chose not to give a statement."

I scribbled my signature. "Is that all, gentlemen?"

"Yes, thank you for your time. And if there is ever a time when you change your mind and wish to give a statement, please, don't hesitate to give me a call."

He handed me a business card, blue and gold, with his name and title on it in fancy lettering. I stood up and left, with the LT following me.

"Where is Legal?"

I stormed out of the building with the LT chasing me.

"Uh, there is a Legal over in CLR-15."

"I'll be over there."

"I'll come with you."

"No, thank you."

"Are you sure?"

She seemed dejected that I wasn't willing to use her services for what was easily one of the juiciest cases she'd had the chance to participate in.

"I'm sure."

I walked into CLR-15's building.

69

September 2010, Camp Leatherneck, Afghanistan

I knocked on the door leading to the lawyer's office. Flyers and informational papers were taped all over it, a messy distraction of untidy clutter. A female captain answered my knock.

"Good evening, ma'am. May I ask you some questions?"

"You'll have to make it quick."

I walked inside her office and sat down on the chair diagonal to her cluttered desk.

"I just have a few questions regarding charges under the UCMJ."

"I'll have to remind you that I can't protect you under lawyer/client privilege."

"You couldn't be my lawyer?"

"No."

"Okay, well these are just hypothetical questions."

She sighed, "Go ahead."

"What charges could someone be charged under, for having sex in a combat zone and with someone not their spouse?"

"Court martial. Usually, a summary court martial. The general order states there is no sex in a combat zone."

"And what happens in a court martial?"

"The accused stands trial and if found guilty, they are sent to the brig and are reduced in rank and are subject to hard labor and other stuff. They don't get a lawyer."

"No lawyer?"

"No.

"Dang."

We sat in silence for a few moments. All of my investigating had told me as much. Jail, dishonorable discharge, and garnishing of wages. If the investigation found out that I was raped by William, and he told them I willingly had sex that first time so he could get my baby taken from me, I would be jailed and stripped of everything I had worked for, and I would indeed be an unfit mother. William's case against me would be easier with a jail sentence. I remembered what he had told me about Amy's mother months ago, how she was crazy, and how he took Amy away from her. He would stop at nothing to make sure he did the same to me.

And where would my child be?

My mind tried not to think of the blood still dripping from me.

None of this can be happening.

"Okay, thank you, ma'am."

Fuck. I can't let them find out it's him.

"Corporal?" The officer stood up to follow me to the door.

"Yes, ma'am?"

"Sometimes punishment is well-deserved."

"Yes, ma'am."

70

September 2010, Camp Leatherneck, Afghanistan

I left CLR-15's building deep in thought. I didn't hear the sergeant calling my name until she was properly upset at me for not responding.

"Come ON, Cannon!"

I followed her into a new building, the command building. My heart began to race.

This can't be good.

The sergeant led me into an office where a female major was sitting.

Jesus Christ, how many females are on this base?!

The two Marines laughed and joked together for a bit, while I stood awkwardly in the doorway and waited for them to finish. The sergeant walked past me with a glare and left me alone with the major.

"Corporal Cannon, I'm Major Bagley, the unit's SARC, the sexual assault response coordinator."

Another one? How many people fucking know?

"I'm here to discuss what is going to happen next."

"Okay."

"First off, how are you?"

Is that a serious question?

"Fine, ma'am."

"Okay, well, since you're pregnant, we need to get you out of Afghanistan. Your unit is returning to America in two weeks. We should probably just send you back with them."

My face was hot and red. I didn't tell anyone but the corpsman that I was pregnant.

His fat fucking mouth ....

The major was gesturing to a calendar on her desk with dates scribbled all over it.

"Okay."

"Have you been checked out by a doctor?"

"The Navy corpsman took a look at me and said nothing, ma'am. But I'm still bleeding."

The major jumped with a start and looked panicked.

"Wait, you're bleeding?!"

"Yes, ma'am."

"How long?"

"About a week, I guess. I can't remember."

"Jesus Christ, you need to go to the hospital!"

She jumped to her feet and rushed out of the door yelling at her assistant. "Go get a vic!"

Oh, so now it's serious?

Numb, I waited while the entire building burst into a frenzy at the female major's yells. I was led to a vehicle, a white truck. The truck drove off quickly in the direction of Camp Bastion, the British base directly attached to the American Camp Leatherneck. The only hospital in the region was there.

"Why didn't you tell anyone?"

"I did."

71

September 2010, Camp Bastion, Afghanistan

The hospital was big, a building that wasn't plywood like the rest. It was concrete, white, and was painted with blue trim. The truck dropped off the major and me on a wheelchair ramp, at what could only be considered the front of the hospital. We walked inside and she told me to sit on one of the chairs lining the walls of the emergency room, while she went to talk to the receptionist. After a while, she came back.

"They need to talk to you. I can't answer the questions."

"Yes, ma'am."

"I need to go back to Leatherneck and keep the CO in the loop about what's happening."

"Yes, ma'am."

"You'll be taken care of here."

"Yes, ma'am."

The major walked out of the empty emergency room and I turned to the receptionist. After I gave her my information, I was ushered into a room where my blood pressure, temperature, and heart rate were taken. My blood pressure was extremely low, dangerously low, and I was asked if I was lightheaded. At this point, I had been lightheaded since July, so I laughed bitterly. The lovely British nurse, with crooked teeth, did not share my laughter. She immediately walked me into a large room, with multiple people swarming around. There was a table with instruments lined neatly on a blue cloth. I saw a shiny metal speculum that is used to force open the vagina, and an ultrasound machine with a wand attached.

"Please lay on the table and loosen your pants so we can access your lower abdomen."

I sat on the table and lay down. I unbuckled my tan belt and unbuttoned my pants. I shimmied my cammie bottoms down and pulled my shirt out of my green skivvy shorts. The dark-haired nurse turned on the ultrasound machine and wheeled it close to the bed. Three other people were in the room, shifting stuff around in a bustle of movement. There was a giant light above my head.

This is an operating room.

The nurse pulled my shorts down to right above my pubic bone with one hand, while she picked up a bottle of blue goo with her other hand.

"Have you ever had an ultrasound before?"

"No."

"Okay, this might be a little cold."

She squirted cold blue goo onto my lower abdomen, placed the wand on my stomach, and began moving the blue stuff around with the wand.

"What is the blue stuff for?"

"It helps conduct the sound waves into your body and gives us a better picture of the baby."

The ultrasound wand spread blue goo everywhere. The screen of the ultrasound machine was facing the nurse and away from me. She was searching, pressing firmly with the wand, moving it back and forth. She found what she was looking for and began typing onto the screen.

"Ah, here is your baby."

"You can see my baby?!"

I tried to sit up to see the screen and another nurse rushed over to gently push me back down.

"Shh, just relax."

The main nurse fiddled with something on the machine and a noise filled the room.

Tha-thump, tha-thump, tha-thump.

The noise was fast and even.

"And there's your baby's heartbeat."

The sound of the baby I had been carrying filled the room and my ears and my heart, as I heard its little heartbeat loud and clear. Here was proof of the life I had been carrying. Here was proof that this wasn't just some horrible nightmare, or mistake, or miscommunication between my pee and a pregnancy test. Here was my baby.

"My … my baby?"

"Congratulations! The baby looks strong."

The nurse smiled kindly at me. My eyes filled with tears and my body began to shake as the tears poured from my eyes onto the table I lay on.

"Was this … expected?"

"No, no, it wasn't."

She studied me as she handed me tissues.

"Well, here is the bad news. You are hemorrhaging slightly, and the baby is at extreme risk right now. So, you'll be medically evacuated immediately."

"What? I'll be medevaced? But that's for people who are dying."

"Well … your baby might be dying."

I was so full of so many conflicting emotions at this point—despair and hope, love and hate—the emotions rolled over me until I went into shock and became numb.

"Is my baby going to die?"

She rolled the wand around to see some more of my abdomen. The baby's heartbeat disappeared from the room.

"It looks like your placenta is detaching from the uterus and that is what is causing your bleeding. But the baby is very strong and is kicking hard, very close to where the detachment is happening. So, the placenta might get worse as the baby continues."

"That's kicking?"

"Do you feel that movement?"

Suddenly, I could match the almost unnoticeable flutters in my abdomen to the whooshing noises coming through the ultrasound machine.

"Oh my God …."

"That's your baby."

She grinned at me, and I sobbed.

"So, you're telling me that my baby is kicking so hard that he or she is helping detach the placenta? My baby is kicking its way out of me?"

"More or less, yes."

"What can I do?"

"Get medevaced. They will take care of you. We will get you into a bed until you are cleared to fly."

"What about my stuff? What do I need?"

The nurse was wiping the blue goo gently from my abdomen.

"Someone will take care of it."

She helped me stand and dress, then walked me out of the operating room and into a bed. She piled blankets on me as I shivered from shock. She hooked up an IV to me and told me to relax and sleep. With nothing on my person, with no books and no people to talk to, and certainly with no cell phone, there was nothing to do but wait. With no responsibilities, no purpose, and nothing to do for the first time in months, I closed my eyes and slept.

****

My eyes shot open. Someone was standing next to my bed. Quickly, heart racing, I focused on the Marines standing there. It was my commanding officer and the regimental sergeant major, the highest enlisted Marine in my parent unit. The CO, the one who had stood outside with me those many months ago, discussing stars and sextants, looked at me with such pity in his eyes that I started to cry again.

The CO spoke. "I'm so sorry."

I turned on my side and closed my eyes, blocking them out, willing their pity and their presence to be a figment of my imagination. When I opened them again, the two leaders of Marines had left.

72

September 2010, somewhere in Afghanistan

I was sent on a helicopter first, I think. I went from Camp Bastion to another location in Afghanistan. It may have been Kandahar. The pilot and other passengers didn't speak to each other, or to me. It was nighttime and the flight from Bastion was brief, or I slept through it, and I don't remember. I was in a daze, with nothing on my person but my military ID card and the thoughts of the dying child I was carrying. Every flutter I could now identify reminded me the baby was killing itself, unknowingly, and I was helpless to stop it. With nothing to occupy my hands, they lay in my lap, clasping each other, white knuckled.

When we reached the next location, the sky was gray with clouds. The buildings on the base were old and I was directed toward a tent immediately off the runway. The tent was a flurry of activity, with Air Force members directing people left and right toward cots and bedding. The majority of the cots were full of men and women sleeping or going through their packs. I tried to catch the attention of a haggard civilian sorting dozens of folders full of paper.

"Excuse me? Ma'am?"

She didn't glance up as she asked for my name. Once I gave it, she said my diagnosis and pointed me toward a cot.

"There's bedding next door."

"Is there a place to eat?"

"Chow hall is across the street. Be quick. Your evacuation can happen at any time."

I walked, empty-handed, across the street. None of the buildings were labeled, so I stopped an Airman and asked where the chow hall was located.

He pointed me farther down the street to a large building. I entered the doors and was swept into a crowded room full of conflicting smells. There was sweet BBQ and what seemed like burnt pizza. Lines of people were piling food high onto their trays. I entered a line and looked at the selection. My heart skipped a beat as I scanned the assortment of fresh fruit and vegetables.

There's salad!

I piled leafy greens and carrots and bell peppers high into a bowl. I grabbed a banana, and I grabbed a small carton of milk, real cow's milk, and headed to a table.

My arm was caught.

"Where do you think you're going without paying?" The Airman scowled at me.

"Paying? Isn't this a chow hall?"

"Yeah, and we pay here."

I looked at those around me, who were staring at the exchange. I began to notice the small pieces of paper in front of every item in line; they were price tags. Mortified, I looked down at the tray of food I was carrying and remembered that my wallet was in Leatherneck, where it hadn't been used in close to seven months. I mumbled. "I ... I don't have any money."

Eager to leave the stares of military members, of multiple branches of militaries from around the world, I set the tray down and started to walk away. The man behind me in line called out for me to come back. "Come on, I'll pay for it. Can't you see she's starving?"

The gentleman, a contractor, admonished the Airman who refused to let something slide just once. He smiled at me as I thanked him, avoiding eye contact while he handed over the cash. I walked off to sit down and the contractor followed me. The eyes of everyone in the chow hall followed me as I walked. I was the only United States Marine in the room. I sat down and the contractor went to sit down across from me.

"Please don't. I'd rather be alone. Thank you for paying."

The contractor seemed stunned and shifted to the table next to me to sit with the people he had originally come to the chow hall with. One of his friends asked me what I was doing on this base. "Marines don't come here."

I shrugged and kept my head down, shoving the salad into my mouth. My desire to eat had left almost as quickly as my level of comfort had. The men kept talking to me from across the aisle. "What do you do?"

I inhaled the salad and shoved the carton of milk and banana into my cargo pockets. Ignoring the question, I stood and left, dropping the tray quickly onto the moving conveyor belt that took trays into another room. I sprinted across the street and ducked back into the tent. When the civilian woman saw me enter, she asked me, exasperated, where I had been.

"I went to eat."

"Well, grab all of your stuff, your medevac is here."

I glanced down at my body and held out my empty hands.

"This is it!"

She'd had enough of my shit. She shoved a folder into my hands and told me to get in line for the plane. I joined a small bedraggled group of men on the tarmac. We stood, some with bags, waiting for the plane. The giant C-17 rolled to a stop in the middle of the runway and we were walked out to it. The back had been dropped. We walked up the steep ramp into the empty craft.

"Sit along the sides!"

Small seats dropped from the sides of the aircraft. I sat closest to the front of the plane. The center of the aircraft was empty. A blonde-haired man-boy was seated next to me. He was still wearing his FROG suit. His baby face was dirty, and he looked in shock too.

"What's wrong with you?"

"I'm hemorrhaging. What's wrong with you?"

"I have cancer."

"No shit? How did they find that out?"

Cancer Boy and I talked for a few minutes. I found out that he had suddenly started itching so badly that he scratched open wounds in the skin on his arms. His doc on Dwyer, the sister FOB to Delaram, had sent off some bloodwork and it came back with bad results. The cancer was evidently fast-growing. He looked so young. I guess we both looked young. Just a bunch of fucking kids at war. This man looked like he had never shaved in his life—a dirty baby-faced grunt who was dying of cancer. "I thought I would die a different way."

We fell silent as movement began at the rear of the plane. Suddenly, airmen sprinted in with gurneys full of men. They locked the gurneys into the plane's floors, hooked up IVs and piss bags, one by one. Each gurney had a team of at least three doctors/nurses/medics tending to the individual on it. Sounds filled the plane, sounds of moaning, and screaming, and crying. Medics shouted to each other, "MORE MORPHINE," while the flight crew began conducting checks. The plane began to move and the medics didn't slow.

The gurney directly in front of me held a man. He was moaning quietly. His face was swollen and beaten. His bag of piss dangled close to my left knee. Blankets covered his body. His medic adjusted a nozzle on his IV, and his moaning stopped almost immediately as he went limp. I strained to look at his body and noticed he was missing a leg.

"Fuck. Fuck."

Cancer Boy sitting next to me was shaking and staring wide-eyed at the spot where the man's leg was supposed to be.

It probably reminds him of one of his friends. Fuck.

"Hey, hey, look at me." I turned his face to mine, breaking his locked gaze. "So where are you from?"

I distracted him for a few minutes with talk about Arkansas and his sister. She would be worried to not hear from him for the last week as he had been shuttled from base to base. The moans of the wounded began to calm and disappear into the noise of the plane as it flew higher and higher. We began to shiver as the temperature of the cabin dropped to match the temperature of the air outside the plane. The medics loaded more blankets onto the wounded. We didn't dare ask for a blanket.

Cancer Boy's head began to drop from exhaustion. I was shivering and tired as well. I touched his shoulder and shook him awake enough to gesture for him to lie on my seat. I stood up and he dropped his head into my seat and fell fast asleep, curled into a small skinny ball.

There was a large roll of cable, about 4 feet tall, along the front of the plane. The top of the cable roll was about a foot and a half wide, sloping down to the floor on both sides.

There are worse places to sleep.

I climbed onto the roll of cable and curled into a ball on my side, with my feet and head dangling down the sides of the roll. I pulled my blouse up around my mouth and willed my breath to warm my body. I fell asleep.

73

September 2010, Ramstein, Germany

The plane landed smoothly. I had expected the temperature to rise upon landing, but I kept shivering while others around me gathered their bags. The back of the plane was lowered, and my eyes took in the most color they had seen in over seven months. The green of the German countryside soothed my desert-strained eyes and my mouth dropped open.

"Whoa .... Look at all of the green."

My words were directed toward no one. The few of us who could stand did so, and we craned to see more. Medics bustled around the unconscious men laying on gurneys, disconnecting wires and rerunning lines, preparing the men for movement. Cancer Boy and I made our way to the top of the ramp at the back of the plane and stumbled down the ramp. I breathed in the damp air. It filled my parched lungs with a heavy moisture, saturating them with relief.

There were maybe five of us who were able to walk. I was the only woman, and as I looked around, I saw how ... horrible we looked. We were all so skinny that we looked like we would break into two with a single breeze. Our sand-covered cammies were dirty smudges against the backdrop of the crisp green trees and grass. Our faces were gaunt and strained. We were jumpy and moved in quick jerks, as the Air Force seemed to glide around us with ease.

The five of us stood in a line at the bottom of the ramp and watched the broken men get unloaded. The gurneys were sprinted into the building behind us. We were shivering and empty-handed. I watched the medevacs with dull eyes.

"Get your shit and come in here!"

A tall and awkwardly happy Airman yelled for us to enter the airport terminal. We glanced around at each other, searching for the bags people kept expecting us to have, before we went inside. We were left alone in the corner of the terminal for a few hours without any knowledge of what would happen to us. We curled up on the floor and slept. I entered a sleep state of half consciousness, listening to the bustle of the military terminal around me while I slept. This state allowed me to be aware of everything happening while simultaneously letting me "sleep." It ensured I wasn't surprised when the Army soldier walked up and loudly announced our rides had arrived.

We were led outside to the curb and motioned to enter the two cars awaiting us. My broken comrade-in-arms and I stood close together and got into a car driven by a man in civilian clothes. The rest of the group piled into the second car. I rode shotgun in the small German car and Cancer boy sat behind the driver. The man who was driving looked like a Marine. He looked how most out-of-uniform Marines look in a garrison environment—clean-shaven, in shape, with the stereotypical hair with the faded cut. "I'm Staff Sergeant Foster."

"Corporal Cannon."

The man dying of cancer didn't answer the staff sergeant. He gazed out of the window in silence as the staff sergeant moved the car off of the curb and exited Ramstein Airport's parking lot. The sky was dark with gray clouds. I hadn't seen clouds in months.

"Where are we going?"

"Landstuhl."

"What?"

"Landstuhl."

I had no idea what he was saying, and I didn't want to repeat myself and look even more like an idiot.

"Oh, okay."

"So, what's wrong with you?"

"I'm hemorrhaging. What's wrong with you?"

He laughed good-naturedly.

"God damn, all of us are the same. A bunch of smart-ass motherfuckers. But hey, at least you aren't here because you want to kill yourself. Those assholes are the worst. They get medevaced for mental issues and we have to make sure they don't off themselves. Meanwhile, real Marines are hurt and dying. I say just let them kill themselves. We don't have time to take care of their pussy asses."

"Oh. Yeah. They are the worst."

"Knew you'd get it. How long were you in the desert?"

"What is today?"

"September 7th."

"A little over seven months."

"Damn, were you set to do 14 months?"

"I don't think so. Other people volunteered to stay longer but no one had gone on R&R yet. No one seemed to know what was going on."

"Typical."

We pulled up into a parking lot. The second car pulled up immediately behind us. Staff Sergeant Foster handed us over to another Army soldier before saying goodbye to us.

"Wait, what are you going to do?"

I was tired of getting shuttled around and dropped off without knowing what the fuck was going on.

He gestured toward the upper floors of the hospital. "I'm going to check on some of our Marines who are dying. That's my job."

He left.

The soldier herded us like cattle into an area of the hospital that was abandoned.

"Here is your meal card. Do not lose it. It will get you three meals a day during your stay at the hospital, until we get you well enough to return to the States."

She lined us up and walked us outside to a trailer. We were allowed, one by one, to enter the trailer. I was first.

It was a shopette, a place to get shampoos and conditioners and every bit of bathroom minutiae to satisfy us during our time in the hospital. I looked at the soldier escorting me through the trailer.

"I don't have any money." Shame filled me. How would I pay for anything I needed?

She handed me a piece of paper. "No one comes here with money. The Wounded Warrior Battalion pays for it."

"Wounded Warrior?"

"That's what you are. Now fill this up with everything you need and want."

She handed me a black and green duffle bag that had Wounded Warrior Battalion's logo—a man carrying a wounded person slung over his shoulder in a fireman's carry—plastered on the side.

Shampoo, conditioner, a loofah (pink), body wash, a razor, a brush, Chapstick ....

I saw the pads and tampon bins and walked past them before doubling back and shoving a bunch into my duffle bag.

Something to stem the flow ....

74

September 2010, Landstuhl, Germany

On the base, we were given bedding and assigned rooms. The room was cold, not very welcoming, and dimly lit from the small amount of light that managed to break through the cloud cover and enter through the window. I had a roommate, a Black woman who looked at me in silence and rolled over to face the wall with her back to me. I was told to put my stuff down and go back to the front of the building. I grabbed a quick shower to wash away the desert before putting my gross cammies back on. I walked downstairs as soon as I was done, and Staff Sergeant Foster was waiting for me. My new friend with cancer caught my gaze and walked up to meet us shortly after I reached the staff sergeant.

"What are we doing?"

"Going to get y'all civilian clothes. The PX isn't very far away. We can't have y'all flying back to America looking like that."

The grunt and I looked at each other, me in my tan cammies and he in his tan FROG suit. We looked like we were still at war and extremely out of place in the calm green of Germany.

"Come on, get in."

"Staff Sergeant, I don't have any money on me."

"They take care of you. Don't worry about it."

Huh?

We traveled down the Autobahn and I listened to the staff sergeant converse with the grunt about various war things. The staff sergeant had gone to Iraq prior to his stint in Europe. When we reached the mall, the staff sergeant handed us over to a Wounded Warrior liaison, who was waiting for us at the front of the mall. She handed us a voucher for $250 and said to spend it on any clothes we needed. We just needed to hand the voucher to the PX checkout clerk and we would be taken care of.

"Be back in three hours. Want a coffee?"

Cancer Boy and I shook our heads at the staff sergeant.

The staff sergeant and the liaison wandered off together to grab a coffee and left us to our own devices. The grunt and I walked into the first store in the mall and slowly drifted from each other as we went to our respective sections of clothing.

I wandered through the clothes and picked out a few pairs of jeans in what I thought was my size. When I went into the changing room and tried them on, I realized that I had lost around 5 inches from my waist. I wasn't overweight before leaving for Afghanistan; I had become that skinny.

I found jeans in a size zero that fit me. I grabbed some underwear, a few shirts, and a pair of black Puma tennis shoes. I changed completely out of my cammies, wearing brand new everything, and took my hair out of the bun it had been in for seven months. My hair was still damp from the shower and fell about my face in blonde waves. I headed to the counter to pay.

The total came to $170. Pleased with my purchases, I handed over the voucher and expected my transaction to be completed. The cashier shook her head. "Go back and get more. Your voucher is for $250, not $170."

"But I don't need anything else."

"Go get something, anything. Get something nice. You deserve it."

She smiled at me and I cringed.

I deserve it? I don't deserve anything.

I went back to the clothes and walked around. I grabbed another pair of jeans and still had money left.

This is a fucking waste.

I went to a kiosk outside of the clothing store. It sold jewelry, mainly gorgeous glass worked into earrings and bracelets. I hadn't worn jewelry in close to a year. A necklace caught my eye, with black and clear glass work. It looked intricate to my unfeminine eyes. The saleslady took the necklace from the counter and placed it on my neck. When she showed me the mirror, I was taken aback by my reflection. I looked like a girl again, not a war-hardened Marine. But my eyes and cheeks were sunken, and I didn't look happy at all.

"I'll take it."

Feeling like a fraud, I took the necklace and turned in my voucher to the cashier. She complimented me on my choice, and I stuttered a thanks.

With my cammies in a bag, I walked back out to the front of the mall. I looked like a civilian but didn't feel like one.

The ride back to the hospital was just Marine Staff Sergeant Foster and myself. I guess the grunt had finished early and had already gone back. During the drive, the staff sergeant kept looking over at me, as I pointedly kept my gaze on the passing countryside.

"You know, if you need anything while you are here, you let me know."

"Yeah, thanks."

He focused his eyes intently on the road. "No, I mean anything."

I snapped my eyes to his and he looked at me, before taking his hand from the wheel and placing it on my knee. I jerked my legs far from his touch.

I don't remember if I said to stop. It reminded me of the time in America when I was a lance corporal and I had caught a ride to the store with my sergeant. He told me to take off my underwear and give it to him. I got out of the car and walked the two miles back to my unit. But in Germany? I was at this guy's mercy. I had to toe the line between acquiescence and retaliation.

His hand went back to the wheel and, with my stomach in knots; we rode the rest of the way in silence.

75

September 2010, Landstuhl, Germany

I had one doctor's appointment with the gynecologist at the hospital that Friday. I went in, expecting to be shamed for leaving a combat zone pregnant. But the hospital didn't care, the nurses were so nice and happy for me. They stroked my hair while I laid back and let them wave the ultrasound wand over my stomach. This time, the nurses showed me my child moving on the screen of the ultrasound machine. Its face was so well formed and perfect. I cried into the pillow as I heard its heartbeat, strong, and saw it kicking.

The hemorrhage was pretty bad, but the gynecologist cleared me to leave Germany and to travel back to America.

"Just don't get too physical, and make sure you have a supportive environment to help you when you get back to America. Immediately check in to your gynecologist in the States. They will probably put you on bedrest for the duration of your pregnancy. You're currently three months along. Do you have someone to support you in the States?"

I thought of my husband.

"Yeah, someone is supposed to be there for me."

"Good. Your health and the baby's health need to be taken care of. You can't get too stressed out or the bleeding could get worse. Take it easy."

When the doctor left, the nurses let me see my baby a little longer. "Would you like pictures?"

My face lit up. "You can give me pictures?!"

She laughed and printed me three precious pictures of my child's face. My name and the baby's gestation were printed on the pictures. I couldn't stop shaking from laughter and tears as I held proof of my child in my hands.

76

September 2010, Nanstein Castle, Germany

Wounded Warrior Battalion tried to cheer up its patients by taking us on a tour of a local castle that weekend. I sat in the back of the car, while the grunt sat up front with Staff Sergeant Foster. Upon reaching the castle, the grunt and I stood beside each other during the tour, eventually wandering off together among the ruins of the German castle. We barely spoke, but we didn't need to. We were sleep-deprived and thrust from combat directly into a cheery little German town to explore a fucking castle. It was surreal to us and we were both shell-shocked as we walked around. It was nice to be with another Marine who knew how weird it was to be surrounded by green scenery and happy people.

We came across a group of children defacing the castle by writing on the walls. We chased them off; the teens were laughing and whooping as they ran. When I saw my fellow Marine's face, it was white with pain.

We sat down on a bench overlooking the town.

"How the fuck can everyone be so happy?"

He sounded angry and I said nothing. I had nothing to say but my own angry and bitter thoughts. I linked my arm through his and we just sat in silence, before we were called down to eat duck in the castle's restaurant.

Fucking duck.

I was issued civilian plane tickets to America for Tuesday. I would land in San Diego, by way of Los Angeles. Once I landed, I would be on my own. I was given orders to report to my command by Wednesday.

Which command?

I tried to call my husband to tell him I would be coming back to the U.S. I used a phone on the wall in the hallway of the hospital that was for public use. As I typed the long number, I kept a mantra in my head:

Please pick up, please pick up, please pick up.

He didn't pick up and he had disabled his voicemail.

I called multiple times before he finally answered.

"Hey!"

"What's up?"

"I'll be landing in San Diego on Tuesday at 1400. Can you pick me up from the airport?"

There was a long pause. "Yeah, I guess I can come."

"Okay, thank you."

There was a long silence.

"Is that it?"

"Yeah, I can't wait to see you."

"Bye, Savannah."

My heart broke knowing that the one person who was supposed to always support me was so upset with me.

It will be better when we see each other in person. We've gone over a year without seeing each other, really. Him coming to pick me up will be good. We can get through this. We can do this.

77

September 2010, Frankfurt, Germany

I had my Wounded Warrior Battalion duffle bag, my ID, and a new bank card to access my money when I arrived at Frankfurt Airport. Staff Sergeant Foster didn't say a word when he dropped me off at the strange airport, in a strange country, where I did not speak a word of German. I had in my hand my one-way ticket to America. I was finally going home.

I navigated the airport, got through security with only a small hold-up for not having a passport. After I showed my military ID, I proceeded to my gate.

Everyone around me looked so happy and carefree. I guess travel does that to some people. I was anxious and jumpy as hell. I walked past a duty-free shop and thought I should get my husband a present from Germany. I couldn't go to him empty-handed. He was a heavy drinker, so what better idea, I thought, than to get him a bottle of Jägermeister from Germany. It was perfect. I bought the biggest bottle I could find, thankful that I finally had access to my money. The saleslady wrapped and sealed the bottle in a duty-free bag with duty-free tape. I tossed the bottle into my duffle bag and proceeded to my gate.

There were U.S. Army soldiers waiting for the plane as well. They were displaying their military status loudly, with boasts and brags, all of them wearing their horrible ugly cammies. Marines are not allowed to be off base in cammies, as it is seen as unprofessional and a detriment to national security if we loudly display our status as protectors of America. The Army does not care and will wear their uniforms in a manner seen as disgusting by most Marines. So, I rolled my eyes and sat in silence to await boarding. While waiting, I watched as the three soldiers were approached by several men and women, who shook their hands enthusiastically, thanking them for their service and sacrifice for American freedom.

What. Complete. Bullshit.

By the time the plane boarded, I was fuming. I knew I didn't look like a Marine. Most female Marines don't look like Marines out of uniform, so we are frequently overlooked, which is fine. We don't do it for recognition, but to watch others hop from one safe military base to another safe military base, out of a combat zone, and get thanked for the danger they placed themselves in, put me in an even worse mood.

Whatever, let's just get home.

I slept the entire flight. It was a strange mirror to my flight to Afghanistan. Sleep; weird airplane food that I scorned on the way to Afghanistan I devoured on the way back; strange civilians instead of my fellow Marines; civilian clothes instead of my cammies, and empty-handed instead of holding my M16 rifle. Angry, bitter, hateful, and scared instead of nervous, excited, anxious, and scared.

I landed in LAX among the loud and fat Americans. It surprised me to see how large everyone was compared to the starving Afghans and military in the Middle East. The Germans didn't look like this, either.

As I approached customs, I placed my duffle bag on the conveyor to the scanner and showed my military ID to the TSA agent. I got through security but was pulled aside with my bag. "What is this?" The agent pulled out the duty-free bottle of Jägermeister from my bag.

"Just a gift."

The bottle was clearly unopened and still sealed within the duty-free bag.

"Give me your ID."

I showed my military ID again.

"You're too young to have this. It will have to be confiscated."

I was still 20 years old, yes. Germany doesn't care about alcohol after the age of 16, so I hadn't been concerned about the alcohol. I had never traveled out of the country before, so I knew nothing about customs between countries. I didn't know it would be found, and even if found, I wasn't drinking it, nor had I bought it on American soil.

"I'm not drinking it. It is still sealed."

"It doesn't matter."

"I'm not trying to drink it! I wanted to get it for my husband!"

At this point, I was desperate.

"I just got back from Afghanistan!"

"No one cares." He placed the bottle of alcohol on his desk behind the conveyor belt and shoved my duffle bag across the table to me.

I bet that motherfucker is going to drink all of that tonight.

"Welcome to America."

78

September 2010, San Diego, California

I stepped off the plane in the tiny Terminal One of San Diego Airport. It is mainly used for commuters on small planes, from LA to San Diego. I walked slowly through the terminal with my bag, looking for my husband. Airports can be weird if you don't know where the reunion place is. You can turn a corner and BAM, there's your family, or you can walk through what seems like miles of airport before getting dumped out into the parking lot.

I scanned the area anxiously, left the baggage claim, and walked outside of the airport. I didn't see him or his car anywhere, so I went back inside to look for a clock.

Maybe I miscalculated the time difference when the plane would land.

Nope, it was 1415.

Maybe he went to park the car and is walking in to greet me.

I sat along the wall outside of the terminal.

1430 ... 1440.

I asked a passerby if I could borrow their cell phone to call my husband. He picked up on the first ring.

"Hey, it's Savannah. I'm at the airport ... in San Diego. Are you close?"

"Oh shit."

"Oh shit? What does that mean? Aren't you coming?"

"Uh ...."

"Adam, seriously?"

I had been so excited to see him after months of feeling so alone, of feeling like I wasn't welcomed in a grunt unit, by the female Marines in the FET, by anyone but someone who threatened and abused me. I was heartbroken.

"I'm on my way, don't worry about it."

"Where are you coming from?"

"Carlsbad."

At least an hour away in traffic.

"You weren't already on your way?"

"I said I'm coming, Savannah."

He hung up and I handed the phone back to the confused stranger, with a quick thank you, before sitting back down on the wall for another hour. I waited, watching men and women in business suits, with their briefcases and busy demeanors, passing by me without a glance as they went about their busy lives.

Adam pulled up in the silver Pontiac Sunfire we had shared over the last two years. Its trunk was still broken from when the latch broke on me while he had been on deployment, and it was held shut with a bungee cord. Nervously, I watched him pull up to the curb and get out.

I ran and jumped into his arms and hugged him with all my might. He kissed me, and I buried my head in his neck as we clung to each other.

79

September 2010, Vista, California

We lay on the bed. I was on my back and Adam was facing me on his side. His hand lay on my stomach. I was so skinny from the deployment that we could see exactly where the baby lay. The baby was low and on the right side of my body.

"Is that it?"

"Yeah."

"What are you going to do?"

"Are you willing to raise another man's baby?"

He was silent, and I sighed.

"Even if you were, he wouldn't let you raise her. We couldn't stay together."

"Her?"

"I have a feeling."

We lay in silence, with him watching me stroke my stomach. He placed his hand on the baby and felt her move.

"I can get an appointment, but it would have to be soon."

"When?"

"Tomorrow. But I need someone to go with me. Will you take me?"

He nodded in agreement, keeping his hand cupped over my child.

I believed his agreement meant he supported what I was planning to do. This was the answer. He would support me. We would move past this; we would be okay. I would be okay.

"Thank you."

****

We drove in the same Pontiac Sunfire that had taken us on a trip to San Francisco, where we had decided to marry, and then it took us through two deployments. We were silent the entire way. When we reached the clinic, we walked up the ramp to enter the waiting room. I had expected picketers or angry crowds. There were none, thankfully.

He sat down while I checked in. Women and families sat in the waiting room in varying states, some visibly pregnant, some holding children. I sat in the blue plastic cushioned chair and waited for my name to be called.

Blood pressure, temp, and an ultrasound verified how far along I was.

They didn't mention that I was already in my second trimester. I was terrified to be turned away. I had gotten the first appointment, once I knew I would be back on U.S. soil and out of the grasp of the military, as a "just in case" option. Even though I had been frozen by indecision for months, I didn't want to be forced in one direction. I wanted to make sure I had all available options. Now I was taking one of those options.

The nurse was kind and patient as she explained the procedure.

"You'll come back tomorrow, and we will continue—"

"What? Tomorrow? I need this today."

"You'll need to come back tomorrow to finish the procedure. Today we just open your uterus."

"Can I change my mind tonight?"

"Once we put this in your cervix, there is no going back. You'll dilate overnight and we will do the D&C tomorrow."

That was it. That was the moment I hesitated. There would be at least 24 hours of knowing my child was dying inside of me, by my hands.

"I can't come back, I can't. It has to be today, all of it."

I was crying at this point, shaking, and wringing my hands.

The nurse touched my knee as I shook and rocked back and forth with tears streaming from my eyes.

"You don't have to do this."

Thoughts of what would happen if I didn't do this, from my career to my reputation, to my future being controlled by the father of this child, someone I was terrified of, played like a movie on fast forward.

"No, I do, I do."

I laid on the table, while something was shoved inside of me to open my cervix.

"You'll be in pain throughout the night. You'll experience some contractions and there might be bleeding."

Adam and I drove home in silence.

"I'm going out." He left for the rest of the night.

I slid to the floor crying and dreading the next day.

****

I was put under some sort of anesthesia that allowed me to remain slightly conscious. Everything was white and woozy. I cried the entire time and noticed the machine that was brought into the room as I lay on my back. I can only remember it looked like a shop vac. And the table was blue.

I wanted to vomit.

Adam drove me back home. I struggled to walk; the drugs were still in full effect. He opened the door for me, and I tried climbing the steps to our bedroom. I had reached the doorway, when I realized he was hanging back. I collapsed onto the bed and waited for him to talk.

"I'm going out."

"Please don't go. Please stay with me, Adam, please."

I started to cry again.

"Please, I don't think I should be alone right now. I feel so sick and I'm in a lot of pain. It hurts so bad, Adam, please …."

He hung in the doorway, and I suddenly noticed his expression had turned into one of disgust.

"I never thought you'd be the one to murder your own baby."

The words slapped me in the face as though he had delivered a physical blow.

"But you said … Adam … I did it for you! So, you would stay with me! So, we could have our own family!"

I had never felt sicker in my life. I had made a choice I thought would keep him in my life based on what we had discussed over the years, and he was choosing to walk away, to leave me still. We had discussed early on in our marriage how our family would continue, even if I accidentally got pregnant from someone else. We had been pragmatic in our discussions, but discussions didn't take into account the realities of pride and pain, the realities of not seeing each other for over a year, of abuse from other parties, of death and deployments, of life.

"Please Adam, please don't go, please!"

I was screaming as he walked out and slammed the door. I couldn't even see straight enough to walk to the bathroom without falling into the doorway. I grabbed the pills and brought them to the bedroom. I looked at the label, knowing I wanted to make sure they would work. I didn't want to not succeed. I wanted to meet my baby as soon as possible, because I didn't deserve to live. I murdered a child for a man and to get out of trouble. How despicable could I be?

I sent a text message to Adam.

I brought the pills to my mouth and had swallowed a few when the bedroom door flew open. Adam whacked the pills out of my hand and screamed at me. He grabbed me by the shoulders and flung me up against the bed frame.

"What the FUCK is wrong with you?! You're fucking crazy! What the fuck!"

He shook me with every word. Then released me, where I lay crying on the bed as he gathered up the pills. I heard him flush the pills before he started to leave again.

I got down on my knees and grabbed his legs. I begged him to stay. I begged him not to leave me.

He pried my arms from his legs and looked at me, again in disgust, before leaving.

He didn't come back.

I had taken the life of a child that I desperately wanted, out of fear—fear of the unknown; fear of abandonment by a man who had promised to love me forever; fear of reprisal from the Marine Corps for adultery and having sex in a combat zone; fear of a future with William, a man who I didn't know and didn't agree with on how to raise a child, who was dangerous beyond what I was willing to admit.

I was so afraid, I took the easiest way out, for a little more than 900 bucks.

80

June 2018, U.S.A.

J. K. Rowling described perfectly in her Harry Potter series with her use of Horcruxes that the splitting of the soul to preserve an individual's mortality can only be created through the taking of a life. I took the life of my child and my soul split forever. I became half of a woman and stepped away from the goodness and wholeness of society when I carried out that decision.

Honor, courage, and commitment—the ethos of the Marine Corps. I had failed every pillar of that ethos tenfold by not accepting punishment and having my child. I didn't deserve the title of United States Marine and I had spat in the face of every brother and sister in the Corps for being spineless and afraid. I should've taken the punishment the Marine Corps would have given me. Eight years later, I'm almost positive I would have just been given an NJP, non-judicial punishment, and reduced in rank, possibly given an "other than honorable" discharge. That's it. Nothing extremely life-altering. Not jail. But as a 20-year-old who was reeling from a combat deployment, I didn't know, and I was too scared to risk it. Is my current honorable discharge worth the everyday knowledge I have of murdering an innocent child? Every day I hold the honorable discharge, I am reminded of how dishonorable I am.

I know that this viewpoint will anger many women who are not ashamed of their abortions. Many don't believe they did anything wrong, and that's fine. I believe it is every woman's right to choose. I'm glad I was given a choice. I just happen to think I made the wrong one, and I think about it daily.

I thought a lot about it when I had a miscarriage in 2013. I thought I was being punished for my abortion. I thought the abortion had ruined my body, as women are warned abortions can affect their ability to retain future pregnancies. I think about it still, when I look at my beautiful son, conceived only a few months after my miscarriage, as he plays today, and I wonder what his older brothers or sisters would have looked like. I think about how perfect and smart they would have been and how bright they would have made my life. I think I might not have had my son, if I had chosen any road other than the one I'm currently on.

Would I care so much about my career, if I hadn't murdered my child to keep my rank, to keep my GI Bill so I could go to school for free? Would I have busted my ass to get my graduate degree without the knowledge I only kept my GI Bill with the trade-in of a child's life? I can't say how things would have played out, but I know life would have been different for me. Every day, I live a tainted life, and I wonder how I'll tell my son about what I've done.

What will he think? What will he say?

"What if you hadn't kept me, Momma?"

81

October 2010, Oceanside, California

I parked the car I had just bought on the other side of the parking lot from Starbucks. I didn't want him to know what car I drove, or from what direction I had come. I was shaking as I walked into Starbucks to meet William.

I had received an email with a phone number and a message saying that he would be coming to the U.S. I was expected to meet him as soon as possible. William knew nothing of what had happened after I left Delaram, about five weeks prior. He thought I was still carrying his child. He needed to know a version of the story that would get him out of my life, but without invoking his anger.

William was dressed in jeans and a nice, soft-looking gray t-shirt. I was, for the first time since he had known me, in jeans and a t-shirt. He stood up as I entered and leaned over to hug me. I'm sure he felt my body trembling as I hugged him back. He told me to sit down, gesturing for me to take the seat that would put my back to the door.

"How are you? How is the baby?"

I could feel my heart start to pound. "William ... I was leaving Delaram and I ... I started bleeding."

He became very still. He studied me intently, waiting for me to continue.

"I got to Germany and ... it was too late. I lost her."

He looked stunned for a moment. Then he reached over the table to grab my hands, which I had curled over my lower abdomen. My voice was quivering, and I wasn't able to look him in the eye.

"I'm sorry, William."

"It isn't your fault. Are you okay though? Did the doctor say when you could have children again?"

"I … didn't ask."

"We can try again. I got a job on Pendleton. I will be living here."

"You live here now?" My heart and mind raced. *He owns a home in Arizona. What is he doing here?*

"Yes, of course. I moved to be close to you and our child. My contract gave me a position near you. Isn't that great?"

"You left your home? Everything? What about Amy?"

"My daughter will be taken care of by my family until we are married and have a home here."

"William … I … I can't do that."

"Why not? We are supposed to be together."

"Because I am just trying to get my life back on track. I'm starting a new job; I need to find a place to live. Afghanistan is a different world, a different place. And the miscarriage has shaken me. I'm not okay."

His voice softened.

"Okay, we can take it slow. But we will be together, you know that, right?"

He reached up to cup my face in his hands, staring deeply into my eyes, as I struggled not to look away. I murmured in agreement, wriggled from his grasp, and walked quickly out the door.

82

October 2010, Vista, California

A week later I walked into the house and slammed the door loudly, not caring if the neighbors heard. I flung myself onto my bed and screamed angrily into my pillow while tears streamed down my cheeks.

I replayed what had just happened over and over again. My husband had gone camping with some friends and I hadn't been invited. In fact, he hadn't even told me he was going until he got to Lake Elsinore. So when I received his text message asking if he could borrow my sleeping bag, I was excited to hear from him. I immediately agreed to drive the hour and bring him the sleeping bag. I had hopped into my car and driven north.

When I reached the campground, his friends stayed at the fire pit and watched us as he came to meet me at my car. I noticed the girl at the fire pit everyone had told me he was sleeping with. I tried to hold my head up high as I handed over the sleeping bag. When I asked if I could stay, he laughed and said no. I looked over at the fire pit and saw everyone laughing.

I saw red. Crying into my pillow, I realized I had acted like a crazy person as I took everything of his from my car and threw it at him. Clothes, CDs, papers ... he could find a way to gather his shit and get it back south. I drove back through tears, and I let those tears of anger and sadness flow.

Now I replayed the last few weeks. They had been hell. He never came home, and I knew he was with someone else. If he did come home, he was buried in World of Warcraft. I downloaded the game and tried finding common ground with him. He wouldn't engage with me at all. So, I tried harder.

We argued about money. He saw me buy my car with cash, $5,000, and he accused me of hoarding my deployment money. He claimed he was in debt because he paid the rent, while I kept everything I had earned on deployment. We had agreed that my deployment money would be a nest egg for us, but evidently, he was struggling to buy food. I asked him how much he wanted.

I cut him a $5,000 check. And the next day he got a full upper back tattoo—the "Angel of Death" carrying a sickle.

He tried everything to get rid of me. He even told me he was gay.

But the sleeping bag was the straw that had broken my metaphorical back. I don't take public humiliation.

I was done.

I grabbed my phone and turned onto my back. I had no texts or calls. I scrolled through my attempts to reconcile with Adam and got angrier and sadder. Closing his messages, my eye caught the name, below Adam's, on the most recently contacted list of texts:

Matrix.

Matrix was a friend prior to deployment. We had met at work, after he had discovered there was a lance corporal in the company who was really good at doing a job he didn't want to do. As a sergeant, he tried to get me to do the work. I had tactfully told him to fuck off as I was in a different platoon and already swamped with my own work. Later in 2009, we ended up on the same target on the range, and he had patiently taught me how to shoot, helping me bring my rifle qualification up from marksman to expert. While on the range, we gorged on the chocolate chip cookies he made every night, in a search of the perfect recipe. He sealed the friendship by not hitting on me once and by bringing me into his family to be his wife's friend. The three of us, and a few others, had spent weekends watching movies, making sloppy joes, having game nights, and exploring Southern California prior to my deployment.

I had discovered on my deployment that Matrix's wife had cheated on him with a "Jody" while he was deployed to Bahrain. "Jody" is a colloquial term for a man who stays in the States and sleeps with a military member's spouse while the military member is deployed. Matrix had allowed this Jody, a subordinate Marine, to room with him while the Marine got his life together. When Matrix deployed, the kindness and trust he had extended to his Marine was repaid with a destroyed marriage.

I scrolled through the messages Matrix had sent me after I had gotten back from my deployment. He had asked me to hang out and catch up and I had told him I wanted to focus on my marriage. He respected that answer, and we hadn't texted since.

I pressed my finger on his name and typed a single word, "Hey."

He was evidently on ship with the Marine Expeditionary Unit, a group of Marines embedded with the Navy on their ships. Working through his terrible cell phone service, we agreed to meet up when he got back to port.

"Can you wait three days?"

I cried and said that I could wait. I could wait for a friendship that had never wavered.

Three days later, I dug my toes into the sand and watched the seagulls fly overhead. The whitish golden sand was so clean that I could see individual grains in their entirety.

Nothing like Afghanistan sand.

Placing my book on the sand, I gazed out at the horizon toward the vast expanse of ocean.

In the distance, I saw a Navy ship.

Epilogue

2018, San Diego, California

I came back to the U.S. in 2010 and spoke to one person about what had happened—Matrix. Within a few months of returning from Afghanistan, I had tried going to Mental Health on Camp Pendleton. My appointments were canceled, not once, not twice, but three times, with a phone call describing an actively suicidal veteran who needed their help more than me. So, I pushed everything down deep. Clearly, others had it worse than I did. I didn't realize until years later how not talking about anything was slowly poisoning me from the inside.

Writing this book was my attempt to talk about my experiences—women in the military, PTSD, suicide, abortion, relationships in the military, and combat deployments—all volatile subjects that are hard to discuss objectively. When we argue topics close to our hearts, we tend to have clouded and emotional reactions. We tend to claim that things are black and white. The truth is never black and white. As a young and emotional 20-year-old on deployment, I saw a lot of shades of gray.

Everyone makes mistakes; everyone makes instantaneous life-and-death decisions with partial or misguided information, and most of us look back and think about how we could have done things differently to prevent bad outcomes. So, if this book helps bring anything relatable to light and helps anyone know that they aren't alone, then I'll gladly take all the anger and disgust that has already been shoveled at me. I expect more to come.

I ended communication with William after the conversation at Starbucks. This was before incessant geotagging, and he didn't know exactly where I worked or frequented. I considered myself relatively safe. I went to great lengths to make sure my locations were kept secret, deleting my location in the Marine Corps' address book so he wouldn't come to my unit. He had accepted a position on the same base as me, so he was always close by. He immediately found someone else who was willing to have his children and he moved back to Arizona. William got the family he always wanted, and I am not the mother of his many children. He still watches my every move through social media and my blog. Anything else between us would need to be in another book.

In November 2010, I checked into the base unit I had requested while in Afghanistan—Marine Corps Base Camp Pendleton. The next two years were a blur of supporting yet another environment that was operational 24 hours a day, seven days a week, 365 days of the year. Some days, I was called into work at two in the morning and I'd work until ten at night, only to repeat the sequence four hours later. I was promoted to sergeant and placed in charge of the Network Operations Center that supported every Marine Corps unit west of the Mississippi River. It wasn't hard for me to succeed; I had always been successful in the Marine Corps. All you have to do is do what you are told. If you want to be more successful, just do a tad bit more. I was an extremely hard worker and threw myself into work, piling everything I could onto my plate. I had a combat deployment under my belt, which was a golden ticket in a unit where most Marines didn't know what a fleet unit looked like. I was above reproach in my actions, or so everyone thought.

The investigation into my rape case was closed after five months with no conclusive evidence because I wouldn't name the contractor.

While in charge of the NOC, I expected perfection from myself and all of my Marines. When one of my Data Marines complained that he had joined to be a grunt, not a Data guy, because Data doesn't even do anything important, I lost my fucking mind, screaming at him how every action we do has implications more far-reaching than his idiot mind could grasp. At 21 years old, I was a tyrant as a leader, with 20 Marines who acted like lost sheep and who didn't know a network switch from a hole in the ground, and they were responsible for communications that affected a large swath of the Marine Corps. My temper was volatile, and I was known for making Marines cry. My humor was rough and crude, like all fleet Marines, and it wasn't until a contractor said I was being a bitch that I began to think about how I was treating people. The transition from a rough deployment environment to a soft garrison environment wasn't easy.

I began working out incessantly, running the Marines six miles in the mornings and then CrossFit training during lunch with government and contractor personnel. I lived for the moment, running so far ahead of the Marines, I could be completely alone on top of the Camp Pendleton hills.

And at night, I cried. Like a pendulum, I swung back and forth between rage and sadness, with tears streaming down the apex of each swing. Matrix sat there and listened for years and tried to help me become more logical and less emotional about my experiences.

My divorce from Adam was finalized in April 2011, and Matrix and I married that October. The military was sending him to Japan and we wanted to remain together.

I left the Marine Corps in 2012 with an honorable discharge after five years of active duty service. I used the GI Bill to finish my undergrad and eventually earned my graduate degree, a Master of Science in Information Technology. Matrix and I spent three years in Japan, where I became a contractor for the Marine Corps as a network engineer, gave birth to a brilliant son, and continued to chase the dreams I had written down while in Afghanistan.

I got everything I wanted—my career, my family, an education, an honorable discharge—but at what cost? Keeping quiet about what happened to me was killing me.

In 2014, I ran into Warrant Officer Rambo while working as a contractor in Japan. He had been commissioned as a warrant officer after finishing his tour as my SNCO in Afghanistan. When we were alone, inside of a loud server farm, he apologized to me for not seeing what had gone on at Delaram and for not protecting me. I choked up and my throat burned. While I was not a Marine anymore, I was still around the Marine Corps, and I was still working in the same field. I didn't know who knew about my time in Afghanistan, so all of my interactions were shadowed by a sense of dread that I would be found a fraud. Rambo told me that NCIS had gone to Delaram and conducted an investigation, interviewing everyone about what they had seen. I wondered what he would think if he knew I had gotten myself in the situation in the first place. Would he still think I warranted an apology?

The commanding officer from Delaram, the major who had ordered people to avoid me, who had ordered people to *not* make me laugh, became Matrix's commanding officer in Japan. He and his wife attended the same small workshop on understanding personality types in leadership that Matrix and I did. His personality type was deemed "green," the analytical one, which is perfect for leading without emotion or appreciating the human factor. This commanding officer's signature is also on the orders that were given to Matrix and me when our son was born in 2014. I see that signature occasionally and wonder if the major has learned to adapt his leadership skills to include more understanding of the nature of man. War is harsh, and leaders must be strong, but they cannot discount humanity.

My interactions with certain characters in the book continue even now, 11 years later.

Samantha Cash, the Marine who was medevaced from Afghanistan seven months pregnant, delivered Jim's daughter on July 8, 2010. Guilliana Rae Cash did not have Jim's name on the birth certificate. Jim laughed at Sam when she asked if he wanted to be named the girl's father. Jules was born with hydrocephalus, a condition where liquid in the brain cavity prevents proper growth of the brain. During Sam's deployment, while pregnant, she was hit in the stomach. The shock waves from the hit vastly impacted Jules' life. Jules was born blind and with a black eye. The lack of proper medical care in Afghanistan, and the time lag before Sam returned to the U.S., meant the hydrocephalus was not caught in time. Sam was given the choice to have a shunt installed to help drain the fluid from Jules' head or to let nature take its course.

Guilliana Rae Cash died November 6, 2010.

I found out about this and more when Matrix asked me to sit down with Samantha, who had been his friend since 2008. We discovered that Jim had lied to both of us, pitting us against each other for years. Sam is a wonderful and strong woman, and someone I am proud to know.

In July 2010, on one of the nights Virkler had stayed late to keep me company, he had chased me around the stacked boxes of communications equipment, finally catching me and tickling me. I laughed and then suddenly fell silent and sad. Virkler asked me what I was thinking about, and I told him to ask me in five years. Sure enough, exactly five years after he had chased me around the TCF, he sent me an email saying: Okay, it has been five years, what were you thinking about? When I asked how he remembered the exact date we had played tag in the TCF, he told me he had changed his passwords to include my name and the date in five years.

After I had returned to the U.S., Virkler called me from Afghanistan a few times. He always focused on how I was doing, and always said everything was perfectly fine and boring on his end. Once he came back to the U.S., he became immersed in his own life, dating someone, and redeploying to a calmer Afghanistan in 2012. We eventually stopped calling and continued our individual lives.

Our friendship rekindled briefly. Once I started writing this book, Virkler and I stayed up many nights talking, via Skype, about Afghanistan, love, and life. And seven years after our time in Afghanistan, he finally told me he had been hit by an IED a month after I had returned to California. He was subsequently ambushed by insurgents while on a convoy to one of the bases we occasionally supported while on Delaram. He survived, and the insurgents didn't. I was furious that he had waited years to tell me something so important.

"Savannah, you had your own stuff going on," was his answer.

Virkler flew out to surprise me, in San Diego, in 2017, and I got to see the man who had supported me in Afghanistan, for the first time in seven years. We went paragliding, we went out on the bay in a boat, we ate real food and drank alcohol. And for the first time, we were able to see each other outside of a combat zone.

He lives on the East Coast, works as a contractor, and continues to support the United States military. He married a wonderful woman in 2021 in a small wedding I was able to attend and they live with Darla, his dog, who reminds him there is a reason to live. Virkler remains a close friend.

Sergeant P dropped off the face of the earth after I got back from Afghanistan. I reached out through military email and discovered he had orders from his unit in North Carolina to Camp Pendleton, where I was stationed. When he answered my emails, he was cold and distant, and I stopped communicating with him shortly after receiving his blunt replies. I reached out a second time in 2012, to thank him for saving my life, and my Facebook message was ignored. In 2016, when my nightmares about Dumaw became too much, I reached out to Sergeant P a third and final time asking him to please talk to me. I needed someone to talk to who understood my nightmares. Then I discovered on his Facebook page the reason for his ignoring me—he was married and celebrating his tenth wedding anniversary. It didn't take a math genius to work out what that meant. Finally, after a scathing message from me about his lack of honesty, he responded. We rekindled our friendship, one full of late-night phone calls. It was great to hear from someone who understood my nightmares and struggles. He told me about his own marriage problems and confided in me about his horrible wartime and personal experiences. But we never talked about Dumaw.

Do you remember the orange he gave me on Delaram? That gesture of human kindness. I learned he had been hit by an IED the week before.

I also learned that the man I had admired for almost a decade, had—after five combat deployments and multiple IED hits—traumatic brain injury and, like many others, was broken beyond what I could repair.

My virtual interactions with Sergeant P taught me that the people we place on pedestals cannot be expected to remain flawless. We all have issues that manifest themselves as actions and reactions to the world we live in, and we have to know when to tolerate behavior that harms us and when we need to walk away. After he was admitted to an inpatient facility for a suicide attempt, Sergeant P told me the only reason he was still alive was because I had always answered the phone when he called, even when he would have a gun in his mouth.

There became a point, however, when I could no longer help him in the way he needed and deserved. Our relationship was complex and draining … I walked away.

Virkler, Sergeant P, myself, and multiple people in this story are all propping themselves up on each other, a bunch of broken and traumatized people breaking down every so often, only to answer a phone call in the middle of the night, hoping to keep a friend alive for one more day. We are navigating the consequences of our actions, the loss of our friends, and a system that deems a veteran who is back in America safe.

We, with our flawed and crumbling lives, want to end our stories with a denouement—a finalization of ideas and characters and events that have taken place. I remember learning the word denouement when I was eight or nine years old. I loved to hear it, loved what it represented, and loved to say it in a horrible French accent, over and over. The idea that stories can be tied up in a neat and pretty bow, with no loose ends, was always appealing.

A happily ever after, if you will. But life isn't like that.

Until someone dies, the story isn't over; their demons remain archrivals to the end. There is no slaying of the dragon, with a cheering arena, like that irritating Marine Corps commercial. That was the whole point of me writing this story—to fight my demons. And writing it did help. Once the words were on paper, they no longer felt like my burden to carry.

My life does not have a denouement, because it continues today. I have a family, I go to work, I continue to make mistakes and I continue to write and learn. I have been seeing a therapist who provides common sense, with a heart-centered approach, and while I still have a lot of unpacking to do (beyond my experiences in Afghanistan), I believe I am getting better in a "three steps forward, two steps back" kind of way.

Life is messy, hard and gritty, and full of regrets and successes. Sometimes people die without knowing the whole truth. The characters keep fighting battles, internal and external. And if we are fortunate, if we have amazing support, we can keep showing up for the next battle.

After Thoughts

The 20-year-long war—the war that has cost me friends through primary contact (gunshots, improvised explosive devices, mortars) and secondary contact (suicide), the war that broke my innocence forever—Afghanistan.

The United States of America invaded Afghanistan in October 2001, less than a month after the September 11 attacks toppled the Twin Towers in New York City, destroyed part of the Pentagon, and took 2,977 innocent American lives. The invasion seemed necessary to eradicate Osama Bin Laden, the leader of the group that planned the attacks, and the rest of the Taliban terrorist group.

Four presidential administrations have dictated the drumbeat of this war: Bush started it, Obama attempted to finish it, and Trump vowed to win it with an increase in troops, before he changed his stance and vowed to draw down troops again. And in August of 2021, President Biden orchestrated the end of the decades-long war in Afghanistan. The sunk cost fallacy of Afghanistan came to a close with an explosion that took the lives of 12 American service members, two of them female Marines.

It is hard to offer commentary on a war that I experienced over a decade ago, one that I decided no policies in, one where I was shackled by the rules of engagement decided by people in faraway places, who didn't know what it was like for the troops and civilians on the ground. I went and did what I was told, in the name of "freedom," which wasn't about freedom to teenage me. Before I was in Afghanistan, it was in the name of "escaping my hometown and affording college." During my time in Afghanistan, it became "in the name of not dying, and not getting any of the men around me killed." It was never about America to me. What does a child care about geopolitics?

The images of Afghan people falling from the airplanes fleeing Kabul are grotesque bookends to the images of people falling from the twin towers in New York City two decades earlier. On each end of America's war with Afghanistan are civilians caught up in the schemes of people who will never look them in the eye and see the terror they have caused, terror that causes men to throw themselves from windows or to cling to the wings of airplanes, knowing in both instances that there is only death below. My stomach churned as I watched both times—at age 11 and at age 31. I have seen that fear in the eyes of the children I aimed my rifle at on the streets of Afghanistan. I have seen that fear in the eyes of broken bodies tortured by the Taliban, bodies I carried.

The war in Afghanistan is over for the American citizens; soon to be eradicated from the news and the holier-than-thou discussions of armchair military strategists. "The war is over! Hallelujah to our tax dollars!" "It is just another Vietnam; a pointless war we lost." However, just like for the Vietnam vets, the war is not over. It continues for thousands of veterans as it has since the day we left the soil of the country where we saw atrocities that leave us gasping for breath in the middle of the night. Every Afghan news story makes us question whether our blood, sweat, and tears were for nothing; the deaths of our friends are data points to be picked apart and weaponized for a future regime. Veterans' wars will continue to be fought on American soil, until we join our brothers and sisters in Valhalla.

Moreover, the war continues for the entire country we left—no, *fled*. It continues for the men and women who helped us when we were in their country, for the ones who gave us foot bread and warm grapes, for the ones who kept us safe, risking endangerment to themselves and their families to do so.

Stone, my Afghan interpreter, was living with his family in Kabul when it fell in August 2021. His family fled, possibly on the same plane that had people dropping from the sky, while he stayed behind to continue helping Americans and their allies leave. Over the next few days, he and I tried to coordinate the escape of a few hundred people through the gates of Bagram Air Base. Veterans all over America sent me the names and stories of friends they were trying to get out before Kabul fell completely. One man had no papers of amnesty; he had an expired DoD ID that could either grant him entrance through the gates to American protection or guarantee him certain death if discovered by the Taliban. Would you hold onto the ID? Everyone begging at the gates of Bagram would become easy targets for the Taliban once the Americans left; why try to leave if you are not guilty and deserving of death?

Other manifests sent to me of endangered allies to America included the families of interpreters and Afghan pilots who were America's greatest aid to killing the Taliban over the years—there were dozens of children. Their names and faces and ages are seared in my mind. The youngest was five days old. They did not get out.

My interpreter posted a video on Facebook two days ago. I watched ten seconds of it before I realized what it was. Four men were holding a man between them, each holding one of his arms or legs. They were pulling him in four different directions to keep him dangling in the air between them. He was facedown. A fifth man had a pipe of some kind and was swinging it as hard as he could down at the man's elbows, breaking them backwards. It had been 11 years since I had seen and carried the bodies of men who died the same way. It wasn't until this week that I saw how it was done.

America has its pretty war bookends. For the people we left, our friends, our protectors, our counterparts, their ending is not one of over-prescribed medicine, nightmares, and therapy. Their ending is getting stretched out and broken, of blood-filled screams and trickles of urine down their legs. Their ending is dying knowing that their American friends left them. Twenty years of relationships formed, and we couldn't even take our friends and their five-day-old babies.

****

With the change in the U.S. administration in 2021, incidents of sexual harassment and sexual abuse in the military are being more closely scrutinized. Social media has played a significant role in exposing the depth and painful effects of sexual assaults, which in some cases lead to death.

Vanessa Guillen was a private first class (PFC) in the United States Army when she disappeared in April 2020 from the Fort Hood, Texas area, less than a week after she reported a supervisor for sexual harassment. The Army didn't begin looking for her for over a month and found another missing soldier's body in the eventual hunt for Vanessa. Eventually, Vanessa's remains were identified and recovered.

This horrible event prompted a wave of female veterans and active duty members to rally around Vanessa's story of sexual harassment in the military, and attempt to raise awareness about the breadth of harassment that we have experienced. #Iamvanessa has been trending, and my Facebook feed is filled with my sisters in arms talking about their experiences, some even naming their rapists. We have listened to each other, encouraged each other to report these men, and continued discussing what we have experienced. The male veterans are appalled that this has happened in their midst with women they served with, and I have seen many men come to the females and say, "How did I fail you?" These are all conversations that need to happen ... but the stories became too much for me. I deleted my Facebook app and went to therapy to discuss my stories ... yes, stories.

My stories are complex.

When I was a private first class myself, my company gunnery sergeant contacted me online after he found out that I was having a—consensual, though not allowed—relationship with my instructor. He proceeded to blackmail me: in exchange for sexual favors, he wouldn't turn me in. A married man, he was exploiting his position of authority against an 18-year-old girl to get what he wanted.

On a field op, a sergeant in my chain of command invited me to go with him to get pizza for the rest of the guys. In the Humvee, he told me I should give him a blowjob on the ride back or he would write me lower proficiency and conduct markings. I avoided his demands, but the ride back was torture. He later died and everyone was so sad. Reading everyone's messages about how terrible it was that he had died, I shrugged. He was one of the smartest Marines I served with. He taught me a lot of what I know about my job. Did I need to put up with sexual harassment to get the knowledge?

Just a few weeks later, another sergeant in my chain of command drove me to the store and told me to give him my underwear or he would leave me on the side of the road. I got out of the car and started walking. He was married, and damn if he wasn't the one who needed to teach me how to configure a Microsoft Exchange Server for the field.

A peer of mine hit on me, grabbing my ass, and when I reacted in an appalled way, told me that my husband would believe him over me so I should shut my fucking mouth.

Another sergeant who was piss drunk came into the room where I was sleeping and groped me. I shoved him off of me and left crying. He said, "Fuck you anyway" and peed on the bed. I told my then husband, Adam, and he did nothing.

A staff sergeant I didn't know, who was taking care of vulnerable Wounded Warriors in Germany like myself, slid his hand up my leg on the way to the hospital, telling me that he would be there to support me in whatever way I needed. I was physically impaired, psychologically broken, without a car or money in a country I didn't know.

Then the bigger stories, like the story I wrote about being blackmailed in Afghanistan by a contractor. Or one that I haven't told many people, about a federal employee in my chain of command who cornered me in the server farm. He told me he loved me. When I didn't leave my fiancé for him, he proceeded to make the last year of my enlistment hell. He would call me into work at all hours of the day and night, called me a lying slut for not sleeping with him, threatened to get my rank reduced when I blocked his phone number because of the horrible texts he sent me. At that point,

I went to the Equal Opportunity Representative and showed them all of the texts and emails, making a record in case something happened. I didn't even consider reporting him officially and getting him taken out of his position. This was 2012 and, without getting told, I knew nothing would happen to him if he was reported. The last day of my enlistment, he begged me to slip my underwear in his pocket before I left. I told him to fuck off and left the Marine Corps.

Why are these stories complex? Because I considered these people my friends, or at the very least my bosses, the keepers of the knowledge, the owners of my career. Coercion, guilt, blackmail, the ol' boy network … All of it melted into situations where I felt I owed something to someone who I cared for as a friend (or my life and livelihood was threatened). These men were supposed to protect me, to mentor me as a young Marine, to build me up. Sometimes I came out unscathed, sometimes I did not. All of those stories happened before my 22nd birthday. I was certainly not weak either, but my career was precarious. A lot of times I froze, succumbing to "friends" and bosses who used their power and my lack of it.

The stories did not stop after leaving the Marine Corps, including getting raped as a civilian. In 2018, I was sexually harassed for months as a contractor. I reported it. He still works with me. Sexual harassment from others continues to this day, most recently this Monday in the form of a very simple catcall. But I can't stand for a "simple" catcall at my workplace. Not when I know the darker side of a catcall.

My name is Savannah, and #iamvanessa.

Glossary

AC	Air Conditioner
AFN	Armed Forces Network
ANA	Afghan National Army
AOR	Area of Responsibility
AUP	Afghan Uniformed Police
CB	Construction Battalion
CENTRIXS	Combined Enterprise Regional Information Exchange System
CO	Commanding Officer
COC	Command Operations Center
Court martial	Punishment under the UCMJ that can result in loss of rank, loss of money, and imprisonment
Drop trow	To pull your pants down
ECP	Entry Control Point
FET	Female Engagement Team
Flak	Vested form of body armor that holds SAPI plates
FOB	Forward Operating Base
Fobbit	Sometimes derogatory term for a person who never leaves the FOB; a play on words with J. R. R. Tolkien's' "hobbit"
FROG	Flame Resistant Organizational Gear
G-6	General Staff Level section of the United States Marine Corps for Signal and Communication (Command, Control, Communications, and Computer Systems)
GBOSS	Ground Based Operational Surveillance System
GI	Government Issue
Grunt	Military MOS with the first two delegators as 03 infantry that includes rifleman, assaultman, scout sniper, reconnaissance, mortarman, machine gunner, baby killer, hard asses
Gunny	Friendly name for a gunnery sergeant, or E-7, in the United States Marine Corps

HESCO	Large structured barriers filled with sand and dirt to protect personnel from blasts and gunfire
Humvee	High Mobility Multipurpose Wheeled Vehicle
IED	Improvised Explosive Device
IFAK	Individual First Aid Kit
IP	Internet Protocol
IV	Intravenous
Kevlar	The helmet issued to military members or the material with which the helmet is made: para-aramid synthetic fiber
KIA	Killed in Action
LT	Lieutenant; pronounced L-T
MATV	MRAP All-Terrain Vehicle
MCI	Marine Corps Institute
MCT	Marine Combat Training
Medevac	Medical evacuation
MOS	Military Occupational Specialty
MP	Military Police
MRAP	Mine Resistant Ambush Protected
MRE	Meal Ready to Eat
MTU	Maximum Transmission Unit
NATO	North Atlantic Treaty Organization
NCIS	Naval Criminal Investigative Service
NCO	Non-Commissioned Officer
NIPRnet	Non-classified Internet Protocol Router Network
NVG	Night Vision Goggles
OOD	Officer of the Day
PMT	Police Mentoring Team
POG	Personnel Other than Grunt
PTAD	Personnel Temporarily Assigned Duty
PTSD	Post-Traumatic Stress Disorder
RAS	Rear Area Security
R&R	Rest and Relaxation
RCT	Regimental Combat Team
River City	State of communications that requires the immediate shutdown of anything to be relayed out of the country; either in the event of a military member's death until immediate family is notified, or during certain missions designated by the CO
RV	Recreational vehicle

SAPI	Small Arms Protective Inserts
Shoot the shit	Aka smoking and joking; to fuck off and not work; to converse with friends and other cohorts typically in a smoke pit and during the long moments of boredom
SIPRnet	Secret Internet Protocol Router Network
SNCO	Staff Non-Commissioned Officer
TCF	Technical Control Facility
TCN	Third Country National
Terp	Interpreter
TTYL	Talk to You Later
UCMJ	Uniformed Code of Military Justice
Vic	Vehicle
VLC	VideoLAN Client
Wadi	Arabic term for valley
White line	Internet connection that is not affiliated with the Marine Corps' network
WPPL	Wireless Point-to-Point Link

Acknowledgements

Publishing a book has been the only group project I've been a part of where everyone pulled their own weight and then some. This book wouldn't have existed if it weren't for the people in my life who believed in me, who listened, and who held me together. My words can't accurately capture the immense love of and awed appreciation for the people who walked with me on this journey.

Thank you, Matrix, for holding me while I cried every day for years, for not leaving when I screamed out of my mind with grief, for staying up late so many nights, walking me through nihilism and suicidal thoughts, for forcing me to eat, and for showing me that I could do anything I put my mind to with your never wavering support.

And obviously, a big thank you to Katherine Duvall for listening to me word vomit this story the first time we were alone in a car together. Yikes. Thank you for being my biggest supporter and best friend. I don't regret trauma dumping on you because look at what we've built over the last decade! You've read every draft and know every word that didn't get written. I love you, Kitty Kat.

Thank you to Paul Dopulos for sitting with me while I wrote and sobbed, who talked me through what happened for years, who always saw what this would become, and who instilled in me a deep appreciation for slowing down and chilling the fuck out. I am grateful for eating pizza for exactly one night and it is the night I met you.

To RJ Virkler, thank you for giving me a chance and for caring for me when I needed it the most. We were two kids just going through some shit, clinging to each other in a tortured desert that we never really left behind.

Thank you to the Marines of PMT who checked my reality and made sure I was okay when Kabul fell. I am honored to be your sister.

To my editor, Neva Sullaway, for being all in and so fiercely so from the moment you read the first chapter. Your patience and belief in me and the story got it to where it is now. I'm sorry I fought you on so much. You put the book into perspective and launched it into the world and I can't thank you enough.

To the team at Casemate, thank you for taking a chance on me and for helping get an important story out to the world.

To the readers of my blog, thank you for following along for that summer. Your interest is what kept me going and showed this could be a book! Y'all are true day ones as this book took shape.

Thank you to everyone who helped Stone escape Afghanistan when Kabul fell. I asked for help and everyone showed up in full force, without hesitation, and in the middle of the night. Jon and Rich, I owe you big time.

I would also like to thank myself. Holy shit.